Dazhan

Secrets of the Cave People

3rd Edition

Douglas Dunn

ESCONDIDO, CALIFORNIA: Word Wizards®

Published by
Word Wizards®
Communications Excellence since 1972
P.O. Box 300721
Escondido, California 92030-0721
United States of America

760/ 781-1227
Internet: http://www.wordwiz72.com

Library of Congress Cataloging-in-Publication Data

Dunn, Douglas, 1950-
    Dazhan: Secrets of the Cave People.

       I. Conduct of life. II. Interpersonal relations
I. Title
BJ1597.D86 1990   170
ISBN 978-0-944363-27-0 (Paperback print edition)
ISBN 978-0-944363-06-5 (Digital e-book edition)

Cover art by **Steven Dunn** and **Jon Wilkinson**

Also by Douglas Dunn: **Extro • Dynamics**, a non-fiction presentation of personal and social strategies for making desires and values work together instead of working against each other. A non-fiction adaptation of principles introduced in the parable **Dazhan**, with extensive analysis and examples that can be applied in our daily lives.

Dazhan® is a trademark registered to Douglas Dunn by the U.S. Dept. of Commerce for lectures, seminars and educational programs.

Contents

Ðazhan: Secrets of the Cave People

Appendices

Others' comments about Dazhan for the 1988 edition

Titles or descriptions of individuals are those applicable when the comments were made.

IN NORTH AMERICA:

Continue with your vital work, because we must change people's outlooks before we can change the world. Your 'pleasurable' approach to compassion makes it all the more possible.

— Leo F. Buscaglia, Ph.D.
Author of "Love," "Personhood," "Loving Each Other" and other books and articles on compassion

Reading *Dazhan* is a delight. The story is so engrossing you don't even realize how much you've learned until you're through. This is self-improvement in a very tasty form.

— Steve Snyder
President, co-founder, Live & Learn

I find the book, lectures and warmth of *Dazhan* to be highly stimulating and a determining factor in furthering students' involvement in compassionate behavior, e.g., working in special projects with the homeless, recovering alcoholics, senior citizens, and so on.

— Gerald L. Hershey, Ph.D.
Chairperson, Psychology Dept., Fullerton College

Want to learn an easy way to enjoy the people in your life? Even strangers? Even 'difficult' people? ... *Dazhan* is a coined word for "compassionate joy." It is also the process which leads to experiencing appreciation and pleasure in sharing life with the other humans around us. ... The simple Steps in the Practice of Dazhan were easy to apply. And they *do work!* They are clearly explained and a variety of examples are given. I tried it. ... The result? A turning point....

The whole package: introduction, adventure, summary, commentary and the examples — all were what I needed. ... I usually consume growth and self-help books like so many bowls of popcorn ... [but] this book has been valuable to me. If you want more joy, empathy and compassion in your life, I recommend you read it and *try it!*

— Jean Mountaingrove
Book review in "Friend's Review," Sept. 1990

Two very intriguing books in one ... The fiction shows, the non-fiction explains. A trustworthy blending of two different forms of definition ... The detailed fictional examination is in the best tradition of superbly crafted utopias. The equally detailed nonfictional side is simple and profound and very clear ... It works.

— The Book Reader
Book Review, March-April, 1990

You may enjoy this interesting book on two levels: First, it is an entertaining story ... on an entirely different level, this book offers a new way of looking at our world and relationships with people ... with practical suggestions for self-improvement.
— Arizona Networking News
Book Review, Winter 1989-1990

A refreshing book. The story is a nice fantasy, but the concepts presented are uniquely appropriate — something we can do as individuals...
— Adell Leslie Shay
Program Administrator, Learning Tree University

IN THE PHILIPPINES:

...It is not far-fetched that I would rank *Dazhan* next only to the Bible in reviving Man's dying hopes and beliefs.

...*Dazhan* is a loud, unabashed, eloquent protest against the materialism, violence, terror, perversions of a technological society — a world of things, not of people.

The author's sensitive eye and penetrating mind and soul have perceived the external world as a creation of high technology which sadly neglects the full and balanced development of Man.

...*Dazhan* is both a symbol and a literary monument to a subject on morality without moralizing. Books in the genre of *Dazhan* seldom appear in our literary scene.

Dazhan is must reading for people buried in the mire of high technology and materialistic philosophy.
— Benjamin M. Montejo, award-winning writer
Book review "The Freeman," Cebu City, Philippines 12-31-88.

Dazhan can be considered as a modern day classic, simply presented in a fantasy/adventure story but conveying a powerful message that attaining full happiness can be possible by being compassionate about others ...

Dazhan is more than a story, it is a technique for how to overcome our conflicts and frustrations... a marvelous book!
— Elizabeth Y. Blardony,
Guidance Counselor, University of San Carlos, Cebu City (Released on behalf of University)

Acknowledgements

Every "single parent" understands the delicate balance of trying to pursue career objectives without denying needed attention to a little one. It is with special fondness that I express appreciation to my daughter, JoAnn, for the closeness and affection she has shared so freely for the many years I raised her alone as a single parent prior to finding a lifetime companion. I have tried to respond in the same way, without sacrificing either domestic or professional responsibilities. With concern for my inadequacies, I am grateful to JoAnn for a child's love, which sees beyond these shortcomings, and encourages efforts toward continual improvement. Now that she is all grown up and a mother herself, she has also become my supportive friend who continues to provide encouragement and ideas.

Special appreciation must be expressed to my sweetheart and lifetime companion — my wife Thelma — for patience, encouragement, hard work on helping take care of details, and sharing many ideas that contributed to the presentation of story development, and for helping me implement the practical values presented in this book in the everyday reality of daily living.

Appreciation also to my son Tracy and daughter Darby in the Philippines, for their years of inspiration and closeness and desire to model these values in their own young lives. I am also especially appreciative of the close relationship with my granddaughters Carina and Ella (daughters of JoAnn) and the opportunity they afford for sharing all that which is closest to me with yet another generation.

Special thanks to my twin brother, Dennis, for many years of suggestions and encouragement, which helped to keep me going and provided much of the guidance and direction which influenced the final form and content of this book. Appreciation also to my brother, Lowell, and sister-in-law Karen, for their ongoing support and encouragement.

A special word of thanks, also, to my family in the Philippines — especially to my sister Marilyn Mantos and my brother Atty. Dionisio Mantos and the many others who have worked so hard with them in sharing **Dazhan** overseas. Their tremendous efforts and enthusiasm have truly helped to make this an international project.

There are many others who have contributed much to this project. I have made various attempts at compiling lists, but in the interest of space and in fear of overlooking anyone, it seems more appropriate to express appreciation to *all* the friends, relatives, and professionals whose input has been so valuable. I can honestly say that every person willing to share their ideas helped to influence the final product. However, there are several whose special and exceptional contributions require special mention, in particular: Jim Newman for energy, and enthusiasm in sharing the project with others and arranging programs and activities; Dr. Gerald Hershey for support in academic circles; Julie Lilly and Bill Belote for assistance with strategies for public relations and promotion; Kim Watkins for many suggestions toward improving and refining the presentation of the message; and Mark Neary for support, advice and arranging many of the other personal and professional contacts whose influence was so valuable in completing and refining this work.

Finally, the most special acknowledgement must be expressed to *you, the reader,* through whose consciousness these little blurbs of ink on paper are made meaningful as thoughts and ideas. Best wishes for enjoying this book, and in discovering the happy feelings of **Dazhan**.

Preface

Each year when spring comes, especially if the preceding winter has been particularly miserable, I have a hard time keeping myself indoors. One bright spring morning, as my twin brother, Dennis, and I were tossing baseballs back and forth at the neighborhood park, we stopped to watch some little-leaguers taking infield practice from their coach. There is a special pleasure in watching children play: watching their childish enthusiasm and the development of adult personalities in embryo.

While watching, I noticed that one of the players, a hopeful but awkward young kid on second base, was having a pretty hard time. And the worse things got on second base, the "tougher" the coach got. With each mistake, this ten-year-old "Babe Ruth" got more frustrated, and the coach got more determined to make him learn it *right*. Finally, I overheard the kid mumble to the player next to him at shortstop, "Y'know, this isn't as much fun as I thought it would be." Apparently I wasn't the only one to overhear this remark, because the coach suddenly stopped and looked up, right toward second base. "I think I heard someone complaining about *fun*. Baseball's not supposed to be *fun* — it's *hard work!* After you learn to do it *right*, then maybe you can have some fun."

It bothered me to hear the coach talk that way, and I hope the boy didn't grow up believing what he was told. Sure, it's great for kids to practice and learn to play well and enjoy performing skillfully. But the real purpose is still more for making life in a hard world a little more pleasant than for producing flawless playing-machines. Baseball *is* supposed to be fun — if it has to teach them anything, it should be how to get along and enjoy doing things together. It just isn't right to make a chore out of it.

Unfortunately, this attitude is not confined just to the baseball diamond. Take a look at the world around, and you will see that we often work hard for difficult goals without considering, often without even knowing, how we may be helping or hindering the Good Life. Our whole cultural ethic has developed this way. Modern technology, for example, has advanced far beyond the wildest dreams of even a few years ago. We have developed more fantastic creations; we can perform more unbelievable miracles; we can think more profound thoughts and discuss more involved questions than the great minds of yesteryear would have dreamed about even in fantasy. Yet, where has it gotten us? Is life in our twentieth-century technocracy really any more pleasant or happy than it was, say, in pre-Western Samoa or Hawaii? Our modern society has also developed more fantastic problems, performed more unbelievable destruction, and ended up with more ulcers, headaches, and tension than even the most sadistic minds of old would have cared to conceive. We have been able to construct from the raw materials of Mother Earth a fantastic network of gadgets and devices — often at the cost of great destruction to the very resources of Nature from which they were spawned. Yet, if Mother Earth strikes back with something as insignificant as a quivering of her crusty surface or a swirling gust of whirlwind, our "great" creations crumble, while something no less than a delicate bird's nest may survive. What is the real worth of all our great creations?

The problem is essentially the same as with the little-league sergeant-coach: the goal has been to improve *things* rather than *people* — to upgrade the game itself without regard for the player. And even though our obsessions started out with a better life in mind (a game to have fun with; conveniences to make life a little easier), we have made the things themselves so important that our values have become mixed-up, and the real goals are obscured. The means are too often confused with the ends, at the expense of both. Thus, in our production-oriented society, technology and achievement have increased at a tremendous rate (which certainly is no problem, if priorities do not become confused or social values obscured), while the level of actual human happiness has remained static. Look around. In many ways, the human race has very little of true value to show, for all its "success" and "achievement" in producing more and better merchandise.

One of the questions I have been most often asked since the first edition of **Dazhan** came out in the spring of 1981, is, "Where did 'Dazhan' come from?"

During my late teen-age years I was sorting out my own values and belief system and exploring the many ideas offered by the great religions, philosophies, and social movements of the world. I was trying to find the best of each, and draw it into my own emerging awareness of values.

One night, as I was relaxing in front of the TV set after a hard day, the eleven o'clock news came to an end, but I was feeling just lazy enough that I remained sprawled out on the sofa and didn't bother to turn off the set or even change channels. I just lay there as the late movie rolled onto the screen, watching with only partial interest the early plot development.

Since I really wasn't paying close attention, I missed a lot of what was going on at the beginning of the movie, but after a while I looked up to see that a small group of people — some who knew each other and some who didn't — had gotten themselves stranded together on a mysterious island somewhere in the middle of the ocean. At this point, my interest was stimulated somewhat, and I watched a little more closely. The plot, as it continued to develop, was all about how these people worked together to build shelter, gather food, and eventually leave the island. It was about the problems of survival and social order that they faced — problems which they were unable to solve as individuals, but which they could eventually overcome by working in cooperation with one another.

When I finally crawled into bed, I lay between the sheets staring at the ceiling. Only moments before, I had been too tired to even turn the TV off, and now I was haunted by a strange sleeplessness as I reviewed in my mind the scenes from the movie.[*]

During this time when I had been giving a great deal of thought to various concepts of human value and social interaction, such ideas gave me the opportunity to consider the process of social cooperation and its relation to the problems of human happiness: how much better it is for people to work together with mutual give and take for the benefit of all than for them to bicker and quarrel and fight and hate and make no progress whatever. It seemed that, just being practical, it was more sensible for people to get along and avoid the unpleasantness of fussing. In my mind's eye I pictured the very origins of civilization stemming from a few primitive individuals who joined forces to work in unity for the common good, and I concluded that this element of cooperation stands at the very core of social development.

But as my weary mind again fell into sleepiness, I further considered that I am certainly not the first person to be impressed with the great value of this kind of cooperation. Most people acknowledge that as a fundamental truth, and my few thoughts of praise surely added no new contribution. With those thoughts, my tired brain submitted to the demands of sleep.

Yet the direction of my thoughts remained unchanged even in sleep as a haunting dream into my mind. That's all it was — just a vivid dream. But it seemed very real:

I saw myself wandering along on a misty plain, groping through a shroud of fog. I stumbled blindly through the cold, moist air, groping through the clouded mist, and reaching out in confusion for something higher — to lift me above the fog — without really knowing what. And yet, I was not really reaching for a higher *place,* but a higher *feeling.* The thoughts and feelings that had been running through my mind earlier were now finding meaning in this dream.

And I was not alone. There were others, groping and wandering through the fog, lost like myself. In the fog, I reached out past all the other faceless bodies, trying, as were they all, to find something better.

---

[*] The movie was *Mysterious Island,* the 1961 Columbia Pictures production based on the novel by Jules Verne.

Suddenly, I felt a firm, warm hand take hold of my outstretched, searching arm. With sureness of direction, it led me forward. My anonymous Friend led me to the slope of a small hill, and drew me with him to its summit.

The little hill extended up out of the fog, and from the top of it I could look out over the fog and I could see, with great clarity, for miles around. The hilltop was sunny and warm and pleasant. After having been mired down in the cold and mistiness of the fog, it was pleasant and beautiful.

I started to say something to my new Friend, but he motioned me to silence, firmly yet gently. He said nothing, but he radiated to me a new feeling of warmth and of close unity. It was this *feeling* that had drawn me up out of the fog. It was an understanding that, as long as I struggled alone, I was stranded in the misty confusion, but that I was able to rise above it only when joined by another.

I realized that all the groping, grasping bodies still down in the valley were like myself. By themselves, they were hopelessly lost, until they could join together and work together to find the Hill. My Friend did not speak, but I understood from him that the name of the little Hill was "Cooperation," because it could only be found and enjoyed with the guiding help of a fellow human being.

And then my dream became even more intense:

My Friend motioned me to turn around. I turned and saw a huge Mountain towering up from the little Hill. He directed me to go to the top of the Mountain, and I sensed from him that, because the little hill of "Cooperation" is of such great beauty and value to those who come up out of the lonely fog, that very few of those who find the Hill ever feel the need to go beyond it to the great heights of the Mountain. He radiated a countenance that assured me I no longer needed his help, directing me to go alone and find new treasures of feeling at the highest summits of the Mountain — treasures which include all value but which no longer require the active participation of, or dependence on, others.

Somewhat puzzled, I left him and ascended, alone, along a narrow, rocky path. This dreamland climb was long and arduous, with the thirsty heat of a barren landscape in sharp contrast to the cold and damp of the earlier fog or the pleasant beauty of the Hill. I struggled over steep rocks and dry, hot, sweaty, bloody thorn bushes; fending off pain and fatigue with weary purposefulness. I could see why those who had found the comfort of the Hill wouldn't rush to leave it and face this harsh journey.

Finally, I found my way to the massive summit of this imposing formation. At the top was a beautiful garden, with rocks and ponds and waterfalls, and with rainbows glistening among the trees and ferns and flowers. And, this garden summit afforded a spectacular view. From this highest height, I could see that the fog and the Hill and all the surrounding area were but minor features in a little valley, and from my new position I could see the **whole world!** I could see **everything!** It was not *just* a mountaintop that I had ascended, but new *perceptions,* synthesized out of all the thoughts and feelings that had been floating around beneath the surface of my conscious mind.

Flowing into my mind was an insight into human social interactions that drew upon bits and pieces of many different ideas, but which — as a whole — was not quite the same as any one of them. It evolved from "cooperation," but was also different, extending far beyond cooperation in the same way that the beautiful and majestic Mountain dwarfed the little Hill. I was so excited I wanted to scream and shout and tell all the people down in the valley — down in the fog — what I had seen. I wanted them to come up and see it, too.

I could see that this kind of compassion is more than a passive, feel-good celebration of "love" and "peace." It does feel good and it is love and peace, but more — *it represents real power!* It was this direct *power of practical compassion in* **action** by which Gandhi brought down the British empire, the greatest empire the world had ever known. It was how Martin Luther King Jr. and Nelson Mandela brought down centuries-old systems of institutionalized racial injustice. And it was how the families and survivors of the massacre at Mother Emanuel AME Church in Charleston, South Carolina, brought down a symbol of hate that others had tried to lower for 54 years, by repaying hatred and violence with love and forgiveness that softened long-hardened hearts. This same power can improve every aspect of our personal, social and productive lives. The *power of practical compassion in* **action** not only brings personal contentment, happiness and serenity, it also makes our lives better and more successful as it brings goals, values and desires into harmony with each other instead of working against each other.

And then I woke up.

It was 3:30 in the morning, but I jumped out of bed and scribbled down some notes so I would not forget what I had seen and felt. I then realized that my Friend had not been with me at the greatest summit to give me a name for the Mountain. Because it grew out of the Hill of "cooperation," and encompassed feelings which were related, but with a different, more broadened perspective, I originally called it "Neocooperation" — a *new kind* of cooperation. This was the name used for the concept of "Dazhan" in the early versions of the writing, before I decided to use a fantasy, fictional setting to *show* how it works. For the story, I coined the term "Dazhan" as a word from the language of that fantasy civilization. It is this expanded offshoot from cooperation that I want to share. I still want the people in the foggy valley, and even on the pleasant Hill, to come up and "see the Mountain."

In one sense **Dazhan** is a fictitious narrative about the cultural shock that arises from an unexpected encounter between two very different civilizations. One is rich in technological wonders, but is plagued by violence, terror, and social injustice; the other is industrially primitive, but thrives in an advanced, harmonious social order. When the Earth is turned inside out and the cave-people of Enrisa come face to face with the Outside world, both cultures are confronted with strange new wonders. But in a fuller sense, it is about much, much more.

Notes on the publication history of **Dazhan**:

Dazhan was first published in 1981 as a pedagogical novel (allegorical parable), using the format of a fictional fantasy to introduce examples and explanations for how a community of people, though primitive in technology, could be far advanced in terms of living in peaceful harmony with each other.

Following publication, a series of lectures was presented based on the concepts introduced in the story by its characters, but the lectures tended to be primarily non-fiction in nature and less about fantasy than how people can really live by principles that integrate values of compassionate joy with practical needs to have successful careers, enjoy financial and economic stability and security, and enjoy life as contributing members of their communities.

As a result, a revised and expanded second edition was released in 1988 to include an extensive Expanded Explanatory Appendix that presented in extensive detail a presentation of the non-fiction values and techniques of **Dazhan**.

As the non-fiction elements continued to expand, it finally became necessary to simply move them into a book of their own, and thus was born the non-fiction companion to **Dazhan**, *Extro•Dynamics,* which was first released in 1995, and has been extensively updated and expanded for a new 2014 second edition updated the following year, 2015 for a revised third edition.

With the non-fiction presentation now in its own book, we are now releasing a third edition of **Dazhan** that removes the expanded non-fiction commentary entirely, and recommend that readers who wish to pursue that aspect of **Dazhan** pursue their interest by exploring the more extensive discussion in *Extro•Dynamics.*

So, once again, **Dazhan** returns to its origins as a fun, pleasant fantasy as the sole vehicle for introducing values of compassionate joy in what one reviewer described as "self-improvement in a very tasty form."

Enjoy!

DOUGLAS DUNN
Escondido, California

Dazhan

Secrets of the Cave People

3rd Edition

Chapter One

Darkness

Without warning, the cave began to shake. Starting as a light rumble, it suddenly erupted into powerful jolts of granite in motion. Rocks began to fall. At first, a few pebbles crumbled loose, but then large wedges of granite came crashing down all around. A haze of dust quickly filled the small chamber. The pounding and crashing continued for a long moment. Then, the noise and shaking and blur of dizzying motion ended as abruptly as it had begun.

A quiet stillness settled through the cave. Clouds of silt still swirled in the dusty air, filtering slowly down upon the rocks.

A solitary human form was draped motionless against the uneven granite floor. The sleek contours of his athletic frame lay battered and helpless. The grimy dust settled into his sandy blond hair and on his skin and clothing. He remained oblivious to it all. He just lay there, crushed and broken beneath the rockslide.

After a while, the Form stirred ever so slightly. His eyes fluttered open.

Darrel groaned, and turned his head weakly. He became aware of a throbbing ache resonating through his head and down the left side of his body. Choking on the dusty air, he started to roll slowly over onto his good side, but was abruptly halted by a sharp pain stabbing through his left hand and arm. He felt like screaming but could only manage a feeble whimper.

Falling limp against the cavern floor, he lay helpless in the pall of silence that hung tomb-like over his stony prison. His mind was drawn to the faint sounds of delicate biological rhythms: his labored breathlessness in the dust-filled chamber; the humming and whining of an over-indulged digestive system making new demands; the throbbing ache that pounded against his head and side in time with the pulsing beat of his heart.

He tugged again at his arm, and another sharp pain shot through his body. Groping around with the other hand, he felt his way to his lantern. He turned it on. Good! It wasn't damaged. A gentle beam shone through the swirling clouds of dust that still hung in the air. He drew the light toward himself, revealing several large stones pinning down against his left side.

Rolling onto his good side as far as he could, Darrel drew his legs under himself for leverage and reached out with his good hand to the largest stone. Grimacing against the constant pain, Darrel managed to loosen it a little before collapsing in exhaustion. He rested a few moments, and tried again. Little by little he was able to dislodge the larger stones. At length there he had made enough space so he could tenderly slide his arm out.

He cradled the battered limb close to himself and positioned the lantern to inspect the extent of his injury. His arm was bruised and bloodied, and badly scraped, but did not appear to be broken. He wiped it with cotton dipped in alcohol from the first-aid kit in his backpack. After the first bite of medicinal stinging, the initial sharpness of pain began to lessen, but still there was the constant throbbing.

Darrel loosened his wristwatch, and slipped it gingerly over his sore hand. Holding the mangled remains of springs, gears, and crystal up to the lantern, it was clear that his expensive timepiece had ticked its last. He tossed it aside. He could buy a new one later. He could afford to buy a whole store of them if he wanted. But for now, he had other concerns.

"What happened!?" he wondered aloud, trying to re-orient himself to his surroundings.

The last thing he remembered was Lee chiding him for wandering off too far on his own. It seemed Lee was always on his case about something.

He remembered the little passageway he had discovered leading off from the main chamber of the cavern. The floor of the little tunnel dropped off in a steep incline away from the main chamber of the cave, with walls that slanted at about a forty-five degree tilt. "Oh yeah," remembered Darrel. He had wandered off into that passageway when the shaking started.

Now, he was stuck inside a deep cave somewhere in the mountains of Canada. "Damn!" he muttered. His first thought was for the great inconvenience to his vacation plans. Something like this could ruin his carefully-planned schedule. "Damn!" he repeated. "What if I'm late getting back? I've got to get ready for that big Reynolds deal coming up a week from Tuesday, and escrow is supposed to close on those shopping center deals a few days after that. Goddammit. I knew this vacation was gonna cut it too close."

He picked up his lantern and guided its beam down into the plunging crevice. A colony of bats stirred to life, fluttering ghost-like through the shadowy chamber. On the stony walls of the narrow passage squirmy insects and strange cave-spiders crawled over the sand and granite, trying to hide from hungry, pale salamanders in the constant balance between death and survival.

A cool chill shuddered through his body as he watched Nature act out its little dramas of life and death. "The world can be a cruel and violent place," mused Darrel, with the realization that he might be its next victim. He felt a strange knot tightening in his stomach. He couldn't believe this was really happening. He began to think of possible consequences more serious than just the loss of his next big deal. He could really die in here!

He was gripped with a pang of sudden terror. "I've got to get out of here!"

No longer pinned bodily under the slide, he was still buried, tiny and insignificant, beneath the vastness of the Canadian Rockies. He had to figure a way out. He had a business to run back in California! No ideas sprang immediately to mind. What if he couldn't get out at all? He had read about things like this. Maybe others, flipping casually through the back pages of their morning papers, would read a cold, factual report detailing the untimely demise of one Darrel Swift.

Other thoughts nagged at his consciousness. His whole life seemed to be crashing in around him. He had been working too hard, too many days in a row, and had taken this trip to get a badly-needed change of scenery. But this was more than he had in mind. He might not even get out alive! And he wondered for a moment if he even wanted to. Successful in his own commercial real estate business and not yet thirty, Darrel was already starting to feel like an old man. He worked all day, figuring new angles to old deals, and then worried about it all night. He never stopped. And it was paying off — for a price. He had money in the bank, in stocks, in money-market funds, and in his own real-estate investments. He could buy anything he wanted. But he was tense all the time. Rushed. Pressured. He snapped at people. He felt a vague emptiness. For all the money he was making, something was still missing. His life of schedules, three-piece suits, and two-martini lunches was a step back-ward from the casual pleasures of playing Frisbee or bumming around on the beach that he had enjoyed as a poor but happy college student.

Now he was too busy. Relationships had come to feel shallow and artificial, and romantic intimacy left him feeling empty and dissatisfied. He had just completed another stormy breakup with his girlfriend, Linda Ferret, who had become increasingly possessive as their two-year relationship of nightclubs and parties deteriorated.

As the world around him grew stale and confining, Darrel had finally agreed to take some time off to sort out his thoughts away from the joy-less compulsions of his real-life monopoly game. With Alan and Lee, he had left his home and business back in Santa Barbara, California, to "get away from it all" — and now it "all" might come to a sudden end.

The immediacy of his own mortality began to set in. Seized with sudden panic, he drew his sore arm close against his body, and with the other clawed frantically against the mass of dirt and rock. He cast the beam of his lantern toward the main chamber of the cave, and realized how completely the rockslide had cut him off from the others. He called out. The only answer was silence.

He had felt no fear or danger in wandering off by himself through the darkness, despite the warnings from his more experienced companions, Alan and Lee. But now he was consumed with a strange mixture of deep regret and panic.

He tried again to yell through the mountain for help, until his voice cracked into frightened sobs. He pounded his good fist helplessly into the granite, yelling and sobbing, until he collapsed in tears against the stones. A few pebbles crumbled loose, but the rockslide remained firm, and Darrel remained trapped. He slumped dejectedly against the stones, whimpering.

* * * * *

"Oh my God!" quivered Alan. "What happened!?" He got no response from the friend at his side. "That's over where Darrel went." He called out loud, towards the rockslide — and his cousin. There was no answer.

Alan grabbed his lantern and shined the light over where Darrel had wandered off. There was a newly-fallen blockage of granite sealing off the little passageway that Darrel had gone off to explore.

Lee, Alan's companion and friend, groaned with disgust. "Now look at what he's gone off and done this time," he complained. "This could really be a problem."

"Lay off the kid," scolded Alan. "You're always picking on him. C'mon, we gotta figure out what happened and try to get him outta there."

"If he's even alive," muttered Lee.

Left unspoken was the fact that it was Darrel, youngest of the three, who was picking up the tab for this little holiday.

* * * * *

After a while, Darrel regained his composure and pressed himself close against the massive granite barrier. Groping with his hands and feet for solid footing, he inched his way up the side of the debris, climbing part way up the rock, still calling out frequently. But this only reaffirmed the extent of his isolation from the main chamber.

Clutching his backpack and lantern for security, he climbed back down to the floor of the passageway. He sat down to think, as his early panic gave way to reason. First, he decided to stop yelling so much. This could trigger another rockslide, or use up what might be a limited air supply. He sat on a rock and turned off the lantern to conserve its batteries. Sitting thoughtfully in the darkness, he considered his options for survival.

Possibly Alan and Lee could go back for help and dig him free. With a morbid chuckle, he wondered if Lee would even permit Alan to try.

But it might take days for them to get back to the nearest village, and even longer to bring back enough men and equipment to dig through all the rock and dirt. His stomach still felt weak. He had no way of guessing the extent of damage, if any, in the main chamber. He could not even be sure that Alan or Lee had even survived the rockslide. He could not depend on the remote hope of rescue aid from them.

He was a businessman. He would take action himself! He took a deep breath. His only hope would be to go further down into the passageway, where it might connect with other caves that could open up to the outside. He knew that the possibility of such an escape route was slim, but looking for it would allow him to keep physically and mentally active. Nothing had ever stopped him from taking calculated risks before.

He opened his backpack and shined his light inside, taking silent inventory of its contents. There was his basic first-aid kit, sandwiches, canned solids and liquids, and some junk food snacks. Closing up the pack, he stood up to make his way down into the tunnel.

Turning away from the boulder-locked opening, Darrel squeezed his way through the narrow corridor of stone, and started downward. As he moved deeper into the Earth, he was amazed at how straight and parallel the tilted walls remained, and how quickly he was descending along its plunging floor.

Hardly aware of time, he pressed his way down between the stone walls a few feet at a time, hour after uncounted hour, until overpowered by sudden exhaustion. He relaxed himself against the slanting walls to rest for a moment. He was so tired. The pain in his arm throbbed relentlessly. "God!" He wished it would just stop. He tried to ignore the dust and grime clinging to the stubble of beard on his sweaty, miserable face. His sandy hair, usually washed and blow-dried, felt stringy and greasy.

He wondered how long he had been descending. Pointing the lantern's steady beam at the bare spot on his sore left wrist, he remembered that he could no longer monitor the passing of time. How far had he strayed from the blocked-off opening of the cave? Did it really matter?

He was a businessman! He was rational and resourceful. He had found success by looking at problems just a little differently than anyone else, and seeing solutions that others might have overlooked. He depended on nothing but his own gutsy independence. *Ha!* Somehow it didn't seem the same. Suddenly he didn't feel so rich, so smooth, so powerful any more. There was no one around to "provide input" for a "game plan" to get out of this mess. There were only cold, empty, silent stones. He felt like a helpless little boy who had gotten lost. His business mind told him to think of ways to get out. But his body just felt like crying.

Gasping for breath, he just wanted to rest for a moment. As he pressed close to the stone wall—panting, sweating, almost sobbing—he imagined that the rocks might still be shaking from the slide. The slightest slippage of Earth movement could send the narrow separation of stone walls crashing together, crushing him into anonymous death deep inside the mountain.

He was haunted by other fears. His mind conjured up visions of creepy organisms crawling toward him through the darkness. What about larger mammal life? Could there be a bear or mountain lion nesting in the dark recesses of this cave, angry at the disturbances within its home? Possibly aroused by hunger?

He was tired, but too apprehensive about the dangers of the darkness to rest for long. Mechanically, he shoved himself away from the rocks and forced himself to go on.

The hours wore on, uncounted. Eventually, exhaustion outweighed apprehension, and Darrel Swift drifted off into the refuge of sleep.

Chapter Two

Light

Alan and Lee sat in front of the unmovable pile of granite. They had tried frantically to do something, *anything,* to move the rocks and debris and find a way through to their companion who had disappeared beneath it all.

"We've got to do something," insisted Alan.

"There's no way we can dig through it by ourselves," responded Lee. "Anyway, there's no way any human being could have survived underneath all those falling rocks."

"*If* he was under them," answered Alan. "We don't know how far he had made it into the cave, or how far the rockslide extended into the cave. As long as there is any chance he could have survived, we have to at least get in there and find out what happened."

"Well, we've tried everything we can do from here," cautioned Lee. "We don't have the kind of equipment to dig through such a rockslide. We'll have to go back to town for help."

Alan shook his head in reluctant acceptance. He knew that it would take *days* to get back to the nearest village outpost, and every moment they delayed reduced the chances of his cousin's survival.

* * * * *

Awakening some time later, Darrel sat up in the cave's dark silence. He started to resume his course through the dark, interminable corridor, but hesitated.

Rested, he was no longer just responding mechanically. "What's the use...?" he mumbled. "I'm going to die here." He quickly reconsidered. The same survival instinct that had motivated a successful career drove him deeper into the cave. Despite the hopelessness, a struggle to the end would keep him active and provide a sense of purpose. And, no matter how remote, it was still his only chance for finding a way out. And he was still concerned about how he would handle business deals waiting for him back home.

He felt hungry. He did not know how many hours he had been groping downward, nor how long he had slept. He longed for some knowledge of time, and wished his timepiece had survived the rockslide. He pulled a sandwich from the backpack. He had been pretty well prepared for a long trip, but his supplies had not anticipated such extended isolation. He could make several meals if he rationed the items thriftily. He ate the sandwich and resumed his journey.

The descent became increasingly steep. Even with the lantern, Darrel could see no end to the plunging crevice. He forged his way downward for hours, feeling greater frustration as his efforts produced nothing more than the same old footage of tired granite.

He thought of Alan and Lee on the outside. He wondered what, if anything, they might be doing to dig through and come after him. He wondered if they were even alive. He thought of various friends and business acquaintances, and how they might react to his disappearance. He even thought about Linda Ferret, the ex-girlfriend he had left behind. He had wanted to get away from an unpleasant situation, but this was certainly over-doing it.

He pulled a small sack of potato chips out of his pack and ripped open the bag. Quickly devouring its meager contents and washing it all down with one of his last Diet Dr. Peppers, he still felt hungry. Wadding up the potato chip bag, he tossed it blindly away. He picked up the empty soda can, and tossed it as far as he could down the passageway ahead. The clanking echo gradually faded as the can bounced further down the cave, reaffirming the constant steadiness of the plunging descent ahead.

He got out a roll of cookies and loosened the wrapping. He paused. He could no longer afford to disregard limitations. He would have to be more cautious in rationing his precious nourishment. He forced himself to twist the wrapping shut. He returned it untouched to his pack and he turned to follow the beam of his lantern deeper into the cave.

The descent continued.

He rested again, and resumed his further descent. The cycles of sleeping, waking, eating, and climbing were repeated over and over, as the dreaming, wakefulness, and nightmares blurred together in a timeless confusion of darkness. He forged his way deeper and deeper into the Earth. The dusty air of the caves took hold of his sweaty body and caused him to feel dirty and unpleasant.

Darrel marveled at the Forces of Nature that could slice such a vast, straight fissure so perfectly through a whole mountain. Was it the fault-line remnant of some ancient earthquake? ...or maybe not so ancient? He shuddered. If the mountain were to move again, another rockslide or quake might send the fissure walls crashing shut, squishing him like a trapped bug.

Sleeping intermittently against the sheets of rock that imprisoned him, he pressed on through the warmth and darkness of the interminable cave passage. And the temperature inside seemed to be rising.

As the heat increased, he sometimes imagined that the tunnel would eventually open up into a great furnace. At other times, he was haunted by that recurring fear of the walls crashing in on him. One way or another, it would take him to Hell.

Eventually the passage leveled off and opened up into a vast cavern. Darrel was weak and tired, and sick of the heat and darkness, but was relieved to be out of the narrow corridor that had imprisoned him.

He stretched his legs. He searched the vast hollow with his light and was unable to see the end of it. Perhaps there would be new passages extending from this chamber. Perhaps this was the end. Darrel stumbled forward, then staggered to the cavern floor. After so long in the slanting walls of the tunnel, this was the first time he could lie down, fully extended.

He shifted the loose rocks into the most comfortable possible arrangement, and sprawled out in his stony nest. Guarding his wounds, he experimented with every position denied him during his uncounted days in the narrow passageway. This wasn't exactly the Ritz, but at least he could finally get some rest, and he lapsed dreamily into sleep.

Awakening later, Darrel was awake and refreshed. His pains seemed less acute. It was the first good sleep he had enjoyed since the rockslide. He wondered how long he had been asleep. He didn't even know what day or week it might be! But at least he felt better. He renewed his determination to find a way out of this dark, sweaty oven, or die trying.

Out of nowhere, Darrel imagined a distant sound.

He sat up. It sounded like the faraway dripping and trickling of flowing water. An underground spring? An opening to freedom? Darrel jumped to his feet. On this level floor, Darrel could move faster. But the uncertainty of odd cave formations also required greater caution, and Darrel had become deceptively sure-footed through long hours in the plunging sameness of the narrow passage.

As Darrel scanned eagerly ahead with his light, he became increasingly excited, and did not watch closely enough the cave floor immediately in front of him. He failed to notice a wide fissure, and suddenly found himself stumbling into empty space.

He let out a yelp as he plunged down through the darkness. He somersaulted in air, and came to rest with a sudden thud, sitting upright in a pile of soft, loose silt. He had lost a little wind, and was shaken up, but was amazingly unhurt. He stood up to walk, and felt a slight limp, but was relieved to have landed so well in such a long fall. Even his sore arm, still bruised and aching, was no worse off than before.

His relief turned to sudden panic when he found he was no longer holding his lantern. Groping frantically around, he was not able to locate it. Perhaps it was smashed on an unseen rock. Perhaps it was intact and hidden very near in the darkness.

Even with his lantern, the darkness had become an oppressive burden. But now it was not only dark, but *completely black* everywhere! He could see nothing at all.

"No! No! No!" he sobbed. Wasn't it bad enough to be trapped under a mountain in the middle of nowhere? Now, with an almost-empty knapsack and not much else, even his limited ability to see was taken from him.

He could do nothing. He was isolated thousands of miles from his California home, and thousands of feet into the Earth, helpless and alone.

Trying not to face the hopelessness of his situation, he returned his attention to his struggle against the caves. The whole thing seemed so pointless now, but he couldn't just lie down and die. He thought of the thousands of sightless people who had learned to live and work through lifetimes of darkness. He did not have the same special training, but he would not go down without a fight.

Unable to see, he focused his power of hearing to the cave's silence. The sound of flowing water was now very near.

He stood up, and waved his good hand through the darkness, groping for obstacles. The sticky softness of a cobweb gathered around his fingers. He shook his hand with sudden quickness, banging it painfully against the top of the cave. "Dammit!" he grimaced, pulling his smarting fingers close to his body and writhing with the sharp, sudden stinging.

He regained his composure and listened again for the water. Inching toward its rushing sounds, his first blind step was into a rocky depression, causing him to stumble. He picked himself up and searched timidly with his hands for any low barriers of stone or stickiness.

He took another wobbly step along the uneven floor, but was so overcome by the uncertainty of total blackness that he had to stop. He felt so blind. So helpless. So *scared*. "Damn!" he muttered, squatting down into a safer position.

On all fours, he crawled toward the sound of the water. He was dirty and thirsty. While the pervasive Darkness had broken him into fearful submission, still he wanted the water so bad he could feel its freshness on his dry tongue and sweaty brow.

Darrel groped blindly forward, following the rough, stony textures that passed beneath his fingertips. Bumping into the cave's hidden formations and seeing nothing but what he could imagine, he finally stumbled into a shallow stream flowing down through the caves.

He shrieked with hysterical ecstasy and splashed in the water. The feel of cool wetness excited him. He washed his face, and rubbed the water in his hair, and drank it. Gently bathing the bruised tenderness of his arm, he savored the coolness of partial relief. Even in the totality of darkness, he imagined the water to be sparkling with beauty. This was the first hopeful development in a long chain of frustrations. Refreshed with new enthusiasm, he resolved to follow his course along this subterranean stream. It would give him a sense of direction — possibly lead to a way out of the caves — but in any case, provide security.

In this canyon carved by the cool flow of water, a pleasant breeze broke up the oppressive heat. Most puzzling was that the cool air seemed to rise from below, contrary to what he would expect. This was a relief, but still there was the darkness....

After a little while and some practice, Darrel could make his way a little better, without stumbling and bumping into things so much. He could even stand up and feel his way through the darkness in an upright position. Hour after uncounted hour, he made his way with increasing tactile proficiency. Still, he longed for even a dim glimmer of real light.

After descending gradually along the stream for some time, drinking often but eating only little of his fast-disappearing food supply, he could hear that there was a sharp drop and a waterfall up ahead. He was apprehensive about climbing down through rocks and cliffs in darkness too thick to allow visibility, but he had nowhere else to go. He approached the edge of the rocks. Remembering his earlier fall, he groped through the darkness one slow inch at a time, feeling for the unseen cliff. Backing over the edge, he climbed slowly downward over the dry rocks at the side of the falls.

As he pressed cautiously downward, he was amazed at how well he had learned to maneuver with just his sense of touch. He quickly realized that the distance down was greater than he had first imagined. Resting where possible on ledges, he maintained his course, unable to measure time or distance, but hoping the rocks would level off soon. He became increasingly concerned as the plunge continued with no end in sight.

Finally, as he was resting on a flat sheet of rock, his foot slipped on a wet spot, and he rolled into a cool spray of water as it streamed across a wide area of the broad, smooth surface. As he sped quickly down the steep waterslide, unable to see, he imagined with panic that this was the end. He could smash into an unseen boulder at any moment, or topple over the side of another deadly cliff.

With mixed relief, he was eventually washed to the side of the main flow and slid to a halt on the smooth, dry rock. In one sense, he wanted to end this terrible nightmare. On the other hand, he was still alive, and not badly hurt for all he had gone through. His clothes were torn, and his side was scratched almost as badly as his arm. But it could have been a lot worse, and he was able to keep going.

A the stream leveled off somewhat, though still downward in a steeper incline than where he had first found it, Darrel paused to rest, and let himself sleep. He awoke much later feeling refreshed, except for the sharp throbs of pain in his side and arm. He ate a little, and washed his face and wounds. The cool water stung with relief.

His attention was abruptly captured by a tiny object from across the stream that made his heart leap. He couldn't tell what it was, except that it cast a gentle, continuous glow of *light!*

Darrel splashed across the stream and stared at the object. It was a small, unevenly rounded fluorescent pebble casting an eerie glow. The tiny stone was not really enough to relieve the ponderous darkness, or even to really allow a clear glimpse of his surroundings, but it was the first time in days that he had been able to see anything at all!

He reached to touch it, but stopped. What if it were radioactive? Or poisonous? "What the hell," he thought, quickly weighing risks against possible benefits. "I'm going to die here anyway. If they ever find my body, this little light will be with it. I won't die in *total* darkness."

He touched it gingerly. It was not warm to the touch, as he thought it should be. It was a phenomenon new to Darrel's experience. He didn't even know what to call it! Scooping it up in his hand, he gathered up the rest of his belongings and resumed his trek down through the caves.

Strange thoughts filled his mind to while away the eternity of the caves. He had taken this vacation to sort out his life, and now he was face to face with death. What good were all the buildings he had ever sold? Where was all that money he had hustled out of his land deals back in California? Who would even miss him? He had never really taken the time to develop close relationships, or cultivate the simple pleasures of everyday living. Friendships had either been casual tools of business, or shallow acquaintances, and family ties were generally remote. Romances had endured only until the novelty wore off. He thought again of Linda, who he had left behind. What would she do when she heard what had happened? Who would even care? "Oh God!" he screamed, clasping his good arm to his throbbing wounds. "Just let me die!" But he was really just beginning to realize how badly he wanted to salvage his life.

* * * * *

Emergency search and rescue crews were quickly assembled in the small Canadian mining town, while Alan took care of the unpleasant task of notifying friends and relatives back in California.

Even so, more than a week had already passed since the cave-in. Even if Darrel could have survived the initial rockslide, there was increasing doubt that he could also survive an extended period of time underground without adequate food, water, and light.

Darrel's old girlfriend, Linda, took the news particularly hard. "He's buried under a *what!?*" she shrieked. "Well, you just better go in there and get him out. You knew damn well he didn't have enough experience to go digging around in caves. If he hadn't been around to bankroll your little trip, you never would have been able to talk Lee into letting him come along. What the hell was he doing wandering off alone? If anything happens to him, I'll hold you two responsible. It might even be criminal negligence...."

"We're doing everything we can," Alan assured her. "We'll find him."

As soon as the rescue party was ready, Alan and Lee led them back over the mountains. With helicopters, mobile equipment, and the latest in available rescue equipment, the journey back to where they had discovered the small entrance to the cave was much faster than their slow, tedious hike from the cave to the town.

* * * * *

Darrel followed the cool underground stream deeper into the fractured layers of the Earth's crust. Climbing, swimming, groping through the darkness, Darrel combined uncharacteristic personal courage with the same drive that had built his business empire, fighting against the odds.

At the base of one small waterfall, he noticed a little cluster of seven small fluorescent stones, which combined to cast the first real sensation of light since he had lost his lantern so long ago. He picked up each little light and set it in his pack except the largest, which was about the size of a misshapen baseball. This stone generated just enough light to let him see the area immediately around him.

In the dim light of the glowing stones, he became aware that the cavernous tunnel branched off frequently into many narrow passageways, away from his cherished stream. He chose to continue following the security of the water, but with growing curiosity about his new environment.

Throughout his cycles of climbing, resting, and sleeping, he remained aware that hours and days must be passing, but without any real knowledge of time or distance. Eventually, his supply of food was exhausted. He cast his empty backpack aside and went on alone with just his little glowing stones.

As food ceased to be available, the fluorescent stones were gradually becoming more numerous. Before long, Darrel was no longer keeping count of each stone, and only carried one large stone. The totality of darkness gave way to the eerie glow of the scattered little stones. To Darrel's eyes, long accustomed to complete darkness, even the dim shadows of these faint little stones were enough to make him feel comfortable. He no longer expected to find a way out of the caves, but as he plunged deeper into the bosom of the Earth, he was motivated with awe and curiosity for each strange new discovery as his descent wore on.

Time continued uncounted. Days passed. Possibly weeks. Darrel forged down through tunnels, through caverns, across underground plateaus, climbing down cliffside waterfalls, swimming across pools of water when the cavern walls closed in too narrow against the stream — moving, sleeping, and hungering in the dim light of the pale glowing stones. Darrel pressed his way deeper into the mountain, hungrily and wearily, with pains in his side and his arm. His clothes and shoes were wet and tattered, and he had only water and pale light to lead him on. Against Time's relentless erosion of his energies, his hungered body steadily felt its strength being drained away.

Desperate with hunger and fatigue, Darrel began to confuse reality with his nightmares. He missed his office. He longed for the security of its hectic pace and more familiar pressures. The noises of crashing, tumbling boulders still resonated in his mind, and he often imagined a sensation of shaking in the now-silent cave. Sometimes he imagined the busy voices of employees at work in his office, and the steady clatter of typists playing percussion to an orchestra of ringing phones, piped-in Muzak, and the hum of office machinery. Sometimes he wasn't completely sure whether it was a cave he was trapped in, or if he was just stuck back in his office. It was only when he turned to answer a question from one of the office girls, and banged his face against a head of stone, that he realized how desperate he was for human conversation — if not the exchange of great ideas, at least a little idle gossip — any kind of involvement with a living, conscious mind.

He stumbled onward, down through the caves. He staggered into the side of a cavern wall, bumping his sore arm. He was weak and hungry. His body throbbed with pain. He felt that death was finally near. He had struggled a long time, but Death would finally win. He sobbed into the stones. He had fought hard for Life, and he had struggled with determination but....

He looked up. Down one of the caverns leading away from the stream there was a huge fluorescent boulder, not more than a thousand yards away. He wasn't imagining it, it was really there. No, it wasn't one of the glowing rocks; it was a break in the rocks, with a flood of bright light pouring in. It was not the dim light of small, scattered little stones, but a bright light, like the outside world. He jumped with renewed energy! Had he defied impossible odds to find a way out of the caves?

Darrel was still aching from pain and hunger, but the bright glow of light gave him hopeful, renewed energy. He stumbled toward it with great effort. Sweat and dirt dripped across his unshaven face, and he splashed through shallow puddles, groping half-crazed with a blend of hopeful energy and the desperation of fatigued starvation.

He pulled himself to the lighted opening, and slithered through the narrow breaks in the rocks. He shielded his face with his hand and flinched with momentary blindness as his eyes reacted to the sudden brightness after uncounted weeks imprisoned in darkness.

As his eyes adjusted to the light, he perceived that it was not the same intense brightness as the sunlight of the Outside. He had not found his way out of labyrinthine caverns. He had stumbled into a vast underground canyon. Millions of huge fluorescent boulders were packed tightly together along the uneven ceiling of the cave, casting a pale and gentle light throughout the Great Cavern.

The pale, shadowy light created a magical aura of otherworldliness. He could see that this expansive cavern extended down into a great valley of rocks, plants, and waterflows. The rocks spread down through many levels of fractured caverns, canyons, and plateaus.

Far below, the cavern floor was broken into layers of caves and grottoes, adorned with gnarled cave-trees, and generously dressed with a lush spray of tropical foliage, nourished by the fluorescent light and watered by crisscrossing streams and ponds that seemed to fall in gentle cascades everywhere. There were rocks and plants of every type — smooth boulders, ragged fractures, oddly-shaped limestone formations and quartzine crystals, covered with every kind of greenery — which seemed to blend with the twisting roots and branches of the cave-trees growing out of them.

Near the waterflows, light from the glowing stones passed through sprays of watery mists and prismatic crystals to generate fantastic patterns of rainbows and shadows around the ponds. Darrel beheld with awe an underground world that seemed to stretch for many miles beyond him.

Darrel's heart sank in not having found a return to the outside world, but he stared in amazement at the panorama of light and vegetation. Not too long ago he would have been seeing the raw materials from which to develop new investment opportunities. Now, the light, water, and vegetation offered nothing more than a chance for survival.

With a hopeful optimism bordering on insanity, but still physically weak, he staggered down into the valley. He straggled over a rocky boulder, lumbered across the knotted, low-hanging branches of surrounding trees, and sloshed through the shallow, cascading ponds. He quickly found his mortal flesh aching again. He stumbled repeatedly, fighting to maintain consciousness. The hunger and exhaustion had been only temporarily relieved by the euphoria of hope.

Slowing his pace, he eased himself onto a rock to rest.

He was startled by a nearby noise in the brush. He looked up. It must be another hallucination.

Through eyes blurred with pain and sweat, he caught the images of two small men, not more than four or five feet tall, with shaggy-hair and smooth, brownish-gray complexions. They were standing a short distance across the brush-covered rocks, staring at him with big, round eyes. One of the little men gave a nimble leap, and landed in a semi-squatting position nearby, staring at Darrel with great curiosity. The other little man hopped into the lower branches of a sprawling, twisted tree, and scrambled out to a position almost directly over Darrel.

Darrel waved his hand at them, to send these new nightmares away. The images did not disappear.

The two small men were pointing toward Darrel and chattering excitedly.

Retreating, the slender, wiry figures moved quickly over the rocks. Dressed in loosely-fitting outfits fashioned from a light, delicate fabric, the two men danced with great agility across the layered grottoes, like barefoot pixies, while Darrel slipped quietly into unconsciousness.

Chapter Three

Discovery

Darrel Swift's eyes fluttered open. The world was a dizzy blur of motion. He could see strange faces hovering over him, staring. Strange sounds swirled in his ears and his head. He felt tired. Weak. He started to sit up, but his body just fell back into sleep.

Some time later, he again awoke. His eyes drifted slowly open, to a dim awareness of granite overhead. He no longer felt any distortions or lapses of perception. He turned his head to the side. Where was he? Around him was a confusing blend of impressions — of cold, rocky firmness blending with gnarled branches and delicate tropical foliage; of colored fabric softness; of delicate fluorescent stones — in bizarre and exotic patterns of arrangement. But for the delicate sounds of musical chimes and gentle woodwinds playing softly in the background, a quiet stillness filled the room. He could hear and feel the steady rhythm of his heart and lungs. His body was surrounded by softness. He patted around with his hands. Someone had placed him in a pile of soft bedding. After a moment, he realized that the incessant throbbing of pain in his arm and side had somehow been made to disappear. But he was not entirely without discomfort. There was a rumbling uneasiness in his belly — a gnawing hunger. That was a good sign. His healthy body, now rested, demanded sustenance.

Darrel was annoyed with himself for having gotten into such a mess. His eyes darted around the cave "room," looking for any clue as to how he might handle this strange, new situation. He groped for his backpack and lantern, but found nothing. He quickly recalled that these had been lost in the darkness of the caves. He felt weak and helpless. But at least he had *made it!* He was *alive!* While he wanted to get up and be *doing* something as soon as possible, still he didn't feel like pushing himself quite as hard as he used to. He would take things a little easier.

His gaze drifted across the new surroundings. He was alone, in a small cave lit by glowing fluorescent stones. Brightly-colored fabrics were draped across the cave-room "walls" in geometric patterns of golden orange, pastel violet, and brilliant lime, blended with a generous spray of delicate primeval foliage growing from the stony sides of the cave. Each perception raised more questions than answers. Where was this place? Who were the "benefactors" that had brought him here? What did they intend to do with him?

Glancing up, he saw one of the little cave-people poke a curious head into the cave. It was a young female, tiny and slender. He guessed she might be about his own age or younger. Her soft brown eyes sparkled with curious delight, and she began to chatter unintelligibly when she saw that he was awake. "Cute chick," he thought, suddenly conscious of just how superficial his reaction seemed. His most immediate concern was in trying to stay alive in this strange place, and in answering the thousands of questions that were flooding into his brain.

As the girl approached Darrel timidly, continuing her strange monologue of foreign sounds, two older men and a little boy followed her into the room. The three stayed back out of the way, in protective readiness.

Darrel studied the cave-people intently. They were clearly human, but did not fit into any of the racial or ethnic stereotypes with which he was familiar. They were somewhat small in stature, like slender pygmies. They were wiry and agile, and moved easily over the rocks and foliage of their cave environment. Their distinct half-gray, half-golden complexion was neither white nor brown nor yellow. Their wide-eyed facial features generated an impression of childlike wonderment.

The girl drew cautiously nearer, talking in soft, reassuring tones a language that Darrel could not understand. She was slender and pretty, with silky brown hair that fell down around her shoulders, and big innocent cave-people eyes. In the pale light, her skin coloration appeared in one moment a golden brown, and the next moment a soft tone of gray. Her pixie figure was accented by the delicate garment that she wore, similar to the knee-length tunics that the men wore, except that her feminine form projected a different image. Darrel noticed that, like the others, she wore nothing on her feet.

When Darrel sat up suddenly, the girl jumped back a step and squealed. Darrel placed his feet on the stony floor, and noticed that his shoes had been removed. The girl turned and whispered to the others, who remained quiet and motionless in the background. Cautiously, she turned again toward Darrel and slowly drew closer to him.

Darrel was still plagued by a persistent sensation of hunger. Back in the outside world, he could have enjoyed the finest meal available, in the finest facilities on the West Coast. But here he was no longer a big shot. In the Outside, he could have anything he wanted. Here, he couldn't even order a cheap snack. He was a helpless stranger, at the mercy of these exotic little cave-people.

But at least he was still alive. And the girl's friendly demeanor made him feel more at ease. He could no longer concern himself with luxuries of the past. He was a progressive, forward-moving person. He must look ahead. As he had done in his own world, here also he would do whatever was necessary in order to make it. He would learn to get along with these cave people and understand them.

The gentle melody of chimes and woodwinds still floated in from somewhere in the background, as the girl continued her unintelligible monologue. What could she be saying? He wanted so badly to know what she planned to do with him. He wished he could just say something, anything, that she would understand from him. Still, he had to try to communicate.

Coming from an outside world of many cultures and nations, Darrel understood the simple problem of a language barrier. Not knowing to what extent, if any, there might be cultural diversity within the caves, he feared the possibility that this civilization may have existed in isolation for centuries, and might have no concept of differing languages. They might consider his babbling to be that of a crazy person.

Darrel looked at the girl and pointed toward his mouth in awkward gestures. "Food," he said.

"Foodah?" responded the girl, uncertain of the strange sound.

"Food," repeated Darrel, motioning to his mouth again, and continuing to make gestures that would convey the idea of eating.

"Food!" laughed the girl, as she understood his meaning. She turned to the trio behind her and babbled something in her own strange language. She returned her attention to Darrel, speaking very softly and slowly, as if her exaggerated enunciation would make him understand. As she spoke, the little boy brought in a stone-hewn dish filled with a light brownish paste. The girl dipped a flattened wood utensil into the paste and lifted a small taste of the stuff to her lips.

"Food!" she exclaimed. *"Zatah!"*

"Zatah!" repeated Darrel, not sure if the word meant "food" or the specific paste-like substance which had been brought to him. The girl placed the stone dish and the same utensil she had just used firmly into Darrel's hand and gave him a broad smile. Darrel accepted his hostess' gracious offering.

He scraped the wooden instrument across the gooey stuff and held it up to close scrutiny. He pinched off a sampling, and rubbed it between his thumb and forefinger. He had no idea what it could possibly be made from. He gingerly melted a little of the brownish paste onto his tongue. He found it bland, but not unpleasant. Desperate with hunger, he wolfed down this *"zatah"* and an additional serving, and found it very appetizing. As he was finishing the paste, the little boy brought the girl some water for him in the same kind of stone dish.

Darrel dipped his hand into the water and sprinkled some droplets on the girl's arm. "Water," he announced.

"Watah?" puzzled the girl. *"Metah! Metah!"*

After his meal, Darrel felt much better, and his thoughts were filled with curiosity about the people and places of this strange underground environment. But he was unable to verbalize even the most simple of his thoughts and questions to his foreign "hosts."

He looked at the girl, and at the others who were still behind her. He wondered what her name was. He wondered if cave-people even had names. "My name is Darrel," he said, speaking slow and clear. "What is your name?" His only answer was a puzzled stare.

He decided to try again. "Me, Darrel," he said, tapping on his chest. "Me, Darrel."

The girl quickly got the idea. "Zhana," she said, pointing to herself.

"Medarrel," she said, pointing to Darrel, very pleased with herself.

Darrel tapped his chest again. "Darrel. Darrel. Darrel." He pointed to the girl and repeated, "Zhana," and then to himself, "Darrel."

The girl smiled.

She took Darrel's hand and led him over to the two men, who were almost as tall as Darrel's shoulder. As they walked, Darrel noticed that the stony floor of the cave was smooth and polished against his naked feet, yet cool to the touch. The girl pressed his hand against her own chest and repeated, "Zhana." Touching Darrel's hand to the first man, she announced, "Rimani," and to the other man, "Laros." Touching Darrel's hand to the little boy, she said, "Jamak." Darrel repeated each name, clumsily aware that it did not sound the same as when Zhana pronounced them.

Standing alongside the others in the tattered remnants of his American clothes, Darrel was ragged and unshaven, and felt dirty all over. Zhana sensed his discomfort. Still holding him by the hand, she led him through a veiled doorway into another cavern "room." There was a shallow grotto pooling with water in the middle and steaming with heat from a natural hot springs, fed by a gentle cascading waterfall, and surrounded by a lush garden of plants set among quartzine crystals and limestone formations. Light from the fluorescent stones filtered through the misting watersprays and prismatic quartz crystals, causing gentle rainbows to shimmer over the pool's surface.

Feeling the firm but gentle grip of Zhana's little hand around his, Darrel at least felt a sense of reassurance that he was not among barbarians who might be waiting to tear him apart. Yet he was still apprehensive. Was he to be a slave? A plaything for the girl? An object of public curiosity?

Zhana brought him a fresh robe, and some strange tools hewn from rock with which to groom himself. With gestures and foreign words, she tried to demonstrate how to use the items, but couldn't make any sense to Darrel. The girl called in the two men, and left.

Back in the outside world, Darrel had no reputation as a prude. But in the uncertainty of this strange place, he turned to make sure the cave-girl was out of sight before undressing. He slipped out of his dirty, ragged jeans and set them carefully beside the small bathing pool. He looked up at Laros and Rimani who watched his every move with intense fascination. Darrel felt somewhat uneasy standing in front of the two cave dwellers without his clothes on.

Stepping down over a small, round stone, and slipping between the feathery blades of silky, tropical ferns, he dipped a toe into the pool to test the water. It was moderately hot, not too far from the preference he would have set for a hot bath at home. He noted that this kind of natural mineral spring might make a good "hot tub" for his use while in this strange land.

He stepped fully into the water and immersed himself. It felt warm and refreshing. He rubbed the water over himself to melt away the dirt and grime, and wished for nothing more than a simple bar of soap. As he bathed, Laros used the odd stones to shave Darrel's face clean like the other men, while Rimani tried to arrange the shaggy locks of his sandy hair.

When the job was completed, Darrel dried himself and put on the robe Zhana had given him. He glanced again at his old, tattered rags. He noticed his wallet hanging out of the back pocket. It held all the money, credit cards, and identification that had ruled his life in the outside world. What use would they be here? Still, after long years of habit, he could not discard such treasures so easily. Certainly he would be able to find some unobtrusive corner where his clothes and effects could be tucked away for safekeeping.

He looked at his reflection in the pool. He fitted the cave-style robe around himself in different poses, to see how he looked. Apart from his height and his fair coloration, he now fit right in with the other people in this strange place. But he was not like the others. He didn't know the people, the mannerisms, the language, or the customs. He paused and grimaced. "What the hell am I doing here?" he thought to himself. He should be modeling a tailored suit from Pierre Cardin and hand-crafted shoes of the finest leather, instead of bare feet and simple garments from these natives. Still, he was alive. And he would have to learn to get along — and get ahead — among these primitives.

His concern lessened somewhat as the girl returned. She made it easy for him to feel optimistic. She looked Darrel over closely, playfully tousled his strange sandy-blond hair with a big smile, and said something that sounded like it was meant to be complimentary. Darrel smiled back. Cleaned and fed and rested, he felt refreshed and truly alive for the first time in recent memory. The last vestiges of his long nightmare had been washed away.

Zhana continued to question the Stranger in her unintelligible language. She spoke slowly and carefully, trying to make Darrel understand.

Dazhan

"Agu dikol enteh ongut?" Getting no response, she repeated the question, with even greater emphasis on each sound. Darrel felt helpless. How could he expect to get ahead if he couldn't even understand the simplest of phrases? He quickly decided that survival and success depended on learning to communicate. And, he wanted the girl to know just how badly he wanted to understand.

Zhana's expression grew suddenly alive with new enlightenment. She excitedly led Darrel into a small cave-room off to the side of the place where he had first regained consciousness. This new room was quite small. In the center was a massive granite workbench that dominated the tiny chamber. The surface of the huge table was polished to a smooth, almost glassy finish. An arrangement of shelves, containing strange artifacts new to Darrel's experience, was cut out of the stone walls. Zhana motioned him over to the workbench, while she went over to the shelves. She presented to Darrel a rigid but tissue-thin sheet of a metallic substance that he could not identify. He set it on the workbench. With a jewel-tipped stylus, Zhana etched a sequence of exotic characters from right to left. Pointing to the foreign script she repeated her question, again with careful emphasis on each sound. *"Agu dikol enteh ongut?"*

Darrel gently took the stylus from Zhana's hand, and pressed it into the thin sheet of metal. "My name is Darrel Swift," he printed in careful, orderly figures. "I am from Santa Barbara, California." He slowly repeated the words aloud in English. He repeated the name "Darrel," which she had already learned, and carefully printed "D-A-R-R-E-L" on the metallic page. He then repeated the name "Zhana" and carefully printed the girl's name next to his own.

Zhana stared at him quietly, with pensive understanding. Then she broke into another wide grin as she recovered the stylus and scribbled her own strange characters below where he had printed his own name. She pointed to her writing and said, "Darrel." She etched a circle around the two words to show that they referred to the same name. She did the same with her own name, reviewing from right to left the sound of each character.

Darrel pointed to various objects and gave their names in English. Zhana repeated each name in her own language, as Darrel listened carefully. Finally, he pointed to one of the little glowing stones. He did not have an English word for the object. Zhana was quick to provide her own vocabulary: *"Kibih. Kibihni."*

"Kibihkibihni?" puzzled Darrel.

Realizing that she had confused Darrel by giving two words for the same object, she tried a different approach. She took one of the fluorescent stones and held it in front of Darrel. "Kibih," she said. Gathering several more of the luminous stones from around the room, she set them in a row behind the first. She pointed to each stone individually and said,

38

"Kibih" to each one. Scooping all the stones together, she motioned to the whole group and said, *"Kibihni."* Darrel understood that she was referring to singular and plural forms of the same word. At any rate, he now had a name for the wonderful little lights which had brightened his world when life was at its darkest moment.

Darrel would soon come to learn that Zhana would be playing an important role as his teacher, and he would learn that her selection for this position was not accidental. Despite her youthful age, she was an important figure in developing and coordinating programs to work with the social and educational problems of children or adults. Back when Darrel was found half dead near the rocky opening of the great cavern, it was under the direction of the highest authorities that he was taken to a little suite of caves near the cave-home where Zhana lived with her parents, Rimani and Lena. Thus, Zhana would be near the Stranger to give personal attention to making his life comfortable and developing communication.

*   *   *   *   *

The rescue team continued its digging and excavation efforts. They had to move slowly, inch by tedious inch, so as not to cause another rockslide, and so they wouldn't dig right through the remains of Darrel Swift if they should encounter them. By now, weeks had passed since Darrel's disappearance, and there was little hope of finding him alive.

The group paused for a break and passed around a six-pack of beers. Alan was in one of his more philosophical moods. "Darrel was an okay guy," he reflected. He had grown up with his younger cousin, and they had gone through a lot together. "Linda? Well, that's between her and Darrel. Who knows how a person is going to react when something like this happens." He finished his beer and resumed digging along with the others. "Oh well, she's paying us to try to find him … at least it's a job."

Suddenly, the massive resistance of the granite barrier fell limp as they poked through, to the emptiness of air on the other side. Alan called excitedly to the others as he chipped away at the opening, widening it enough for grown men to pass through. After long weeks of tedious labor up on the mountainside, they had finally tunneled through the rockslide. But the real task was just beginning. They still had to find whatever might be left of Darrel.

Alan and Lee and the others crawled through the granite tunnel and were amazed to discover the same slanting passage that had intrigued Darrel so many weeks ago. Pressed between the narrow walls of stone, they followed downward along its plunging floor.

"There's no sign of him," noted one of the men.

"Maybe he's buried somewhere under the rockslide," suggested Lee. "We can't dig through all the granite in the cave!"

The beam of Alan's lantern caught the reflection of something further down in the passageway. It was an empty can of Diet Dr. Pepper, with junk food wrappers scattered loosely around. It was clear that Darrel had at least made it as far as this slanting passage.

"Let's go a little deeper," Alan decided.

* * * * *

After Darrel's brief initiation to the problems of language and literacy, Zhana led him upward through several levels of cave-rooms whose arrangement was too orderly not to have been carved out by deliberate human hands. Finally, they ascended through a short inclined tunnel and out into the floor of the great cavern that Darrel had first seen from its cliffside opening far above.

Outside the carefully carved out cave dwelling, the stony surface was no longer smooth and gentle against Darrel's bare feet. He felt the prickling and poking of each rocky point. He wondered if his feet would toughen through time, or if he should try to find his discarded footwear.

Now, down in one of the valleys of that Great Cavern, he looked out across the multi-layered plateaus and canyons, covered with foliage and extending out to the endless reaches of the expansive grottoed cavern. He was amazed that such a place could exist thousands of feet into the depths of the Earth, and wondered silently how many other tunneled homes might be below the visible surface.

Far above, millions of fluorescent kibihni combined to generate an unending profusion of light. The light, rainbows and generous flows of water created a lush subterranean garden.

As Zhana pointed descriptively toward the scenery, explaining everything in beautifully unintelligible phrases, an agile figure leaped over the rocks and plants, landing barefooted on the rocks, and gripping the stony formations with his toes as he crouched nearby. The man was promptly joined by a woman, and followed quickly by others until a small crowd had gathered on the nearby rocks and in the lower branches of surrounding trees. News had spread fast, and they all wanted to see and touch the Stranger.

The little cave-people crowded around, pointing towards Darrel and chattering noisily. Darrel looked into the excited faces and pointing fingers of the gathering crowd, frightened and embarrassed. His first impulse was to run, but where could he go? Remembering his resolution to take things easier and get along with the natives, he tried to relax. He turned to Zhana for reassurance. She was busy holding back the crowd, while taking obvious delight in babbling the whole story of her experiences thus far with the Stranger. Darrel chuckled at the humanness of his hostess.

He again looked over the faces of those gathered around. This was no "angry mob," and he felt there was nothing to fear. They still chattered noisily among themselves, with curious fascination. But they meant no harm. There was a festive air, as if they all knew each other.

As additional people gathered, a small band of musicians settled into the group, playing their simple melodies of chimes, woodwinds, and with the accompaniment of simple percussion instruments. There was a simplicity in the technology of their music, yet a graceful, melodic elegance in the patterns of harmony that they created. This was a happy people. They did not seem to threaten any harm. More than ever, Darrel was certain he could survive well if he could learn their customs and get along with them.

While Zhana was describing her account with wide-eyed enthusiasm to a still-increasing crowd, the people suddenly became very quiet, and backed off slightly in unison. The musicians stopped playing. Zhana stopped speaking and looked up. Darrel turned to see what might have caught the attention of the cave-people so completely.

Carried on the backs of four husky youths was an open carriage with a shriveled old man capped with a brilliant flash of white hair. The Old Man bubbled with kindly enthusiasm for the crowd, smiling eagerly in all directions as if to touch each face that drew respectfully near. He wore a simple tunic of pastel green, and received total reverence from the hushed crowd.

Darrel, standing and watching in silent awe, felt the strong presence of a person who was clearly a figure of great prominence.

The youths cleared the crowd back enough to open a space near Zhana, and set the carriage down on the ground. The Old Man motioned her to come near. She squatted down next to him on the rocks. He smiled gently as he spoke, and radiated a sweet feeling of peace to Darrel. As Zhana and the Person continued talking back and forth at great length, Zhana finally beckoned Darrel to come closer and sit down with them. He did.

The Old Man stared at Darrel for a long moment. His round, piercing eyes broke into a sparkle of delight as he smiled softly and gave a little laugh. Darrel felt a greater sense of reassurance from the presence of this man than at any time since he had come into the caves. The Old Man spoke some words that Darrel could not understand, and his wrinkled face again bubbled over with compassionate joyfulness. He seemed to smile so easily. A murmur raced through the crowd as the Old Man touched Darrel's face gently, and then drew the Stranger close with both hands in an affectionate embrace.

Darrel followed as Zhana resumed a standing position, and the Old Man was carried quickly away. The music again flowed, and a pleasant chatter again rippled through the crowd. More than ever, Darrel wanted to know what kinds of thoughts and feelings motivated this strange community of beings who had never seen real daylight. Zhana was still talking to Darrel in her unintelligible chatter. She led him back into the maze of underground rooms, and the crowd outside slowly dissipated.

Chapter Four

Unfolding

Darrel wiped his brow. A happy crowd of little cave-people closed in around him, greeting him joyfully as the first loads of dirt were drawn out from the diggings of a new cave dwelling for one of their neighbors.

A system of levers and pulleys engineered by Darrel, along with modifications in tools, greatly speeded up the efficiency of digging and removal of debris.

Darrel was the hero of the moment. He was making progress in his determination to befriend the subterranean community on whose mercy his survival depended. Several months had elapsed, uncounted in the timeless continuity of the bright fluorescent stones. Darrel planned every move carefully. He was learning the ways of the cave-people as well as he could, trying to imitate their mannerisms and habits, and blend into their culture as unobtrusively as possible. He was even adapting to bare feet and unending brightness. His feet had toughened enough so they no longer hurt each time he walked over the stony cavern floor, although he still could not grip the uneven surfaces of rocks or branches with his toes as the cave people did. The timelessness of the caves was still his most difficult adjustment. A hectic schedule of clocks and calendars had dominated his previous existence. His one advantage, which he sought to exploit at every possible opportunity, was his more technological back-ground, which he could use to carve out a position of unique value for himself. And the cave-people, with a curious fascination for the tall Stranger, were always eager for new insights into his culture and technology.

There was no shortage of opportunities for him to share. While each person here seemed to excel at his or her own particular trade, no one seemed to have a "job." The mild, protective environment of the caves generated abundant resources of food and other necessities. As needs arose for particular skills, everyone joined in to help. There was a spirit of community social fun as people shared in creating works of fine craftsmanship, with pride in the artistic quality that was happily added to even the most mundane creations.

In the unwavering steadiness of kibihni "daylight," the formality of Time was unknown, and the "rat race" nonexistent. Everything was relaxed and informal. Even work was like a hobby. Darrel's overwhelming perception was one of incredible spontaneity among the cave-people as they worked and played so freely together. And with the same determination that had driven him to success in his business, Darrel always made sure he knew where the action was, and came prepared with some original contribution to help it come off better.

As work progressed on the immediate project, a little man came up and embraced Darrel with the cheerful enthusiasm of the caves.

Rattling off a rapid-fire sequence of meaningless syllables, he expressed some kind of appreciation, which Darrel could only partially understand. Darrel slowed the man way down, and the native repeated himself in simple words and phrases within Darrel's limited vocabulary. Time and effort had not passed entirely without reward. Darrel had developed sufficient fluency to carry on awkward conversations with patient listeners on general subjects. With slow, frustrating effort, he was making progress toward his objective of getting to know the people whose world he now shared.

Still, Darrel was not entirely satisfied with the way things were going. Even now, as work progressed on the project Darrel had helped put together, he felt himself being gently squeezed out from the real center of activity. It was the same thing that always seemed to happen. Once he managed to get something started, they would manage to keep it going very nicely without him. Sure, they were nice about it. The cave-people were always nice. Smiling. Happy. Always so appreciative. They were so considerate of Darrel that after he would get things started, they would protect him from having to get his hands dirty in the real work of building cave-homes or whatever else they happened to be working on. But for now, what Darrel really wanted was to get in there alongside the others, working and sweating and learning how they talked and what kinds of things they thought about. But it never seemed to work out quite that way.

On most such occasions, Darrel would keep on trying even after he began to feel that he was being eased out of what they were doing. He would stick around, chatting with whomever he could, hoping for a chance to become more involved. But this time, feeling somewhat discouraged, he turned unnoticed and headed toward his own little suite of caves.

Making his way across the rocks and underbrush with a great deal less agility than the nimble cave-people, he met a somewhat older group of men and women gathering some of the fruit that grew wild in the almost tropical foliage of the Great Cavern. They were kindly and cheerful, like all the natives, but spoke little as they passed.

While some of the natives accorded him curious respect, as an alien being from outer-someplace, others saw him as a poor, uncultured barbarian in need of their patient understanding. Sure, these people were nice to him, too. Everyone here was. But they talked down to him, as if his intellect were as primitive as his speech, the way one might address a precocious child who might be very smart for his age but who hasn't learned his manners yet. Darrel knew only too well that he was, indeed, having some difficulty mastering the natives' very refined cultural ethic. He was awkward, and too often painfully aware of social blunders without always knowing exactly what he had done wrong. It *was* sometimes disheartening. It was especially clear when he would show his temper or express his frustrations. Such behavior seemed so foreign to the simple joyfulness of the cave-people.

Although he was never held accountable for his miscues, he did feel that, whether he was shown appreciation for his technical contributions or feeling the kindly but condescending patience of those willing to tolerate his awkwardness, there was a gulf separating him from gut-level interaction with the little cave-people.

He paused to look at his reflection in one of the ponds near his own little dwelling. He certainly didn't look like the cave-people. He was taller, and lacked their distinctive half-golden, half-gray complexion. He smiled wistfully as he tried to imagine how funny his English-accented attempts at their language must sound. With his foreign culture and mannerisms, and the subtle but elusive quality of joyfulness enjoyed by the natives, which Darrel couldn't quite put his finger on but clearly sensed he was lacking, he must really seem strange to them. "Why shouldn't they keep their distance?" he thought, revealing something of his own social perspectives.

Well, at least they were nice about it.

In silent pensiveness, Darrel completed the last steps to his own rock-hewn dwelling. He made his way down through the little cave-rooms, to the "study" where he had spent so much time struggling to understand the caves' foreign mysteries.

He paused at the entrance of his "study." Stretched across the opening was a brightly-colored banner, cut from dye-stained fabrics and etched in a sequence of the foreign characters that he was just beginning to understand. "Kibihni are bright, but not as sweet as your own human light. Be happy!"

He had little doubt as to who might have placed it there.

As the months had passed unmeasured, Zhana had worked long hours to help Darrel develop his current limited vocabulary. With slow, frustrating effort, she was also helping as he wrestled with the cave-peoples' strange script.

Zhana was a sharp, alert teacher, with clever ways of making meanings come alive for one struggling with the simplest basics. In addition to more systematic "lessons" in producing the strange characters onto the firm but tissue-thin metallic plates, she would often sneak in and decorate either his "study" or his living area with simple notes or banners which would be within his limited understanding, and fun for him to figure out. Zhana always seemed to sense just what was in his mind, and geared every action toward the perspective from which Darrel would receive it. The results were impressive. Darrel credited much of his early success in mastering the fundamentals of the language to Zhana's creative efforts in working with him. As with just a few other key natives with whom he shared frequent interaction, he did not feel separated by any "gulf" in getting along with her, and he only wished that kind of acceptance could be enjoyed more widely with the general community.

Darrel was still feeling a little discouraged from his latest failure at real acceptance by the natives. "How would I handle this as a business problem...?" he mused, with no quick answers leaping to mind. In typical fashion he resolved to try even harder. Yet, beyond mere survival or even ambition, Darrel's recent brush with survival had led him to a vague restlessness about other concerns that he couldn't quite pin down. And he sensed in the cave people that calm, quiet enjoyment that he did not understand. Perhaps there was something more than social acceptance that he wanted from his subterranean hosts.

His eyes drifted up from the little banner to a shelf piled high with metallic volumes. He decided to practice a little on his own, using native literature not selected by Zhana's careful choosing.

He noticed a sheaf of metallic pages, which was prominently placed, but invitingly small. He pulled it down. He set the volume on the glazed surface of his granite workbench and unloosed the binding with a clanking sound. He studied the title. Reading the phonetic characters from right to left as Zhana had taught him, he sounded out a single word: *"DAZHAN."*

It was not a word he had learned yet. He glanced through the text, recognizing individual characters and occasional words, and quickly realized that this material was much too advanced for a beginner.

As he was puzzling over the document, Zhana burst enthusiastically into the room. She was carrying a pastry and presented some of it to Darrel. Darrel grinned, and with a mouth still full of pastry acknowledged the cute banner that had greeted him.

Darrel looked over Zhana's delicate figure and imagined something more than mere friendship. As they became closer, he often wondered how she felt about him, and if he could ever be more than just a fascinating creature from another world to her. He fumbled with words to make a more aggressive move ... he hesitated ... "Cool it buddy," he told himself. "Don't spoil a good thing." He needed to make sure if such a move would hurt or help his chances of getting ahead. And he did not want to risk unknown consequences for whatever might be thought of as an improper act.

Instead, he inquired about the reading material that he had been unable to decipher. Perhaps it would provide a clue toward understanding this people who now provided the social framework in which he had to operate if he ever again hoped to get ahead.

Zhana gathered it up and returned it to the shelf. "That is the Ancient Text of *Dazhan*," she explained, careful to select words from her language within Darrel's understanding.

"Ancient Text?!" His eyes lit up. This might be just the tool for gaining better insight into the cave-peoples' outlook on life — additional awareness that might help him in getting ahead. But he was also self-conscious about his frequent social blunders, and hoped he had not been irreverent. Still, he wanted to pursue this new discovery a little further. He fumbled with the task of formulating a question out of his limited foreign vocabulary: "*'Dazhan'* — what does it mean?"

Zhana smiled, and attempted to explain the word. "*Dah*" was interpreted as meaning "joy." The Book presented the joy of human happiness as the ultimate standard of value. "*Zhan*," from which his hostess' own name was derived, was explained as "compassionate." In the grammar (with adjectives following their nouns, unlike English) the contraction "*Dazhan*" formed a new word to describe the happy feeling enjoyed in certain types of compassionate interactions. The book itself was a brief summary of how those interactive processes operate.

Darrel was suspicious about any concept of true "compassion" or anything that claimed people could ever do something without ultimately expecting something in return for themselves. Still, he kept a straight face. He must not let his hosts perceive anything less than total enthusiasm on his part. And, in any case, he did feel a genuine curiosity about the little "book." He might find their myths and legends fascinating, and he did need to understand them better if he ever expected to get ahead.

Zhana looked into Darrel's eyes, and was not sure exactly what she saw. But, whatever his motives, she could see that his interest was genuine, and she would never turn away a sincere inquiry about the fundamental values of her people. Still, she was not sure how to go about explaining values and ideas acquired through a lifetime of education and conditioning, using simple vocabulary, to a full-grown man who was still having difficulty with the language.

"Even a person fluent in our language reading this Text for the first time as an adult would not be able to understand it," she cautioned. "It is a *summary* of concepts and conclusions, without containing adequate explanation or commentary."

"If I want to understand these People, then I have to understand what *Dazhan* is," insisted Darrel.

Zhana hesitated a moment, but couldn't resist Darrel's enthusiasm. She began by trying to explain the cave-people's view of the universe. She presented two more words that were new to Darrel's vocabulary: *"Koruh"* and *"shintuh."* These represented the distinct dimensions into which Nature was divided. *Koruh* was explained as the "external dimension" of the physical environment. *Shintuh* was explained as the "internal dimension" of thoughts, feelings, or consciousness. The cave-peoples' system of values was based on perceptions of how these dimensions interact.

When Zhana tried to explain further, it was evident that Darrel was struggling to keep up. He became hopelessly confused with vocabulary too specialized for his beginning level of fluency. Zhana fumbled for simpler words, then reconsidered. She suggested that a more gradual exploration might be more effective in helping him eventually learn about *Dazhan*.

Darrel nodded in reluctant, temporary acceptance.

*   *   *   *   *

Additional months had passed, and as the mid-summer calendar stretched into late autumn, rescue efforts had been unsuccessful in finding the remains of Darrel Swift. While occasional scraps of litter had been found here and there, they always seemed to lead down dead-end tunnels in the unending maze of passages that branched out in every direction. Eventually, the official rescue efforts by civil agencies had to be called off. There was virtually no chance that a human being could survive without food supplies for the time that Darrel had been underground, and there were not adequate resources to support an unending venture to explore a possibly interminable cave-system.

Linda Ferret was outraged at the Canadian civil rescue forces, and threatened to sue. In the meantime, she organized her own financial resources to arrange for a continuation of the rescue effort.

Alan and Lee agreed to continue. Alan still wanted to find his missing cousin, and Lee agreed to remain with his friend because he needed the work, and because Linda was still threatening him with responsibility for the accident.

While Linda could not afford all the heavy machinery that had been used previously, the heavy digging was mostly behind them, and they organized a carefully-selected crew of spelunkers to explore the caves. But it was still no easy task. There were many branching tunnels in every vertical and horizontal direction. It seemed the little party of vacationers had inadvertently stumbled into the discovery of a massive new cave system, to rival Mammoth Caverns of Kentucky, Carlsbad Caverns of New Mexico, or any system in the world. It could be an exhaustive study just to explore all the levels of passages, much less to find the decomposing remains of an erstwhile hiking buddy somewhere among the tunnels. And Darrel's careless disposal of litter, often tossed away from himself toward passages leading in other directions, confused the searches more than aided them.

*   *   *   *   *

In Darrel's prolonged visit to this timeless land of no day or no night, where the only measure of time was in the annual rise and fall of the waterflows, he was finding as many questions as answers about where he was and who the people were. As he fumbled with basic language skills, he began to realize that the cave-people were just as curious about his own existence and origins as he was about theirs.

Through the centuries of their recorded history, there were scattered reports of bodies or bones found with strange artifacts in the dark peripheral caves, which the natives called *"Timera"* — the outside limit of their known universe. Legends had evolved to explain the mysterious beings from beyond Timera, but the Enrisans had no real answers.

Darrel, strong and healthy, and driven by his determination to survive, was the first of these Outsiders ever to have found his way alive into the Great Cavern, known to the natives as *"Enrisa."* And it was evident that the highest levels of Enrisan administrative power were determined to provide him with every comfort, and develop communication so that his origins and experiences might be fully explored.

As Zhana continued to teach him about life in Enrisa, she simultaneously gathered information about his own background, and learned with astonishment of a vast world beyond Timera. As Darrel struggled to become familiar with the subtle customs of Enrisa's small, homogeneous civilization, Zhana was fascinated with his stories of many diverse nations made up of huge populations of differing colors, customs, and languages. She listened dreamily to endless descriptions of technological and mechanical gadgetry, becoming enthusiastically confused as she tried to visualize the strange procession of vehicles, machines, and conveniences. Darrel tried to explain the workings of a universe closely regulated by patterns of days, nights, and seasons, but such ideas were difficult for Zhana to grasp. Nor could she understand the vastness of wide open spaces filled with noises, lights, and the rushing of chaotic crowds after a lifetime of confinement in the quiet beauty of the caves. Darrel wished it could someday be possible to take her to the Outside so she could really see how different it was.

Zhana's curiosity about life in the Outside even led her to dabble in learning a few simple words and phrases in English, and even learning to write her name in the strange characters which Darrel himself still used with a feeling of security. She quickly realized how difficult it was to relate, even superficially, to Darrel's strange language and customs. Yet

Dazhan

Darrel had to become intimately familiar with all of the subtle details of Enrisan culture and communication, not for fun, but to survive! This awareness led Zhana to become all the more patient and conscientious as Darrel's teacher and friend. And Darrel enjoyed the real give-and-take of honest cultural exchange that he wished he could share more universally with the other Enrisans.

Darrel became increasingly fascinated as he slowly unraveled the mysteries concealed within these strange caverns. The great cave of Enrisa, in its physical layout, was an elongated diamond-shaped rupture laced with gardens and grottoed pools. The population of several hundred thousand was unevenly distributed into seven tribes based on the natural topography of plateaus, valleys, canyons, and other natural divisions. Zhana and her family lived in the largest of the regions, on the main floor of the central valley.

Because the total population of all the regions was only about the size of a large rural county, complex formal institutions were not necessary. The affairs of each regional tribe were loosely coordinated by the seven Chief Divines, with assistance from local Divines. Each of the Chief Divines presided over a palatial Sanctuary, where the myths and morals were taught from the pages of *Dazhan*, and all disputes were resolved.

At a central point within the Great Caverns, where the valley merged with plateau and canyon regions at the point of a great cliff, the greatest of all the Sanctuaries was hewn from granite and generously adorned with kibihni. Secluded in this majestically templed palace lived Nolak, the Most High Divine — the gentle Old Man who had come to see Darrel during his first hours of consciousness in Enrisa. Though the Old Man was mentally alert, and actively involved in the affairs of the people who loved him for his spontaneous but compassionate humor, he generally remained in confinement for reasons of physical weakness. Thus, most Enrisans only looked with awe upon the towering Most High Sanctuary from afar. Few but the Divines ever gazed upon the mystery-shrouded inner walls.

With little hope of ever returning to the outside, Darrel forced himself to accept this strange new environment as his home. He liked the new friends who were so kind to him, and enjoyed the paradisiacal stone-bound garden.

Still, Darrel couldn't help but miss some of the comforts of his old life. He missed the softness of carpeting, and the plush furnishings of his previous affluence. He wished the Enrisans had developed functional restrooms, or at least soft toilet paper. He wished he could go into a fine restaurant and order the best cuisine from around the outside world. The food here wasn't bad, but he would have liked something with the sweet taste of home. Even a "Big Mac" would have been appreciated. He missed being able to sprawl down in front of a TV and revel in the mindlessness of programmed entertainment. He missed the secure progression of days and nights in cyclical regularity. He wished he could trade all his erstwhile riches to see just one more golden sunset along the California coastline. He missed being able to enjoy a neon-lit nightlife of movies, nightclubs, discos, or just the simple enjoyment of a home game at Dodger Stadium.

Still, life in Enrisa was not all that bad. Darrel Swift was glad to be alive at all.

Early in his experience underground, Darrel came to realize there was no orderly system of practical day-to-day timekeeping. He found the timelessness of unending brightness a devastating personal adjustment. But the Enrisans just took it in stride. When they were hungry, they ate. When they were tired, they slept. Here, there was little concern for time or schedules in the affairs of human behavior.

Gradually, Darrel began to develop his own cycle of individual activity. Despite occasional moments when he desperately wished to know the hour, the date, or even the month, he slowly grew accustomed to behavior based on function rather than timing. Except for sleeping.

Unlike the Enrisans who were impervious to the steady light of the kibihni, Darrel hated sleeping in "daylight." In the Great Cavern, there was no escape from the constant brightness. But deep within his own private chambers, illuminated by kibihni stones brought in from the main cavern, he could just cover the glowing stones to darken his room for sleeping. When rested, he could uncover the little lights and restore the room to brightness.

Much of his waking time was spent practicing and developing his language skills. Depending heavily on Zhana to make sense out of puzzling foreign complexities, or just to break up the loneliness of isolated study, he would arrange his cycle of activity to accommodate her availability. He also continued to seek involvement with other Enrisans in their work projects or other social activities.

He learned that mealtime was determined only by a consensus of hunger. Not exactly a master chef in the outside world, he was even less able to get along on his own in a world without instant foods or TV dinners. Enjoying the kindness of his friends, he would often join Zhana and her family for the sharing of meals. Darrel was fast becoming accustomed to the strange Enrisan delicacies. While a scarcity of larger animal life caused meat to be generally unavailable, there was no shortage of exotic fruits, vegetables, or grains that were prepared in odd dishes that Darrel learned to enjoy. He discovered that the odd brownish paste first served to him was a staple in the Enrisan diet, often served with other foods to balance meals.

On one occasion, while Darrel was eating with Zhana's family, he thought he noticed a brownish speck in his *zatah*. He scraped up a bite of the stuff and held it up for closer examination. "Hey, I think a little bug got into this," he announced, as politely as possible.

Zhana tried to suppress a chuckle.

"Well, as long as he's not still wiggling...." answered her father, Rimani, with a pleasant grin.

Darrel tried to enjoy their playful response to his plight, but wanted them to understand that he wasn't just kidding. "I think there really is a bug in here," he said. "I can't eat this!"

Zhana's mother, Lena, reached across to gently touch his hand. "It's okay," she assured him. "Insects are not thought to have any real process of conscious experience, so they feel no pain when we eat them."

Darrel gave a frozen stare. He thought of all the *zatah* he had eaten — and enjoyed — in his months underground, and his tummy began to feel very nervous. Zhana, recognizing another intercultural crisis, took his hand and led him down into a little cave-room where family food supplies were stored. It was here that each family member took turns blending ingredients to be served. Lifting the lid of a metallic container, Zhana revealed a crawling, moving mass of Enrisan cave-insects. She scooped up a handful of the wiggling creatures, and set them into a smaller sieve-like container. She rinsed the contents in a bath of cool water, and mashed the lid against the sides to strain out the contents into a stone dish. This was blended into a mixture of grain and other powdery substances, to make the familiar brownish paste. Zhana startled him further by explaining that protein was included in the Enrisan diet by adding similar insect preparations to many of the foods he already enjoyed. By this point, Darrel was numb to further shock. Zhana smiled knowingly, confident that he would quickly overcome this initial revulsion and reacquire his taste for the cuisine.

Continuing his individual cycle of activity, Darrel would sometimes seek out activities with the Enrisan children. He had a special affinity for Jamak, Zhana's little brother. Darrel guessed the boy would be nine or ten years old by the measurements of the outside world. At least with the children there was no sense of social blundering. They were all learning Enrisan social values together. Darrel felt the same real acceptance that he enjoyed with Zhana and the few others he had come to know well. Darrel enjoyed the playful enthusiasm of the Enrisan children, and marveled at the way they had learned to express their youthful energy creatively, in a cheerful awareness of others. All the Enrisans were like that. They seemed to respond almost automatically to the experiences of those around.

Determined to learn the ways of the cave-people, the competitive businessman from the outside world found himself becoming caught up in the contagious enthusiasm of the happy Enrisan community.

Chapter Five

Concept

"I'm afraid it's hopeless," Lee announced with uneasy caution.

"No one could have survived this long underground," agreed Alan. His forehead glistened with beads of sweat from the autumn sun above and from the pressure of the moment. "It's been months since he went in there, and we can't seem to make any progress finding our way through that maze of caves. We really have no choice but to call off the search."

Linda Ferret just glared. "It's my money, and I'll make the choices," she fumed. "We will not give up until we find Darrel. You bums should be glad I'm around to keep you employed. Without Darrel to support you, you'd both starve...."

"Darrel is dead," insisted Lee. "We're not gonna find anything in there. We'll be lucky enough just to find his bones...."

"Then don't come back 'til you do," stormed Linda. "Now get back up on that mountain with the rest of the team or I'll have to pay someone else who will. I've got business to take care of back home."

Linda went off to catch a plane back to California, while Alan and Lee joined the others up on the slopes to try and find what was left of Darrel.

* * * * *

Far below, in the strange subterranean gardens, Darrel Swift was surviving very well indeed. As additional months slipped past, he was becoming able to communicate more easily with those around him.

Darrel sat on the rocky shore of one of the ponds, where he had brought Jamak to play. Zhana's little brother crowded in close, watching wide-eyed as Darrel scraped off carvings from a piece of stick and fitted it carefully into pieces of other sticks he had carved, to make a little boat. Repeating the process, and showing Jamak how to do it, the duo worked together until they had a small fleet of little boats.

"Let's go down by the water and see how they float!" suggested Darrel.

They set the boats afloat, guiding them around a shallow area in one of the ponds, with Jamak listening in fascination as Darrel described great ships sailing upon vast oceans of the Outside World.

As they played, several children wandered over from nearby. Curiosity and fascination shone in each child's wide, innocent Enrisan eyes.

Darrel always enjoyed watching how the boys and girls played together without the pushing, shoving, and do-or-die competition of

American children. At an American playground, the kids might be organized into carefully-structured, formalized competitive games supervised by dictatorial coaches. Here in the caves, they just scampered over the rocks, playfully clambering through the foliage.

Without hesitation, Jamak gave each little boy or girl one of the boats, with Darrel's first-made and finest boat going to one of the smaller children. Jamak kept only one modest toy for himself.

Darrel was amazed, but still he did not want his little friend to come out on the short end of the deal, either.

Calling Jamak over, he suggested trading back so that he could still share his toys, yet keep the best for himself. "Best?" answered Jamak quizzically. "I have a boat I made myself. I'm having fun. Why would anyone care which boat is *best?*"

"Suppose you want to have a..." Darrel hadn't learned an Enrisan word for *race* "...in case you want to see whose boat is fastest — then you should have the best one, so you can win!"

"Why does anyone want to know which boat is fastest if all the kids are having fun?"

Darrel just smiled, and Jamak scrambled off to show the other kids how to make more boats for themselves.

Left with a moment of solitude, Darrel squatted in the shadows of a low, uneven stone cliff made up of large, round boulders, uneven fractured rocks, and quartz crystals, on a ridge overlooking the main valley. Nearby, the pond rolled off into a delicate cascade. As light from the many kibihni passed through sprays of watery mists and prismatic quartzine crystals, patterns of shadows and rainbows danced over the nearby rocks.

Looking out over the valley, and watching as the children played, Darrel did not see Zhana descending in graceful silence down the face of the cliffside behind him. With a quiet laugh, she dropped catlike to the ground and embraced the startled Darrel. She sat down next to him very close and rested her head on his shoulder.

"I'm glad you came!" he mumbled lazily, in English-accented Enrisan. "Isn't this a beautiful garden!"

Darrel and Zhana snuggled up close together, laughing and talking in the tropical rainbow beauty of the garden. There was some small talk. There was a pause.

Through the passing months, Darrel and Zhana had come to know each other well as individuals and as representatives of mutually bizarre cultural systems. They had shared many thoughts and feelings. Yet the basis of all Enrisan values, which Darrel felt was so critical to his goal of understanding the cave people, had been conspicuously neglected. Now, after a little more chitchat, Darrel carefully guided the conversation into a discussion of *Dazhan.* Darrel was more concerned about gaining insights into the lives of the cave people, which he could use to get ahead, than with learning how the physical dimension of matter *(koruh)* and the dimension of spiritual energy, or consciousness, *(shintuh)* fit together into a system of values based on compassion as he had learned earlier.

With Darrel's continued improvements in language fluency, Zhana agreed he was ready to learn more about *Dazhan.* Also, she had given more thought as to how to present the ideas and values of *Dazhan* to someone who was already an adult.

Looking for some common ground between the values of the cave-people and his own background, Darrel picked up on the idea of "compassion." In his own life he was too practical to worry about such idealistic qualities, and was ready to take advantage of those "bleeding hearts" who did. Hmmm. If that's how the cave people were, he would have no trouble getting ahead here. Still, he had to focus on common ground for discussion.... He repeated to Zhana some of the clichés he had learned as a child in Sunday school: "Love your neighbor as yourself. Love your enemies. Turn the other cheek." He thought about how the same message from his non-religious friends, youthful radicals in the 1960's: "love, peace, brotherhood." In college, a similar message was echoed in the academic setting, in philosophy, the social sciences, humanities, and psychology. The value of love or compassion seemed to be a universal ideal. He expressed to Zhana the similarity of those shared cultural values.

Zhana seemed surprised. "Are the people in your world compassionate? Are *you* compassionate?"

Darrel thought of the people he knew, mostly like himself. Except for their radical fling in the 60's, most people weren't compassionate at all. A few people he knew, or had heard of, worked long hours of sacrifice in the name of compassionate service as volunteers for those in need. But most were too busy trying to earn a living and get ahead, so they could have a little pleasure in life. They couldn't just devote themselves to some obligation to a duty of compassion. With surprising candor, he expressed those thoughts to Zhana.

"So everyone in the Outside talks about 'compassion', but only a few really do it?" Zhana questioned, raising an eyebrow. "Maybe the problem is that people in the Outside hear the *words,* but they don't really know *how* to feel compassion. They say, 'love your enemies', but *how* do you feel good towards someone who tries to hurt you? You say you're too *busy* to be compassionate? You have to make a living? You need to have a little pleasure — you have to *make yourself happy?"*

"Is it wrong to want to be happy?" Darrel was careful not to let the tone of his voice become too challenging.

Dazhan

"Remember what the word *Dazhan* means? It is a contraction of two words. It means *'Compassionate Joy'*. Compassion *and* happiness. It *is* important to have a happy life. Must happiness be incompatible with compassion? Must it be a duty or obligation? The emphasis of our *Dazhan* is more than just an idea. It shows *how to enjoy* a compassionate lifestyle." Zhana could see the expression of skepticism on Darrel's face, no matter how hard he tried to suppress it. She smiled in return. "You just want to be happy, right? Why waste time with the compassion part? You just want to go out and make yourself happy?"

Darrel just grinned.

"Your way — does it work? How many watercycles of your life have you sacrificed your ideal of compassion in trying to make yourself happy? Tell me, Darrel Swift, *are you happy?*"

"Well..." he paused. He thought about all the pressures in his life — his work, his shallow relationships, all the messed-up values he had gone on this trip to get away from. The harder he tried to make himself happy, the more shallow he felt his life becoming. For all his money, his life was not really more happy or pleasant than the simple, cheerful existence of these primitive cave-people. But he couldn't come right out and say it.

"Well," Zhana continued, "if you can't follow the model of compassion that you claim to believe in because you have to 'make yourself happy', then you should at least do a good job of it. You should at least understand what happiness is. Do you even know what it is?"

"Well ... of course ... it's a feeling — an emotion," Darrel responded hesitantly.

"You mean, like a rock?" asked Zhana, with a smile.

"A *rock?* What does a *rock* have to do with happiness?" This time, Darrel's voice clearly revealed his irritation. He wondered if maybe it wasn't really possible for an educated American to discuss such matters with a primitive native.

"You mean there's a difference between objects or things, and feelings or processes of consciousness?" Zhana asked triumphantly. "That's the difference between *koruh*, that aspect of the Universe which consists of physical, inanimate matter, and *shintuh*, the dimensions of consciousness."

"Of course, that's obvious..." Darrel stuttered.

"Well, it's obvious when you think about it," agreed Zhana, "but the reason people work so hard to try to make themselves happy, without achieving happiness, is that they get those two dimensions mixed up."

"Huh?"

"Yeah, you try to go out and get 'happiness' the same way you would go out and 'get' an object or a thing like a rock. Tell me, if you think it's so obvious, what *is* the difference between *koruh* and *shintuh?* What is the difference between *objects* and *consciousness?"*

Darrel had to stop and think. It made him feel he was back in school, taking a test. But he had to prove himself. "First of all, objects or things are tangible, physical. You can touch them, hold them. A feeling, or a process of consciousness, is abstract or intangible — a *process.* It's *energy."*

"Good. What else?"

Darrel had to think again. Coming from a Western civilization, he drew on his exposure to science, and the laws of physics that govern objects. "Well, by themselves, objects are inactive, whereas consciousness is active, ongoing — never stops 'til it's dead. But objects..." He tried to paraphrase the axiom "...an object at rest tends to remain at rest...," but he couldn't find the right words in the cave people's language. "Nothing happens to an object unless some *external* force acts on it to move it or change it."

"Good. If you put a rock on the ground and leave it there, how long would it stay there?"

"If nothing caused it to move or change, it would stay there *forever,"* answered Darrel.

"What about consciousness?" asked Zhana. "What if I put a tiny child here and told her to stay. With no outside interference, how long would she stay there?"

"She's already outta here!" mused Darrel.

"So objects, unlike consciousness, really exist independently. What about food or water? If I don't feed it or water it, how long will the rock stay there?"

"By itself ... forever," Darrel repeated.

"And the child? No food, no water, no air ... how long does she stay there?"

"No food or water? No air?" Darrel shuddered.

"And why doesn't the child want to stay in place?"

"She's bored."

"And if you smash the rock, it will suffer pain?" persisted Zhana.

"It wouldn't care. It doesn't have any feelings," Darrel concluded.

"And, in contrast, the consciousness does *not* exist independently?"

Darrel thought a moment. "I'll go along with that. Consciousness is *not* independent," he agreed. "The active *process* of consciousness does depend on its surrounding environment for sustenance and stimulation. I still don't see the point. What does this have to do with happiness?"

"The point is this," answered Zhana. "When you try to go out and *make yourself happy,* you're trying to 'get happiness' the same way you would get an object or a thing. You make two important mistakes:

"First, as you said, happiness is not physically tangible the way objects are. You can't just reach out and grab it. It's an active process of energy, not a static object; happiness is the *journey,* not the *destination.* If we think of the physical environment as being dark and consuming, to represent its lack of feelings or consciousness, and the dimension of feelings or consciousness as being little dots of light within living minds, we quickly see that there is a vast, non-feeling dimension of physical objects which encompasses and consumes the sparsely-scattered dots of light.

"The second mistake is that, as you said, unlike objects or things, consciousness depends on its interaction with the surrounding environment for stimulation and sustenance. It has to reach *outward,* — away from itself — into the environment, to meet those needs. When people focus inward towards themselves, trying to make themselves happy, then the attention is focused in exactly the wrong direction. This is the 'paradox of happiness': The human consciousness is not capable of satisfying its own desires through direct pursuit of its own happiness. *The harder you try to make yourself happy, the less successful you are.* When you want something, and you get what you want, the *active process* of consciousness has to move on to the next thing. If you stop to dwell on it, it is never enough. There is never enough to satisfy the continuous gulf between expectation and disillusionment."

"Doesn't that put us in kind of an impossible situation?" wondered Darrel, as he felt his old skepticism returning. "If we can't find happiness by pursuing it directly, then where *do* we look for happiness?"

"Don't be so negative!" teased Zhana with a cheerful smile. "Don't look for the answer in what happiness *isn't* — look for the answer in what happiness *is.* You gave the description of happiness yourself..."

Suddenly there was an interruption. The boat Jamak had given to the smaller child had drifted away, and none of the children could reach it. Jamak came running to Darrel for help. "Darrel!" he yelled. "The boat got away! It's heading toward the cascades! It's the best of all the boats!"

Zhana put her arm around the child to console him. "Just make a new one!"

"But it's the one Darrel made. It's such a good one!"

As the little boat drifted farther across the wide pond, Darrel grew impatient. "Why don't you just..." he realized he hadn't yet learned a word for *swim* "...go into the water and get the boat, instead of talking here while it moves farther away."

"Darrel!" protested Zhana. "That water is deeper than the height of a person! Whoever goes in there would die!"

Darrel looked into the pond. It couldn't be more than eight or ten feet deep. The water was fresh and clear, and he could see all the way down to the rocky floor.

As Zhana and Jamak gasped in terror, Darrel plunged into the water and dove to the bottom. Swimming gracefully, easily, through the rocky pool, he surfaced near the cherished toy. Pushing the treasure with one hand, he floated it back across the surface of the water.

Zhana and Jamak stared at him in such astonishment that he realized this civilization, from its earliest days, must have cultivated a deeply-rooted cultural fear — a reverenced awe — of the many waterflows. They had no concept of human beings being able to swim through water.

"What kind of magic...!?" Zhana was amazed.

Darrel continued to enjoy the refreshing exercise, and the chance to show off a little. Finally, he climbed out of the pond and sprawled out, dripping wet, on the lush floor of the garden. "Are you all right?" asked Zhana. "How did you do it?"

"In my world from beyond Timera, anyone can swim," he explained, using his own word "swim" and adapting it to fit an Enrisan pronunciation. "Children much younger than Jamak can learn to *swim.*"

"You mean you'll teach me to swim!?" exclaimed Jamak with a shriek.

Darrel laughed. "Sure!" he responded. "Not right now, but we'll do it!"

"What a wonderful thing!" exclaimed Zhana. "Swim."

Zhana was very excited about the possibility of humans swimming through water, but Darrel was still curious about the Enrisan concepts of *Dazhan,* and he brought the conversation back to his question about how to find happiness if it couldn't be achieved by direct pursuit.

Darrel relaxed with a sigh, and stood up. He was dripping wet, and wanted to get some dry things on. He pulled Zhana up by the hand and headed homeward. He continued to inquire about Dazhan as they walked. He was curious about the secret of Enrisan happiness. He thought of the cave people. They *did* seem to be happy and cheerful. Certainly more so than himself. Even the children could play together with a real sense of fun, but without fighting or American-style competition. "Hmmm," he wondered, "maybe there really is something to this!" Maybe these "primitive natives" were more advanced than he ever could have realized before.

Zhana slipped her little hand into Darrel's as the topic of their discussion moved on to *how to achieve* a happy lifestyle. "As you said, the consciousness depends on stimuli and sustenance from outside to provide perceptions and experiences," she explained. "So even though it all happens within the *shintuh,* it has been crystallized into meaningfulness from its origins elsewhere. The *shintuh* cannot survive alone. While certain basic personal needs must be taken care of, the individual must ultimately reach *outward* toward the environment...."

Arriving at the opening to Darrel's living area, Zhana gave him a little kiss. "Get some dry things on, and come over for something to eat."

Dazhan

As Darrel entered his own living area and sought a dry change of clothes, he continued to reflect on what Zhana had said. "...crystallized into meaning from its origins elsewhere..." He tried to relate the nature of human consciousness to something less abstract. He compared it to a television set. "The experiences passing through the conscious mind are like the images, sounds, and colors that pass through the TV set. Before a TV can even begin to operate, it must be in good mechanical repair. Likewise, the body, which allows the Consciousness to operate in a physical environment, must be in good condition. Skills and talents should be developed to allow the Self to express its will effectively. A positive self-attitude helps the individual to appreciate the inherent value of the *shintuh*. But all this attention to Self is only a starting point." Darrel imagined that a person buying a particularly nice set might admire the intricate beauty and complex workmanship of the set itself. But no matter how well-crafted the set may be, the real use goes beyond the physical equipment. It must be *turned on* so that images, colors, and sounds are brought in *from the outside* and crystallized into focus within the little mechanical box! Likewise, Darrel considered that the inherent value of the Self could be enjoyed by inner reflective feelings, or in savoring memorable experiences, but that the Self must ultimately respond to *outside* stimuli, which can be crystallized into meaningful experience. The Self must get "turned on" by reaching *outward*. No one would buy an expensive set and just stare at the blank screen, without bothering to open up the vast world available at the touch of a switch. He was starting to feel a real excitement for the Enrisan concept of happiness, and a desire to learn more about how to use it not only for "getting ahead" in Enrisa, but for really learning to develop the same peaceful, cheerful sense of happiness that sparkled in the lives of the cave people.

As he finished dressing and hurried over to Zhana's living area, his thoughts turned toward his own life, which had been filled with glitter and fast-paced action, but which was really so hollow. Maybe there was more to this *Dazhan* than just the local superstitions of the "natives." How many "TV sets" had he bought in his thirty years without ever turning them on? With all his money and time, he had never really reached outward. Now, he wasn't sure if the "set" would even work.

Darrel persisted in his exploration of this idea during the meal — now with a legitimate curiosity for its real value as a practical tool for enjoying a richer, more rewarding life. His questioning took on a deeper level of inquiry as he cultivated additional reasons for wanting to understand the cave peoples' book. "How do you reach outward?" he asked. "Which way is 'out'?" He thought of the many channels on a TV. Which should he watch?

Zhana could sense the slow emergence of deeper feelings in Darrel. She smiled. "There are many ways out. There is the whole environment!

We can enjoy a variety of many outward interests. The variety itself may generate a happy feeling of zest for life in general, and for each new situation in particular. You can become 'lost' in a pleasant or interesting activity; or feel the creative excitement of a new discovery; or enjoy moments of spontaneous playfulness; or enjoy the absorbed interest of a special hobby or work project — any diversion that leads your concerns outward, away from Self."

"But consider this," added Zhana. "Each consciousness is not alone. It is surrounded by the environment, but that environment also includes other consciousnesses. Each one represents a complete dimension of experiences as intense and radiant as your own. If we can reach outward toward these spiritual dimensions, there is a combination of interactions. There is the inherent value of each shintuh individually, plus the value which is added to each when it is brought into the experience of the other. The internal values of the two shintuhni feed on each other, breeding new responses in unlimited possible combinations. This is why human contact is so fundamental, and why relationships with other human beings are so necessary."

Zhana felt that enough new material had been covered, and steered the conversation to other subjects. "Of course, we still haven't talked about the relationships themselves yet," she said, closing the subject. "Later we can review the practice of *Dazhan* itself: how we reach out to other consciousnesses to relate in spontaneous experiences."

"You mean we're still on the introductory concepts?" wondered Darrel. "You mean we haven't gotten to *Dazhan* yet?"

"Not yet," laughed Zhana. "But we'll get to it next time."

* * * * *

A short time later, Darrel was alone in his own living area. Covering up the larger kibihni to partially darken his room, he undressed and sat up on his "bed." His thoughts were of Zhana, of Dazhan, and of the people who were so simple and childlike in many ways, yet so profound in their own kind of spiritual sophistication. He got up to cover the rest of the kibihni so he could sleep in darkness.

As Darrel was getting ready to cover the last kibih, a willowy shadow appeared in his room. A female silhouette slipped across the small cave and squatted on the side of the fitted bedding that was nestled into the carved-out rocks. It was Zhana. Darrel lay down on the bedding beside her as she guided his head into her lap. Her hand brushed through his sandy hair, and she gently caressed his face. "I was thinking about you," she whispered, "and I needed to come and see you."

Darrel sat up a little, resting his face against the back of her neck. She pressed her cheek very close against his face and quivered a deep sigh. Her body trembled as Darrel's mouth embraced her lips gently but very firmly. His hand brushed across her loose robe, which tumbled easily open as he eased her down onto the bedding beside him.

Darrel had been in the caves of Enrisa for many months, without intimate feminine companionship. His life beyond that was just a faded memory; a distant dream from long ago. Now, holding Zhana closely, stirrings of desire were quickly reawakened. There was an excited blur of touching, fondling, caressing — and of penetration — as Darrel squeezed Zhana close to him in a sudden eruption of ecstasy.

Zhana was somewhat disappointed that everything was over so quickly, but she was understanding. As Darrel rolled over on his back, she rested her face on his chest and caressed his body. "I love you very much, Darrel," was all she said.

Darrel sensed her disappointment, which caused him to feel self-conscious. He could sense the real spiritual love she radiated, and it made him feel even worse. He started to explain, "The first time is..."

"Each time is better," she interrupted, nestling closer. "I really do love you."

Still embracing, they turned over to sleep. But neither of them felt sleepy. Talking and touching, they shared thoughts, feelings, and experiences as they reviewed the incredibly different backgrounds that had brought them together. Darrel fondled Zhana's small, tender breasts as they talked, and stroked his fingers across her tummy. In the dim light of a single kibih, the half-golden tones of her flesh radiated a magnetic, sensual beauty.

They continued to explore each other playfully and completely, as sensations of arousal began to return. Darrel rolled onto his back, and felt himself being gently consumed in Zhana's tight, passionate closeness. Now relaxed, he was able to enjoy prolonged sensations of complete intimacy. Darrel groaned with pleasure; Zhana remained quiet and intent, savoring the total experience of the closest possible human embrace. Together, they shared the explosive burst of energy that climaxed through both of them.

They continued to hold each other closely — embracing, talking, caressing, and continuing to explore a complete spectrum of physical and spiritual feelings. At length, they snuggled up very close together and fell into a happy, peaceful sleep.

When Darrel later awoke, Zhana was perched over him, grinning. Her robe was pulled tightly around her. The room was bright from the luminous kibihni she had uncovered. He embraced her enthusiastically and wrestled her playfully onto her back. She laughed, and wriggled loose through the tangle of disarrayed bedding. Giggling, she raced into the next room, with Darrel following nakedly behind.

He caught up to her and pulled her close. She braced her hands against his chest to hold him back. Her face showed an unexpectedly serious expression, which caused Darrel to grow suddenly concerned. "Darrel," she began, "there is a great difference between physical attraction and true spiritual love..."

Darrel's stomach began to feel weak.

"In the darkness of sleep, we had a beautiful and sensual experience..." she continued.

"But it was much more than that!" protested Darrel. "I have felt very close to you for a long time. This was ... well ... a new dimension to our experience together. It was the first time I really felt such a powerful combination of spiritual and physical closeness, and I thought..."

Zhana appeared relieved, and pulled herself close to Darrel. "Oh, I love you so much!" she sighed with a tight squeeze. "I have also wanted this closeness for a long time. But after the excitement is over, people don't always feel the same. I didn't know how you would feel. I just don't want to sleep alone anymore."

Darrel held her close. "I don't want you to sleep alone, either."

Chapter Six

Inquiry

Sprawled out alone in the soft, mossy hollow of a tiny cavelet near one of the ponds, Darrel continued his studies of Enrisan literature and language in the beauty of the garden. Reading from increasingly advanced levels of material, and scratching foreign characters onto thin metal plates to write, his closeness to the culture of this timeless place continued to deepen. He glanced up from his studies. He gazed out over the valley, and glanced toward the still waters of the ponds.

Suddenly, with a blur of motion, Darrel found himself smothered by a tangle of robes and the sounds of laughing young voices. Caught by surprise, Darrel struggled a moment to get free from the web of fabric. He saw Jamak and one of his young friends scampering gracefully up the rocks. Jamak waved Darrel's stylus teasingly, as the other child clutched the metal plates. Darrel's eyes followed to where they had climbed up the cliffside and out onto the gnarled branches of an old Enrisan cave-tree overhanging the cliff. Perched in the safety of its ancient, moss-covered boughs, the two boys laughed with glee.

Grinning, Darrel followed more slowly up the wall of rock. As he finally reached the tree, the boys split up in opposite directions, still enjoying their playful antics. Darrel chased after his friend Jamak. As Darrel approached, Jamak carefully unraveled a thick vine that was wrapped around the limbs of the great tree, and lowered it down toward the garden floor. When Darrel was dangerously near, the boy eased himself off the branch, laughed, and scrambled downward along the vine, climbing quick and monkey-like, with hands and feet. Darrel braced himself securely against a fork in the branches, and pulled the vine upward hand-over-hand while Jamak was still trying to climb down. The boy was agile, but slight of build like the other Enrisans, and Darrel could easily pull him up with the vine. Jamak was still laughing, but Darrel was laughing harder, as he plucked the boy off the vine and held him tight so he couldn't escape.

"Oh, no!" moaned Jamak in mock terror. "What are you going to do now?"

"You're in big trouble now!" cackled Darrel playfully. "I can't climb back down and carry you at the same time, so I'll just have to throw you into the pond!"

"Yippee!" shrieked Jamak. "You mean you're going to teach me how to swim now?" That sounded like fun for Darrel, too, so they lowered the vine back down, climbed down to the garden floor, and raced over to the edge of the pond.

Jamak stepped timidly into a shallow area of the pond where the water was no deeper than Darrel's waist. With a curious blend of caution and excitement, he waded to Darrel. Awed by the recent memory of watching Darrel swim, and encouraged by Darrel's assurance that "anyone can do it," Jamak was eager to bring the aquatic experience to the Enrisan people. Darrel only hoped that a lifetime fear of water could be outweighed by Jamak's optimistic sense of adventure, and his trust in Darrel.

"First you gotta get wet!" explained Darrel, holding his breath and dropping briefly to the shallow bottom. "Now you try it."

Jamak hesitated, and made a face. But with encouragement from Darrel and assurance that nothing could hurt him in this shallow area of the pond, he took a deep breath and dunked himself in the water. He came back up, sputtering and laughing. "I did it! It's easy!"

Darrel showed the boy how to hold his breath, go under water, and slowly exhale, releasing a flurry of bubbles. Jamak tried it excitedly, and continued to immerse himself repeatedly.

As Jamak played and splashed, becoming not only comfortable in the water but actually enjoying it, Darrel suggested a new idea. "What do you think would happen if someone went into the deep water and *didn't* swim?"

"He would sink to the bottom!" answered Jamak. "He would die!"

Darrel swam out to the deeper water. Treading water, he called to Jamak, "I'm going to stop swimming now. Watch what happens!" Darrel let his hands and legs go limp, and his face slipped below the surface of the water. But he did not sink. His body remained suspended in the water, near the surface. He bobbed around in the current for a few moments, and then swam back to Jamak.

"People don't sink," Darrel explained. "They float near the surface. It's natural to float. That's why swimming is so easy. Your body will float naturally, and you just add a little direction by pushing against the water with your hands and feet!" He gave a demonstration.

Darrel watched as Jamak practiced letting himself go limp and floating in the security of the shallow area. After several tries at free-floating, he started paddling with his hands and kicking with his feet, to swim short distances under the surface of the shallow water. He was awkward, and couldn't make it work the first time he tried. Darrel had to help him remember exactly what to do. When Jamak thought carefully about each movement, he could do it— awkwardly, slowly, but he could make it work.

After swimming successfully several times, Jamak climbed excitedly out of the pond, laughing and dancing with an enthusiastic sense of achievement. "I'm going to tell Zhana!" he exclaimed as he scrambled away. "I'll be right back!"

Alone, Darrel plunged to the depths of the pond, exploring the jagged features of its secret chambers and crevices. Darrel enjoyed the peaceful beauty of the watery environment as he drifted silently among the underwater formations.

Jamak soon returned with Zhana, accompanied also by Rimani, Lena, and several local children. Jamak plunged into the pond and swam a short distance under the surface toward Darrel, who quickly joined him back in the shallow area. Rimani and Lena gasped with amazement and delight. Zhana was surprised at how quickly and easily her little brother had mastered the simple basics.

Zhana removed the outer robes of her toga-like garment and gingerly approached the pond. Darrel took her by the hand and led her into the shallow water. She splashed a little, and snuggled up close to Darrel. "Do you think I could learn to do it?" she asked. Darrel smiled and led her out to waist-deep water.

With significantly increased personal contact, Darrel repeated for Zhana the same teaching process that had worked so well for Jamak. He found a greater resistance to the water, as her fear of it had become more deeply rooted through a longer lifetime of conditioning. Still, her enthusiasm for the discovery of this new adventure, and her confidence in Darrel, allowed her to see beyond previous limitations and enjoy new challenges.

Just like her younger brother, she found the first attempts awkward and unsuccessful. But with repeated efforts and more practice, it was only a short time before she was swimming underwater in the shallow area with Jamak. Darrel knew it would be only a short time before they were swimming on the surface as well, and in all areas of the ponds.

The other children were now yelling excitedly. Each wanted to learn how to swim. But Darrel had been in the pond several hours by now, and was tired. He was also concerned about accepting responsibility for children not as well known to him.

As Darrel climbed out of the pond with Jamak and Zhana, a lone figure emerged from the crowd that had gathered, and headed toward Zhana. He was one of the tallest Enrisans Darrel had yet seen — just a few inches shorter than himself.

Ignoring Darrel completely, the man spoke to Zhana. "Don't make a fool of yourself," he warned. "It's bad enough what people are saying, but you don't have to make a spectacle in public like this! Zhana, you know I still want you back..."

67

"Rezak," answered Zhana, drifting closer to Darrel, "please don't...."

"He's not even Enrisan!" continued Rezak. "Look at that pasty white skin. He looks funny and talks funny. How will you ever...."

Zhana's parents closed in on the man gently but firmly, resisting his muted objections, and quietly directed him away. Darrel was glad to see him disappear into the background, but was haunted by the uneasy feeling that he might encounter this tall Enrisan elsewhere.

Darrel gathered up the robes that Jamak had playfully dropped on him earlier, and blotted himself and Zhana dry. Still, the inner robes they had worn while swimming were not so easily dried, and as they headed homeward, the outside air — usually so pleasant and temperate — pressed cool against their wet clothing.

"Who was that?" wondered Darrel as they walked. It was the first time he had seen this kind of outburst among the gentle Enrisan people. Although there had never been anything from Zhana to justify a lack of confidence in her, the incident was threatening to a relationship, which had become very special to Darrel. Made vulnerable by so many recent assaults against his generally confident nature, he was surprised to find himself struggling with feelings of spontaneous jealousy.

"That was Rezak," answered Zhana, sensing Darrel's uneasiness. "I used to be very close to him. He is well known for his craftsmanship with metals. He is able to make many beautiful things, but somehow he has never mastered the spiritual understandings of our people. We had a brief and exciting attraction, but there was a basic difference in values. It could never work out with us, but he can't accept that." Zhana continued to reassure Darrel as they climbed downward, emphasizing that Rezak's personal bitterness did not reflect feelings held generally among the Enrisan people. Darrel knew Zhana was right, and he appreciated her tenderness and understanding. But while this may have been the first display of any outright hostility, the metalworker was certainly not the first to have noticed how different the American was.

Zhana followed Darrel into his chambers, where she had since moved most of her personal belongings. Zhana was annoyed with the clingy wetness of her robes, and was eager to get dried off. Darrel loosened the damp garment and dropped it to the floor, gently caressing his lover's figure. Zhana snuggled close to him and removed his wet clothes. Holding him close, she whispered in his ear. "I love to swim with you. I love everything with you."

After a playfully intense sexual interlude, Darrel and Zhana lay silently tangled in each other's arms. In the peaceful afterglow of pleasant togetherness, Darrel was haunted by a remote feeling of discomfort, which he couldn't quite put his finger on. He wasn't sure if it was a lingering reaction to his encounter with Rezak, or if it was something nagging at his newly-developing moral awareness.

To Darrel, Zhana had come to represent a commitment to the highest standard of ethical values. The values of Dazhan and of the whole Enrisan social ethic seemed central to her lifestyle, yet her spontaneous sensual playfulness, which Darrel enjoyed, seemed inconsistent with traditional moral standards as Darrel understood them. Not that such questions had ever bothered Darrel in the past, but something just didn't seem quite right.

"Is it wrong for us to do this?" he wondered aloud, breaking the goldenness of silence.

"Huh?" responded Zhana dreamily, pulling Darrel closer. "Did I do something wrong? What...?"

Darrel repeated his uncertainty about the moral aspects of their relationship. Zhana sat up a little and gave him a funny look. "Why should anyone really worry about it?"

Somewhat confused, Darrel explained his understanding of traditional moral values, which did not permit sexual experience outside of formal marital relationships. He also explained that there was a great deal of contemporary opposition to such values by those favoring more variety in the pursuit of sexual pleasures.

"Why would an ethical person be concerned about physical pleasure as a moral question?" repeated Zhana.

"Well, the Enrisan social ethic is based on a concept of relationships," continued Darrel, feeling somewhat awkward in the role of justifying traditional values. "I suppose the point could be made that the most special of relationships should be protected by formalized, institutional safeguards."

"Did you say *'special'* or *'sexual'?*" laughed Zhana. "Your outside world sounds awfully strange. Everybody's worried about sex!" She again insisted the whole thing had nothing to do with "right" or "wrong," as he would see after he had heard the rest of Dazhan.

"You have a whole civilization that has never even heard of Dazhan, yet they argue about morality in terms of sexual relationships! Those who are preoccupied with promiscuity and those who are preoccupied with virginity are on opposite ends of the same moral hang-up. Each side places a 'special' moral value, pro or con, on sex. Yet if you asked someone what made their relationship 'special,' I don't think it would be sex. It would probably be some romantic kind of tenderness — some– thing they *do* explore, very carefully, before 'marriage'."

"But which side is right?" persisted Darrel. "The exclusive lifetime commitment, or a free exploration of various relationships?"

"The whole question is silly," answered Zhana. "Which is morally right, a pink robe or a yellow robe? Arguing about which kind of relationship is 'right' is like two kids arguing about whose favorite color is the prettiest. They will never resolve the question, because it is a matter of *preference*, not *morality*. There are also *practical* issues, such as questions of pregnancy, or of avoiding sexually-transmitted disease. But it has nothing to do with Dazhan, as you will see later.

"Some people, like my parents, need the depth and security that comes in sharing the close intimacy and total exploration of One Special Friend. Others need the variety of enjoying several special friendships. What is 'right' can be found at both extremes of the continuum and every point along the way. And maybe the same person is at different points on that line, at different times and in different situations. Perhaps people need to find whatever is right to fulfill their need for 'completeness' — either in one person with whom to share the same 'wavelength' of feelings, interests, lifestyle and values, or in various partners who contribute portions of that 'completeness'. A person must look inward first, to determine their own real needs. Then they can reach outward to develop honest relationships accordingly. Sex itself, like any other abstract thing, has no inherent value either way. It all depends on how these feelings enrich or impair our relationships. Of course, it's wrong to 'use' another person sexually — but it is the 'using' which is wrong, not the sex. If there is any 'immorality' it would be when a person who needs to be free gets trapped in the demanding confinement of a close relationship, or when a person who needs depth and security feels betrayed because they are 'used' for someone else's brief moment of fun."

Darrel held Zhana close so he could feel the warmth of her exposed flesh. "Have you looked inward?" he whispered. "What kind of relationship will fit *your* 'own real needs'?"

Zhana answered cautiously. "All my life I have thought I was like my mother," she said. "I have always felt that I would need the personal security of sharing my whole life and values with One Special Friend. But each time I began to get close to someone, I soon became either incompatible or bored, and I eventually began to wonder if I really needed more variety instead. But, Darrel, every time I see you or think of you I get this exciting sense of fascination — of completeness, of wholeness, of harmonious blending — whether we are discussing ideas, involved in activities, or sharing physical pleasure. In an entire lifetime, Darrel, I could never fully explore all the wonderful mysteries of you and your strange world. So I guess I always knew what I wanted. I just needed to find the right person, Darrel Swift."

Through his last affair with Linda Ferret and all his other mixed-up relationships in the distant Outside, Darrel had never thought about it in quite those terms. But he knew that Zhana was central to all of the exciting discoveries that were still being added to his life, and he did love her very much. He enjoyed the mixture of different kinds of feelings which they shared; a spontaneous blending of friendship and romance absent that was missing from earlier experiences. He pulled Zhana close, and they snuggled up to sleep for awhile.

Some time later, they were awakened by the sounds of a visitor announcing himself from outside. Zhana quickly dressed and hurried up to the entrance, as Darrel, dressing more slowly, followed behind. At the entrance was a young man dressed in a bright green outfit. Zhana recognized the outfit representing Nolak's personal staff, and explained this to Darrel.

Identifying Darrel to his satisfaction, the messenger presented a metallic certificate, and departed. It was an invitation for Darrel to present himself before Nolak, the Most High Divine and highest authority in Enrisa. It was not a command, and was expressed in pleasant terms. It was clearly more an invitation than a summons. The message was very clear as to where to go and what to do. Darrel was instructed to "...present this invitation for admittance into the Most High Sanctuary." But one question was left uncertain in Darrel's mind.

"*When* should I be there?" Darrel asked Zhana, noting that no time was specified, and not wanting to be untimely in his appointment with Enrisa's highest leader.

"What do you mean 'when'?" puzzled Zhana in reply. "You should be there when you are ready to go and meet Nolak!" It was still difficult for Darrel to adjust to the timelessness of the caves.

Darrel was somewhat uneasy about the invitation. "After everything you have told me about the Ancient Text of Dazhan," he explained, "we never got to the practice of Dazhan itself. How can I face the spiritual leader of a whole population when I don't even know about his most fundamental beliefs?"

"Think of the opportunity you have!" responded Zhana excitedly. "All the people of Enrisa learned about Dazhan from their parents or teachers. If you ask the right questions, you can learn about it directly from the Most High Divine himself."

Darrel still wanted a little more background, which Zhana agreed might prove beneficial, while still reserving discussion of the real essence of Dazhan for Nolak himself in the Most High Sanctuary.

"Dazhan is based on a natural kind of pleasure in reaching outward — away from self-preoccupation — and enjoying the dimensions of experience that exist in the other people around us," she said.

"It may be 'natural' in Enrisa," suggested Darrel, "where such responses are conditioned from early childhood. But in the cold reality of the Outside world, where people grow up with a very different kind of experience, these feelings aren't natural at all."

"Social interactions — relationships in some form or other — are still basic to human experience, even in your world," continued Zhana. "But

Dazhan

maybe they haven't developed in the same way. Even if this natural flow among human consciousnesses becomes corrupted through an environment of frustration or antagonism, it might manifest itself in negative ways such as practical jokes, pranks, or a morbid delight in anticipating the suffering of others. In some form, the inborn desire to relate to others' feelings would still be there. But in a more positive form, this natural awareness allows us to enjoy pleasure from others. Without being cultivated, this pleasure might be nothing more than 'people watching'. Such a feeling requires no 'give and take'. Because we are directed *outward* this feeling, which is the basis of Dazhan, does not expect or demand anything in return. We become so involved in someone else's feelings that our interest is in seeing them happy. Our interests are merged with those of another person through this natural linking-up of feelings, even though that person need not be actively involved in the process and may not even be aware of it."

"Oh, I see!" exclaimed Darrel. "Dazhan is like a very high level of cooperation!."

"In a way...," nodded Zhana, with some reservation. "However, we make a distinction between cooperation and Dazhan. Cooperation means that several individuals work together to accomplish separate, non-conflicting goals, or for a common goal, in which abilities and efforts are combined for greater results than what they could have achieved on their own. Cooperation means working together, expecting to get something in return. This is certainly a valid form of interaction for many of our goals or relationships in which we have to depend on others." Darrel briefly considered situations such as business or romantic involvements in which legitimate expectations cause us to be selective in choosing partners.

"Dazhan is something different," continued Zhana. "Dazhan allows an individual to become so involved with the feelings of someone else that he draws them into his own emotional perspective. Dazhan is a merging of our interests with those of another human being with no demand for anything in return. It is a step-by-step process of enjoying whoever we find, however we find them.."

"But what, how...?" Zhana's explanation had only raised more questions in Darrel's mind. But he could see that she had come as close to Dazhan as she wanted, and did not pursue the matter. The rest would be left for Nolak.

Darrel snuggled up close to Zhana and they went back to sleep.

Chapter Seven

Enlightenment

Darrel gazed up the towering cliffside. One narrow path meandered upward, carved out of the sheer face of stone. Far above towered the Most High Sanctuary. It was an imposing structure, carved high and deep into the granite cliffs. Generously adorned with kibihni and colored banners, it glittered like a jeweled temple.

The young American shrugged, and started up the stony path. Alone, Darrel forged his way upward along a steep series of switchbacks. Except for sparsely-scattered shrubs, the trail was dry and barren, in contrast to the lush, tropical foliage and flowing gardens of the valley floor.

Beginning his ascent at a brisk clip, Darrel trudged upward. He eventually began to realize the distance of his climb as time wore on and he gradually became weary, while the distant palace seemed no closer. He paused to rest. Leaning against the cliffside, he gazed out over the valley. Except for the local Sanctuary, he could see none of the hollowed-out tunnels that crisscrossed beneath the surface.

As he climbed, his thoughts wandered often to this *Dazhan* that Zhana had introduced him to. He was looking forward to a deeper, even more engaging exchange with the one person among the cave people who should know it most intimately.

Pausing at intervals, he continued upward. At length the Sanctuary seemed to be drawing closer, and this gave him renewed energy to press onward toward the glittering stone fortress. Uncounted hours passed before he rounded a final twisting switchback and stood facing the imposing majesty of Nolak's massive citadel. He stopped, and pondered for a moment the awesome wonder of the Most High Sanctuary.

As Darrel completed his final weary steps, the Earth began to tremble slightly with a delicate rumbling sensation. Fearing the onset of a subterranean quake, Darrel pressed himself close to the side of the cliff and turned his face toward the Sanctuary. In anticipation of the arriving pilgrim, the massive stone gates creaked ponderously open. Several of Nolak's aides lined the opening behind each gate, offering Darrel a cheerful but cautious greeting. Darrel stepped briskly up to the gate, and presented his invitation to one of the aides. The green-robed officer studied the document briefly and ushered Darrel into the Most High Sanctuary. He entered, and the massive gates rumbled shut behind him.

Dazhan

Standing in a great hall, Darrel gazed around dreamily. The center of the hall was dominated by a lush garden, watered from flows that rolled down across the sides of a carefully-arranged ridge of decorative stones. Bright rows of pastel green banners, set in front of sheets of kibihni to make them appear luminous, lined the frontal walls of the great hall. Several yards before the far end of the hall stood a row of huge rectangular granite tablets. The entire text of *Dazhan* was melted in metallic script into the face of the great pillars. The simple yet richly harmonic music of chimes, woodwinds, and simple percussions floated through the vast chamber from the energies of unseen musicians somewhere in the background.

Darrel drew his attention to the rear wall. Set between the two centermost pillars rose a tremendous glow of flame, which cast a flickering shadow of eerie light throughout the main chamber. Seated in a humble cut of stone at the end of the hall, directly in front of the fire and the row of inscribed tablets, was a frail figure with a shock of snowy white hair, attending vigorously to present matters of business.

It was Nolak.

The Old Man was busily absorbed in piles of metallic "paperwork" when Darrel was presented. Setting his work aside, Nolak looked up. His eyes sparkled through the wrinkled, cheerful features, and he greeted the Stranger with a gentle laugh. Hesitantly, he balanced his way up into a standing position, enjoying the humor of his difficulty. He took a feeble step toward Darrel, and stopped to compose himself. Advancing another cautious step, he faltered, and collapsed forward into Darrel's arms. He held the Stranger in an affectionate embrace as his bony fingers pressed close against Darrel's back. He was still bubbling with his warm, genuine kind of enthusiasm.

"Oh, thank you for coming to see me!" exclaimed the Old Man, with a pleasant, infectious smile. Darrel was amazed. "Come right over here and sit down!" Nolak continued. "We have so much to talk about!" Leaning on Darrel for support, the Old Man guided his visitor to where the two could sit closely together, facing each other.

With a spontaneous, sometimes irreverent style that put Darrel at ease, Nolak explored the full range of his visitor's experience. His questions were deep and probing, but expressed so casually that Darrel opened up freely. Physical weakness belied the Old Man's alert, sensitive nature that allowed him to quickly develop a close rapport with his guest. As the Old Man looked into Darrel's eyes, the young American felt the Spirit of the Enrisan leader touch his own. More than at any other time since coming to the caves, Darrel felt that there was a richness and value and power in what the Old Man had to share. It was more than just survival, or of "getting ahead." Darrel wanted to learn what it was that made the soul of this Old Man burn with such an intensity and fullness of *life*.

After a while, Darrel remembered what Zhana had suggested earlier. Gradually, he worked the conversation around to an inquiry about *Dazhan*. In the presence of its highest authority, facing the complete text in bold metallic script on massive stone pillars, Darrel continued his search for the feelings and understandings of the Ancient Enrisan Text. Darrel expressed an interest in finding out more about the practice of Dazhan that allows a person to reach outward toward the spiritual value in the beings around them.

The Old Man laughed. *"You* are the Dazhan!" He clasped his hands around Darrel's head, and the tone of his voice grew subdued. "Oh, Darrel," he said. "Within my two hands is the whole Dazhan. This treasure! You must start here, within yourself."

Darrel was puzzled. So far, he had learned about the need to look *outward*, and now the Most High Divine was telling him to *look toward himself*. Darrel was not one who was generally intimidated by the presence of authority. But he felt a great sense of awe, or respect — or *something* that he couldn't quite put his finger on — toward the Old Man. Cautiously, Darrel expressed his confusion.

Nolak just laughed again. "Of course you want to reach outward! Of course you want to touch other experiences! But how can you enjoy the value in others if you have not tasted it in yourself? How can you enjoy the simple joy of many treasures if tensions, pressures, frustrations, and unresolved emotional needs *within yourself* force your attention inward?" This caused Darrel to reflect again on his earlier thoughts, comparing the dimension of consciousness — the shintuh — to a TV set. In order to receive value from outside itself, the "receiver" must be in good repair.

"Think about yourself," continued Nolak enthusiastically. "Think about the unique pattern of experiences that have combined to form the special dimension of value which you alone represent. It is exciting for me to meet you and visit with you, Darrel Swift. In a brief moment, I am exposed to a whole new horizon of spiritual value. *YOU*, in fact, are someone unique and special and very important."

Darrel listened quietly, as the Old Man continued. "Consider for a moment just how important you actually are and how intense is your world of feeling," he said. He looked deep into Darrel's soul as if he had known Darrel through uncounted years and unnumbered cultures. "Think back to when you were a little boy. Think about how important your peer group was in your experience. Think of a time when you tried to impress them and it all went wrong and you embarrassed yourself in front of your friends. Think about the sudden flash of embarrassment that stung your consciousness — how intense it was; how real it was."

Nolak paused to allow Darrel a brief moment of reflection, then continued. "What about other feelings? Disappointment in love? Think about the empty pit in your stomach as you sat in silent loneliness, reflecting on happier moments from a crumbling relationship, no matter how right the end may have been. Still other feelings? What about fear? Pain? Uncertainty? Consider how real your feelings are, and how much you are willing to do to protect them. You are willing to cover up your real feelings and conform to weird fashions or repressive lifestyles, and do all kinds of silly things just to fit in with the 'right' crowd. Of course, not all feelings are negative. In romance, there is probably much joy you can remember. What about success in making special achievements? Enjoying the awe and wonder in the beauties of nature, or the subtle, reflective pleasures of quiet introspection?"

Darrel reflected on his own feelings. He thought of times when he had felt so happy that he thought he would burst with joy, floating through a cloud that no one else could understand or appreciate. He also thought of times when he had suffered traumatic loss or personal tragedy, when he felt as if he had been singled out, that no one else could ever have suffered so much; when he felt like crying out, *"Why me?"* He recognized how unique and special and intense his own feelings were, and how he could celebrate the special value represented by his own internal dimension.

"So, Darrel, the first step in the practice of Dazhan is to cultivate and enjoy the special value of the unique dimension of feelings and experiences that you alone represent. You must love yourself. For many people, this step may be easily begun. For others, it may be a very difficult step, wrestling with feelings of inadequacy or unresolved emotional needs. It may even require special help from professional teachers or counselors. But even when a mastery of self-love is achieved, there will still be times when you may want to kick yourself over some silly blunder you may make, but that's because you aren't perfect. Love does not require perfection; it only requires *love.*"

Darrel continued to listen intently. The Old Man's piercing features glowed with vigorous enthusiasm. "Now, we can start to move outward, beyond self. Sometimes this is difficult because, even when we begin to reach outward, our experience is still confined to our own perspective. We need to develop a more objective viewpoint through which to filter these perceptions. Try to look from a perspective *outside yourself.* Look around you, and visualize the surrounding environment." Nolak paused. Darrel took the cue and gazed around the huge, cavernous hall. The Enrisan leader continued: "As you look around, imagine that you are looking, not through your actual viewpoint, but from *outside yourself.* You not only see the people and objects around you, but you also see *yourself* from a detached, neutral perspective — as *part* of the environment rather than as the *observer* of the environment.

"The second step of Dazhan is to move outside yourself, into a state of detachment which accepts and honors yourself, but is not centered around yourself. In some ways, the second step is the easiest, because it is so simple and straightforward as we move into a perception where we are a part of, not the center of, the surrounding environment. In other ways, it is the most difficult, because the mental habits that confine us to that self-directed perspective may be stronger and harder to break than we imagine. It is the gateway to freedom from imprisonment within ourselves.

"Now, from this objective, detached frame of reference, we are able to move into the third step and integrate the values and perspectives of the first two steps to build the bridges to other consciousness.

"Glance around toward some other person. Anyone. Watch the person very closely. Realize that within this being there is a special world of feelings and experiences just as real and just as intense as your own. Think of the fears, the desires, and even the mistakes of this human brother or sister. In every person there are ongoing conditions of difficulty that have to be dealt with, as well as the joy and happiness unique to that individual's experience, which make them special. Are the feelings any less real because they occur within another mind? Here is a whole dimen-sion, which has developed its own fascinating pattern of experience, and you might only have been marginally aware that it even exists! Just like you, his world is very important. Just like you, his feelings are valuable *for their own sakes,* and not for what you can get out of them. Just because you can't actually crawl into this mind and actually feel those experiences doesn't make them any less real. Pain is pain, and happiness is happiness, and it is the same whether it is in your consciousness or someone else's. Relax and smile. Let yourself feel receptive to the Spirit of another consciousness. Recognize the "little lights" of consciousness as being distinct and separate from the 'darkness' of the surrounding physical environment. Let yourself be openly receptive to seeking the value inherent in each such light. So, Darrel, *feel* the awareness that each other person represents a dimension of spiritual value as real and intense as the great value developed through the sequence of experiences in your own existence."

Darrel recalled the celebration of his own feelings — the depth and intensity of both positive and negative feelings. Now, considering the equal value in other consciousness, he realized that every person had such feelings. They can't be exactly the same ones, but every other person has their own uniquely intense joys and sorrows. He wondered what the *"Why me's"* of other people might be. He began to consider that, as unique and special and intense his own feelings were, he could also celebrate the *equal* value represented in someone other than himself.

Nolak continued: "In the first step, you let yourself be aware of — and enjoy — the value of *your own* unique process of conscious experience; in the second step you explored from an outward, neutral perspective, the *same value* in the unique perspectives of another person; in the third step you will merge those two separate perspectives of value into a combination that is greater than what each could ever be on its own, where they can interact to multiply the effect of those separate perspectives."

The Most High Divine paused a moment before continuing the explanation of his Holy Book. "Among human beings there exists potentially a bond of feeling that can bring separate dimensions of personal value together. It is a natural flow of emotions between the internal dimensions of the shintuhni as they interact. When an individual encounters another person in an emotion-charged setting, it is common to get a strong feeling for the other person's experience, and identify it with the experience of the Self in a bond of *empathy*."

Darrel reflected briefly on the nature of such feelings. He considered the way a vivid picture of starving, neglected children can arouse strong sentiments, as people who are otherwise very comfortable feel the child's suffering themselves, through the vicarious experience of empathy. He recalled how "smiling is contagious...." He considered how this natural emotional process was used to make big money in Hollywood: a skilled writer presents a set of fictitious experiences portrayed by talented actors, which seem so real that the audience perceives those feelings and experiences as being real, and feels the feelings of experiences which never actually happened at all, through a natural process that allows a "linking up" of the otherwise separate spiritual dimensions.

When Darrel was ready, Nolak continued. "When this natural, basic kind of *empathy* is combined with the other steps in the practice of Dazhan, there is an intense, deeper level of awareness which the human consciousness can enjoy.

"This is how it works: After a person has developed a real love of his own self, and an appreciation for the intensity of value and feeling within the shintuh of his own experience, he directs his attention outward, toward another person. He focuses his awareness on the intense, inherent value of that other person, perceiving that value as being important for its own sake, and equal to his own spiritual value.

"In this setting begins the third step of Dazhan. Instead of looking at the world through *your* point of view, as in the first step, or from a *neutral* perspective as in the second step, look through the vantage point *of the other person*. Look into the eyes of the other person. Imagine yourself as occupying the physical place where he is. Visualize various objects as they would appear from his vantage point. Try to imagine subtle differences in the way things might appear from *his* perspective instead of *yours*. Try to imagine how *you* look to *him!* And don't limit yourself to the way things might *look* differently. How do they sound? What does that person hear? What is he smelling? What perceptions of *touch* do they feel? Feel the sensations of air on their skin. What are they touching? Holding? Take the time to thoroughly explore the immediate *physical* environment as it would appear through the perspective of another person's senses."

The Old Man paused to let Darrel catch up with him. "Then, carefully evolve your way into an exploration of his immediate *emotional* environment. Imagine all the little thoughts and feelings that might make up his present experience. Try to visualize the operation of the outer environment on his present moment of consciousness. Let yourself recognize conditions of mood that color the brightness and flavor of that little "light" of consciousness. Is it happy? Content? Angry? Frustrated? Be aware of those *transitory* aspects of consciousness that we can often discern clearly by watching for them receptively. But also be aware of the great extent of unique lifetime experiences and deeper levels of real personality beyond your superficial observation, and be aware of how much brightness and value you are exposed to, beyond what you can perceive. And without having to know specific details, let yourself feel curious about the traumas, crises, and conditions of difficulty, as well as the joys, pleasures, and conditions of happiness that add up to weave an ongoing process of experience that is special and unique.

"Get inside his mind until you identify his feelings with your own and make him almost an extension of yourself. Feel his feelings! Reach out, and really share the spiritual value of another being."

"That's a lot of effort!" considered Darrel breathlessly. "Won't some people resent this intrusion into their private consciousness?" he asked.

Nolak again chuckled. He seemed to laugh so easily. "The feelings of Dazhan do not require anything that would make someone else feel uncomfortable. This is your own experience. It imposes nothing on the other person. While you can draw value into yourself from outside, you are still confined to your own consciousness. Dazhan will open up new potentials for spiritual value, but it will not make you a mind reader. You can reach outward to the perspectives of other thoughts and feelings, without intruding into specific details.

"Up to this point, the practice of Dazhan is only your own experience," continued Nolak. "The other person is an important part of it, but, so far, has not been directly involved. This, Darrel, is the fourth step of Dazhan: seeking in each situation what you can actually *do* to reach outward and make a contribution to the experiences of those around you — developing an appropriate behavioral response, as part of a *universal practice* — moving from passive observation to direct interaction.

"In this step, you continue to maintain the mental perspective of the other person's frame of reference. Be positive, cheerful, and let yourself *smile*. The intense spirit of linking yourself to the value in another's consciousness will generate a compelling desire to *do* something that reflects that value. Imagine and visualize ways in which your interaction could add to the cheerfulness, happiness, playfulness — or at least to reduce any unpleasant feelings. Let your actions flow in harmony with those feelings. But let yourself remain attuned to *that person's* perspective. If that person can enjoy what you have to share, then you can be as direct and intense as possible. But often they are not in the same emotional place at the same time and, if we truly wish to reach outward to *their* perspective, we must respect their need for distance, and use restraint so as not to intrude into their privacy or make them feel uncomfortable. Dazhan is a simple sharing of happy feelings, not something to be imposed on others.

"And consider this," suggested Nolak further, his aged features again wrinkling in a friendly grin: "Interactions with others are a part of *everything we do.* It doesn't make sense to sometimes feel good about people and sometimes bad. The true practice of Dazhan is not just in sharing this complete involvement once in a while, but in using these simple steps to draw out the unique personal value from *each encounter.* Dazhan is really just a cheerful habit of enjoying the people around us. Mastery of Dazhan means you can glide through life's daily pattern of interactions, freed from the constraints of self-preoccupation, while being continuously recharged by all the spiritual wealth that surrounds you."

"That seems so natural — so easy — for the Enrisans," mused Darrel. "But how does a person like me get that way?"

Nolak gave another gentle laugh. "The Enrisans begin practicing these steps as children," he answered. "With practice, these steps — which we present and discuss as if they were four separate steps — are blended together into a smooth, automatic practice. For those who become used to it, it is a quick and simple and automatic way in which to approach each interaction with another person. For you, it is a whole new experience. It takes time to make it a habit. The steps themselves are easy. The only difficulty is in overcoming the resistance to a change in habits. That can only be done by practicing the steps, on your own, and also perhaps with feedback from others who have mastered them or who are also learning them. In the beginning, conscious effort may be required through each step. It is like learning any new skill. This may detract somewhat from the same enjoyment as when it becomes a spontaneous part of your lifestyle, but you have to start somewhere."

The Old Man remained enthusiastic. "It is only awkward at the start. We start teaching our children to go through these steps at about the same age we are teaching them to dress themselves. And in both cases they start out awkwardly, but it soon becomes a childishly simple process. It is the same for you. Set aside specific periods for practice. Identify specific individuals and, unknown to them, go through each step of the process. These people can be people you know or people you don't know; they can be men or women; they can be grownups or children —

any size, shape, color, or background — anyone who is a person. All are important, and they all have consciousnesses and feelings you can enjoy.

"Over a period of time, these practice experiences become a natural part of all your moment-by-moment feelings, directing your perceptions outward as you leave a trail of cheerfulness wherever you go. Eventually you will not need to consciously monitor the steps. It becomes a smooth, automatic approach to interactions with others, going through the steps quickly and spontaneously. What is most important is that you not just think about Dazhan as an idea — an abstract concept — but that you actually go out and practice, so you can start doing it!

As he continued responding to Darrel's questions and ideas, Nolak gradually eased the conversation into lighter subjects. And when the frail Old Man eventually became aware that young Darrel was tiring, they broke for a rest. A fine meal was served, and afterward Darrel was led to a private chamber in which to stay during his visit to the Most High Sanctuary. Then Nolak, still bubbling with enthusiasm, was helped away.

Darrel felt physically and emotionally drained from trying to keep up with the Old Man, yet as he rested alone in his room, his mind was still racing with new thoughts and ideas.

As Nolak's teachings gradually gelled into intellectual understanding, in a blend of new insights and unanswered questions, Darrel lay in silent introspection. He no longer felt any sense of skepticism or doubt about *Dazhan*. He felt as though he had been transformed into a new person, hungering for a deeper experience of this new treasure. He wanted to explore the full value of what it offered, yet it was still so new, so foreign. And Nolak was right: the real key would be in going beyond *ideas* and *values* into a *practice* of daily lifestyle habit.

In his mind, Darrel reviewed the step-by-step practice of Dazhan — first, self-esteem; second, recognition and appreciation of the equal value in every other individual; third, an empathetic "linking up" with others; fourth, an appropriate behavioral response in each situation, leading to a universal practice of all the steps in a habitual enjoyment of interpersonal interactions. He tried to imagine how it would work in real life. "Hmmm," he thought, "it might not be *so* hard. It's just a matter of having good feelings about yourself, and keeping yourself in good shape; then reaching out to the same value in someone else — a merging of self-value with that of the other person to share *their* feelings from *their* perspective; and then find cheerful ways to contribute something positive to that moment of interaction. Anyone doing that couldn't help but enjoy feeling good about others — *of course* their lives would be happier!"

Darrel's mind wandered back to his life before Enrisa. He recalled the frustrations of sitting in his car, stuck in traffic. He thought of all the faceless, nameless drivers sharing the same dreary space of highway, passing in and out of each others' lives in brief, anonymous moments, interacting only in the angry exchanges of real or imagined offenses. Could it be possible to find enjoyment in the sullen faces of these frustrated drivers? Because this unconditional compassion was not based on expectation of anything in return, Darrel reasoned that good feelings could be drawn even from those who intended otherwise. In fact, the outward perspective of Dazhan might be the key reversing such tensions.

Darrel tried to imagine what *Nolak* would do in such situations. He imagined for a moment that he could *be* Nolak, and it gave him a warm feeling. He considered the possibility that visualizing qualities of Nolak's goodness in himself might help him in the most difficult situations.

He thought of his office. He could see employees not merely as tools for achieving his own goals, but as complex patterns of experiences and feelings, with hopes and aspirations of their own. He thought of all the things a person in his position could do to create happiness for these people, and how much *he* could enjoy sharing in *their* positive reactions through this vicarious empathetic synthesis. He thought about business associates and clients in the same way. He had always known the business value of gifts and favors and a general treatment of respect for such people, but could now see the added enjoyment in sharing *their* reactions. It made him consider other possibilities of use in business situations. He thought of how much more rewarding his work could be if he really got involved with his clients' and associates' experiences and applied his creative energies in fulfilling *their* expectations to generate positive reactions which he could share. Not only would business be more fun, but it would actually make him more valuable in his trade....

Darrel groaned in self-disgust. Here he was, just getting into this, and he was already thinking about what he could get out of it. Yet, such personal benefit did not seem entirely inappropriate, either. After all, he still had certain legitimate expectations from his employees, associates, or clients. He considered the complex network of everyday transactions made possible by expectation, agreement, and fulfillment in all areas of business and personal interactions. He recalled Zhana's earlier explanations of *cooperation* as a valid process of interaction for many goals or relationships involving others, but different than Dazhan, which involves no expectations. He wondered if the reciprocating nature of such interactions might interfere with such purely unconditional perspectives, but hoped it might still be possible to combine both experiences. Perhaps a special surprise, an unexpected extra kindness, or a truly compassionate awareness of personal feelings *beyond* expected benefits could result in a greater intensity of both processes.

He would ask Nolak about it later. For now, he was tired. Sleepy. His body was physically exhausted; his mind could no longer entertain conscious thought; his soul was lonely for Zhana.

Chapter Eight

Confrontation

Darrel was awakened by the movement of his rock-hewn bedding, and sat up with a start. Was the Earth moving? He turned around as Zhana locked her arms around him and pulled him close. Nolak, sensitive to Darrel and Zhana's relationship, had sent a special invitation for Zhana to come to the Most High Sanctuary. She had accepted enthusiastically.

At length, two of Nolak's aides appeared to escort Darrel and Zhana to Nolak. As they wandered through the palatial corridors, Darrel imagined that this was not the same way he had come after his earlier visit with the Most High Divine. Shortly they arrived at a great wooden door, set back from the corridor. It was the first time Darrel could remember having seen wood used in Enrisan architecture. It must have been carved from one of the many gnarled old cave trees that grew among the rocky cascades. On each side of the door, in the space where the entryway was recessed from the hall, there was a stone pit in which a small fire burned, and which cast an eerie glow on the wooden door. On the door was carved the image of a burning stone.

In front of the door stood Nolak, smiling.

Looking around at the furnaces, the carved wooden door, and the Old Man himself, Zhana gasped. "The *Chamber of Fire!*" she exclaimed. It was a mysterious, highly-revered realm that she had heard about since childhood. Not open to regular visitation by the general community, it was spoken of only in whispers, and was the single most reverenced site within the hallowed walls of the Most High Sanctuary.

Zhana was struck with awe, and her reactions caused a sense of respect in Darrel, as Nolak's aides lifted open the massive door. They faced a narrow stone staircase, winding sharply downward into an obscure dungeon. Nolak cheerfully instructed his aides to remain behind, as he bid only Darrel and Zhana to follow him into the Chamber of Fire. There were no kibihni lights to brighten the way down. At regular intervals pairs of torches lit each side of the ancient stairwell, and this was the only source of light. In spite of the Old Man's physical weakness, he was surprisingly able in descending without assistance, as though he had hobbled up and down these steps so many times over the years that he could stumble along with little conscious effort.

At the base of the winding steps was a small circular room, dimly lit by twenty-seven torches spaced evenly around the perimeter of the circular stone walls. Beneath each torch was inscribed the text from one section of the *Dazhan*. The ragged edges of granite preserved a sense of primeval beauty, and carved in the walls beneath each of the torches were shelves filled with ancient metallic volumes of all shapes and sizes. In the center of the room was a small stone altar, about three feet high, with a flat surface about three feet across and three feet wide. On the flat surface was an intricately carved *Dazhan,* etched in elaborate Enrisan script. Behind the altar was a granite throne, and facing the throne from across the altar were seven similar stone seats grouped closely together.

"This altar," explained Nolak, "is set directly below the massive pillar of flame in the Main Hall. Symbolically, this altar generates spiritual heat that keeps the Great Fire blazing eternally. In the Main Hall above, the *business* of Enrisa is completed. In this Chamber, the *spiritual* institutions of our people are developed, as the seven Chief Divines meet with me at the beginning of each Watercycle."

The Old Man beckoned Darrel and Zhana over to the altar. "Touch the Book," he suggested enthusiastically. Reverently, Zhana lifted the intricately carved metallic cover and spread open the "pages." She and Darrel delicately fondled the elaborate work.

"This," continued Nolak, "is **THE DAZHAN**. This is the *original text* of the sacred writing, entrusted to the safekeeping of each of the Most High Divines down through the centuries of our recorded history." Darrel drew back at the thought of defiling an artifact so ancient, and Zhana likewise backed away from the sacred treasure. A smiling Nolak put them both at ease. Beneath his lighthearted manner, the Old Man radiated a deep, spiritual affection.

In the musky shadows of the torch-lit chamber, surrounded by wondrous ancient relics and the awe of being within the center of Enrisan spiritual culture, Nolak continued to teach from the pages of *Dazhan*. Answering Darrel's questions, and offering new explanations of old ideas, he finally concluded by again stressing the need for positive action beyond the mere acceptance of Dazhan as an idea. He stressed the need for setting aside regular sessions to practice each step of Dazhan, first with deliberate, conscious effort, finding ways to express compassionate feelings through appropriate behavioral *action* in each situation, and gradually developing a smooth, spontaneous and automatic habit of enjoying other people as a natural approach to every social interaction.

Nolak continued to host Darrel and Zhana in the Most High Sanctuary through several cycles of waking and sleeping, teaching them, sharing ideas and continuing to provide stimulating new perspectives. Yet throughout the visit, Nolak never seemed to fall behind in his responsibilities as the highest spiritual and administrative authority in Enrisa. Darrel was continually amazed at the vast spiritual power in such a feeble old man.

When it was finally time to leave the Most High Sanctuary, Darrel radiated a warm, spiritual glow. He felt very much the gift of compassionate love that Nolak had bestowed on him. Zhana was pleased to note how much Darrel had changed since the first time she had found him as a confused, helpless wanderer in a strange land.

Darrel had really come to believe that the simple practice described by Zhana and Nolak could add deeper meaning and happiness to his life. And he remembered Nolak's admonition that merely understanding or accepting the *idea* of Dazhan would not really change his life or feelings unless it was expressed in action through the *practice* of the four simple steps. He would need more than mere intellectual acceptance. He would have to *do* it.

As he walked outward through the great hall on his way out of the Most High Sanctuary, he paused to consider the various other people that were around. At the rear of the Great Hall, where the text of *Dazhan* was etched on the granite tablets behind the pillar of flames, Nolak remained, bidding cheerful adieu to his guests. At the exit-gates in front of him were various aides waiting to assist those entering and leaving the Sanctuary. In the main garden area were various others — some who seemed to belong as permanent aides to the Sanctuary and others, like himself, who were pilgrims in search of spiritual treasures.

He looked around and saw an Enrisan man in the garden area of the Great Hall, seemingly about his own age (although age was difficult to determine among these timeless people). He decided to try the "steps."

He took a deep breath. His first reaction was one of discomfort — it seemed silly. It was a departure from the cool, dispassionate lifestyle carefully cultivated over many years in the Outside. His mind believed it might really work. But his spirit wasn't quite sure yet. Still, Darrel was strong and determined. He forced himself to just plow forward and try the first step. He stopped for a moment to try and remember the sequence of the four steps. First, appreciation of self value; second, awareness of the equal value in another person; third, blending the perspectives of the first two steps by "looking through the eyes of another..."; fourth, appropriate behavioral response in the development of a universal practice.

Yeah — he remembered them — it was easy.

He began his attempt, but ... as he started to try the first step, he remembered there was a lot more than just "appreciation of self value." Nolak had guided him through a very detailed description of what that meant, but now his mind went blank as he tried to recall Nolak's explanation in greater detail.

He turned to Zhana, and was surprised to see that *she* was watching *him*, and smiling. Sheepishly, he confessed awkwardness in trying to practice the steps, and having difficulty remembering exactly what to do.

"Remember when you taught me and Jamak how to swim?" Zhana said with a smile. "It didn't work the first time we tried it. Even when we made it, our movements were slow and awkward. We had to consciously think of each movement. But now that you've taken us swimming a lot of times, it's easy. We can do the movements automatically — without having to think about each one. Not only is it smooth and easy, but we can also swim much better! Learning Dazhan is much the same. At first you have to really think about what you are doing. It is not smooth or spontaneous. But if you do it enough, it becomes a natural approach to interactions with the people you encounter."

Zhana re-explained much of the same material that Nolak had taught him before. An aide provided Darrel with a jewel-tipped stylus to use in scribbling brief notes on a thin metallic sheet, while Darrel wished he could just have a simple pencil and piece of paper from his old life in the Outside. He tried to write a few brief notes that he could keep for quick reference when he wanted to practice the steps.

After Zhana helped him refresh his memory and compile some simple notes, he looked again for the Enrisan man he had selected as the object of his attempted practice. By now the man had moved over to the edge of the Great Hall's garden area, where the cascade of water spilled over the rocky landscaping.

Darrel quickly reviewed his notes and made another attempt. He remembered what Nolak and Zhana had said about conscious effort detracting from the smoothness and spontaneity of early attempts. They were right.

As he had done before under Nolak's direction, and referring frequently to his notes, he began with an appreciation of his own value as a person. He took a moment to consider his own importance, and to really appreciate his own worth. He tried to think about those occasions where he had strong experiences with his feelings, both negative and positive.

He thought of embarrassment: he remembered the time he was playing shortstop for his high school baseball team in a key game, and made a clumsy error on a key play, which cost them the game. He remembered the flash of pain and fear when it happened, and how sensitive he was to the ribbing that continued for weeks afterward.

He thought of awe and respect for Nature. He visualized natural wonders of beauty he had enjoyed in the Outside world, and new ones he had come to enjoy in the caves of Enrisa — the cascading mixture of granite and crystal rocks flowing with water and dressed with leafy foliage and gnarled trees, adorned with rainbows and limestone formations.

He thought of romance: he thought of his first teenage love and the heartbreak and pain that lasted for weeks when it didn't work out. He thought of other loves — how some had ended in that same tortuous agony and others, like his recent break up with Linda Ferret, had ended with a sense of relief. He also considered the joy of romance. He thought of Zhana and how lost he would feel if he ever had to face the prospect of life without her. He had tasted tantalizing bits of that joy in each of his earlier relationships, no matter how good or bad. Now Zhana had brought so much depth and fulfillment into his life as they shared not only romance, but also friendship and involvement in each other's feelings and activities.

He re-lived the excitement and pride of his business and career achievements, and the joys and fears of other situations that made him unique and different from any other human being. He paused to consider that he was, truly, a uniquely special light of consciousness.

He turned again to look at the Enrisan stranger he had selected, who was just going about his own business. Darrel paused to relax. He let himself smile and feel receptive to the spirit of compassionate joyfulness. Darrel did not know anything about this man — just a fellow traveler within planet Earth. He gazed very closely at this anonymous human brother. He tried to consider that within this being was a special world of feeling and experience as real and intense as his own. He thought of the fears, joys, pains and desires that might be within the experience of this stranger. He did not know what they might be, but tried to keep in mind that these feelings and experiences were no less real than his own just because they occurred within a different consciousness. He let himself be drawn into a feeling of warmth and closeness to this anonymous Enrisan.

Darrel looked into the eyes of the Enrisan. He tried to visualize how the world might look from his point of view. The Enrisan was standing alongside a wooden railing in the garden area, where a gentle trickle of water ran down from the ridge of stones beneath one of the illuminated green banners. Darrel tried to imagine how that idyllic view might appear from the other man's vantage point instead of his own. As Nolak had suggested, Darrel tried to imagine how *he* might look to the other man. Darrel tried to imagine the sensations of touch as the main rested his bare forearms on the wooden rail, and the feel of the air on his skin. He tried to imagine the sounds of trickling water that the Enrisan might hear.

As he slowly and thoroughly explored the immediate *physical* environment as it might appear to this other man, he carefully developed an exploration of his *emotional* environment. Again, without knowing specific details, he imagined all the little thoughts and feelings that might make up the present experience of this other man. He considered the temperate climate in the Great Hall and the beautiful scenery, and felt a mood of contentment mixed with anticipation in the Enrisan. He tried to draw on that spiritual energy to feel the perspective of the present moment as the Enrisan might feel it — to get a sense of blending his consciousness into the spirit and viewpoint of his anonymous friend. Considering that mood of contented enjoyment of the physical and spiritual beauty in the garden area of this Great Hall, Darrel could draw that same feeling into himself.

Darrel looked at his notes. He hadn't felt the need to refer to them in the third step, which seemed to flow naturally from the first two. But he knew there was still a fourth one. "Behavioral response." He must seek from the present situation what he could *do* to reach outward and make a contribution to the experience shared with this anonymous stranger. What could he do? If he walked up to a stranger and just started doing *anything* it might seem weird or uncomfortable. Or maybe that's what people in Enrisa expected. What about in the Outside world? Would Dazhan be practical back home in California? Darrel decided that it would be. He also decided that sometimes the appropriate behavioral contribution might be the choice *not* to do something; not to intrude — to enjoy the sharing of spirit but also to realize that, in some cases, what another person may need is to be left alone. For now he would not act directly. But he would consider other possibilities, too. If a comfortable opportunity presented itself, perhaps he would try to get acquainted, or talk, or something. He would see.

For the moment, Darrel was satisfied. Although an awkward "first attempt," he was able to go through the steps. And it really wasn't hard. It was only hard to make he take the initiative and actually *do* it. But once he got going, it wasn't really difficult.

Of course, this first attempt was very "safe." It was in a situation that was neutral and anonymous. There was nothing negative to cause resistance, nor positive to create expectations that would conflict with Dazhan. What if he had tried to practice with someone who disliked him? Could he overcome the resistance? What about someone from whom he had *expectations,* even legitimate ones? Would he be able to practice toward someone he knew, such as Zhana, apart from — or in addition to — his interest in enjoyment of the relationship?

As they left the Sanctuary and traveled along the trail down the face of the cliff, Darrel was unusually silent. The time passed so quickly. Perhaps downward travel is always easier. Perhaps it was because he was consumed by the thoughts and feelings of his recent experiences. Perhaps it was because he could enjoy Zhana's companionship.

As they reached the floor of the main valley, Darrel gave Zhana a little kiss. "You go on alone," he said. "I need a few moments to myself, to sort out my thoughts."

Zhana smiled softly. "I understand."

With a lingering spiritual afterglow remaining from his encounter with Nolak, Darrel wandered silently toward the ponds. His thoughts were mixed. His mind was alive with spiritual excitement, and at the same time strangely peaceful.

Suddenly, there was a soft, ominous growl that shattered Darrel's thoughtful reflections. Perched on the top of a nearby rocky bluff was Rezak, Zhana's jealous ex-lover, waving a sharp, gleaming weapon, which the skilled metalworker had been able to produce.

"It is wrong for a demon of the pale flesh to touch Enrisan women," he called out threateningly, advancing slightly from the top of the bluff.

Darrel's first reaction was fear, then anger. Quickly, though, he considered Dazhan. Could Nolak's spiritual treasure really work to ease the tensions of confronting a jealous lover?

Darrel backed off. To succeed in this situation would require a more experienced practitioner of *Dazhan*. For now, Dazhan would have to wait. Darrel's immediate concern was for his own physical safety. Though Rezak was one of the tallest of the cave people, the wiry Enrisan would still be no physical match for the big blond American — except for the gleaming weapon, which he wielded menacingly.

Darrel broke into a run toward the ponds. But on the uneven rocky surfaces of the garden landscape, he knew the agility of the nimble cave dweller would quickly overtake him.

Despite an early lead, Darrel soon found Rezak closing in on him. He paused for a moment, with his heart pounding, as he faced the thought of senseless physical terror that Rezak hoped to inflict on him. He turned, and made his way as quickly as possible up the rocky fractures of the subterranean surface, hoping to advance as far as possible before Rezak reached the end of the level ground.

Rezak arrived at the rocky edge as Darrel reached the branches of a great tree growing out over the pond. Darrel was dismayed at how quickly Rezak danced over the rocks. Darrel ambled up through the branches of the tree, but it was clear that he was no match for Rezak's natural climbing advantage. Rezak drew ever closer, wickedly brandishing his weapon. Darrel considered the irony of surviving weeks of darkness in the outer caves only to lose it all in a deliberate act of violence.

He inched further and further out into the extremities of the small branches, which swayed under his weight, glancing hopefully downward at the ponds below, as Rezak scurried quickly up the tree.

As Rezak drew to within striking distance, Darrel pushed himself out of the tree and fell into the safety of the water, where the non-swimming Enrisan would be afraid to follow. A rush of victorious excitement, tempered by cautious relief, swept over Darrel as he splashed into the temperate pond and glided into the security of its refreshing depths.

Unseen by Darrel, the sudden release of his weight caused the branches to flip upward violently, throwing Rezak loose from his perch. The alert Enrisan was barely able to grab the endings of another, smaller branch nearby. As Darrel returned to the water's surface, he saw Rezak struggling to climb back into the tree on the tiny branches which were clearly not strong enough to support him. There was a slow cracking sound, as Rezak let out a terrified scream and tumbled into the water below in a torrent of fragmented leaves and splinters.

Darrel's first thought was an impulse of relief for his own personal safety. But the spirit of Nolak's gift was still with him, and as Rezak thrashed about in the water, hopelessly trying to remain afloat on the twigs and leaves surrounding him, Darrel's feelings extended beyond mere desire for his own survival. He watched the expressions on his enemy's face and recognized the agonizing sensations of terror that seized the consciousness of the non-swimming Enrisan. What would it be like to grow up with a lifetime fear of water, not know how to swim, and then fall into a watery pool, facing the threat of certain death? He imagined a little light in the water. Could he stand aside and let this little light be extinguished? He thought of his own past sorrows in romance, and considered the violent throbbings of emotional pain that could drive a man to such extremes of behavior. He felt sympathy for his helpless attacker. Maybe Rezak had brought this calamity on himself. Maybe he deserved what he got. But that wasn't important. Darrel felt concern for the plight of a helpless human brother. It wasn't a full-blown excursion through the joyful steps of Dazhan, yet Darrel felt a sense of deep spiritual warmth as he made his way toward his helpless attacker.

Swimming quickly to Rezak's side, Darrel gently pried the weapon loose from the metalworker's fingers, and let it drift to the depths of the pond. Rezak grabbed toward Darrel, grasping frantically for survival. To avoid being smothered by the hysterical Enrisan, Darrel positioned himself behind Rezak, and reached around one of his attacker's arms so he could tow the man in a partially immobilized condition.

When Darrel finally released the man in shallow water near the rocky edge, the Enrisan staggered toward the security of the edge, and fell into the rocks, sputtering and choking. Darrel rested his arm around the man's shoulder to comfort and reassure him, not apologetically, but with compassion. When Rezak shrugged him away, Darrel backed off. Noting that a crowd had gathered to watch the action, and that other Enrisans were already coming forward to help, Darrel swam away in solitude.

The Enrisans were yelling and waving excitedly on the rocks, beckoning him back to shore. He wasn't sure what to do. His encounter with Rezak was his first hostile confrontation with an Enrisan. How would the rest of these happy cave people view such a confrontation between an outsider and one of their own? How much of the encounter had they seen? What conclusions would they draw from the incident?

As he continued floating and treading water in the pond, Darrel also realized that he couldn't survive forever alone in the water. Sooner or later he would have to return to the shore.

At length, as he watched the gathering on the rocks, Zhana burst through the crowd, calling to Darrel. He was relieved to see his sweetheart, and felt a sense of safety in returning to the one who had guided him through all of his previous crises in this foreign place. As he headed toward the shore, Zhana removed her outer robe and stepped into the shallow area of the pond. Gingerly, she swam out to Darrel, as he had taught her.

Zhana embraced Darrel in the water. "What happened?! The people are all very excited, but no one seems to know what's going on," she said. She noticed Darrel's uncertainty. "There is no reason for concern," she continued. "I think you are truly wonderful." Darrel was still apprehensive, but Zhana led him back to the rocks and shielded him from the others until she could bring him safely into the living area they shared.

Squatting on the floor of their stony domicile, Darrel explained the details of what had happened, and expressed his concern that in such a confrontation, local sentiment would eventually favor the Enrisan. Zhana completely rejected such an idea. "Our people can only respond to you as an individual. They will not 'judge' you on any other basis."

She explained that while the cave-people had built a successful social order based on the spontaneous interpersonal awareness of Dazhan, every sizable community must expect its share of failures to surface as delinquents. While the cave-people may have had few failures, Zhana conceded that this was certainly not the first show of antisocial behavior in the caves. She continued to assure Darrel that his background would not result in being judged unfairly. "You are Enrisan now," Zhana insisted. "I know my people. They have seen that you are learning to practice Dazhan."

They were interrupted by the sound of a visitor announcing himself from the outside. Inviting the visitor inside, they were greeted by a messenger dressed in an outfit similar to of Nolak's aides. But instead of the bright green of the Most High Sanctuary, the robe was white, to represent the local tribal Sanctuary. This was a representative for Kerreih, the regional Chief Divine.

As the leader of the most populous of the seven tribal regions, this youthful woman was the second most powerful official in Enrisa, and the most probable successor to the aging Nolak. Kerreih's messenger presented a metallic document to Darrel, and departed.

Darrel glanced at the document and passed it to Zhana.

Zhana read the text quickly and stared in disbelief. "It can't be!" she stormed, dropping the metallic plate on the floor. It was the strongest reaction Darrel had yet seen from his gentle sweetheart. Darrel could see that she was struggling to hold back tears of anger.

Rezak had formally petitioned Chief Divine Kerreih with a request that Darrel be confined to long-term institutional treatment for his failure to adjust to the values of the Enrisan social order. Specifically, Rezak accused Darrel of having attempted to drown him in the ponds. As a further general complaint, the metalworker alleged that Darrel was incapable of adjusting to the spiritual values of Dazhan that were so foreign to him. A hearing would be held before Kerreih and a council of the local Divines to determine the matter, and Darrel would be summoned when he was to appear.

Darrel was amazed at how much faster the wheels of justice turned here in the caves than in the Outside.

* * * * *

In the outside world as well, there was mixed speculation as to the long-term fate of Darrel Swift.

"Can you believe the money that sucker is gonna blow on a bunch of bones!" Lee was openly contemptuous of Linda Ferret's little enterprise, but opportunistic. "What the hell. If she wants to spend that kinda dough, with my name on the checks, it's okay with me."

Winter had passed. In the harsh weather of the Canadian Rockies, the exploration for Darrel's remains had been suspended. But now, as the weather became milder, but still with a great deal of snow on the ground, Linda had insisted on resuming the search.

No one but Linda expected any possibility of Darrel's survival. And, as they descended deeper into the maze of previously unexplored caves, it became improbable that they would even find his remains, with all the possible places where they could be dispersed in water, buried at the bottom of an unseen pit, or otherwise lost in the caves' darkness.

Still, they searched relentlessly. If nothing could be found of Darrel, there was still much else to be found. As they made their way down into the lower passages, they stumbled into discovery of the underground waterflows and, like Darrel before them, were astonished by discovery of the little fluorescent stones.

As they made their way deeper into the bowels of the Earth, it became clear that exploration of the caves might lead to even greater discoveries. Perhaps there might even be greater riches than the paychecks from Linda Ferret.

Chapter Nine

Justice

Popping up out of the water, Darrel swam over to the rocky edge of the pond where Zhana was sitting. "Still can't find anything," he said.

Zhana slipped into the water next to Darrel. "It's got to be down there somewhere!" she answered.

Once again, Darrel pushed off from the side of the pond. He drifted down through the depths, carefully scanning the floor of the pond beneath the spot where he had rescued Rezak. The uneven features were obscured by billowing underwater greenery drifting breezily with the gentle current. Specific details of the rocky bottom seemed impossible to define. Darrel glided over the roughness of the stones, straining to see, and groping along with his hands. Just as he was running out of breath, the motion of his arm swept away a loose drift of sand and revealed the sharp blade of Rezak's weapon. Darrel wriggled it loose from its wedge between two stones and darted to the surface.

Bursting up from the water, he drank a great swallow of air and waved the trophy. Zhana shrieked with delight. Now, they would attend the formal review of Rezak's with some verification that Darrel had not only saved the life of the Enrisan, but had done despite Rezak's threat against his own personal safety.

Returning to their subterranean dwelling, Darrel and Zhana worked up a strategy for presenting their evidence with maximum impact in the coming "trial." Darrel prepared an elaborate defense, as if to face an American courtroom. Zhana, confident in the compassion and fairness of her people, felt Darrel's precautions were somewhat extreme, but she could understand his uncertainty. He was still unfamiliar with Enrisan formalities, and was not acquainted with the young ruler who was to be his judge. Also, he could not imagine what kind of "institutional treatment" he might be confined to in this strange place, and he did not really want to find out.

The time finally came when white-clad aides of the tribal Chief Divine, Kerreih, appeared to bring Darrel to the hearing. Zhana was permitted to accompany them. Darrel was genial and cooperative, and the aides responded in kind. They were cheerful and pleasant, yet alert in case greater firmness became necessary.

Zhana was polite and friendly, and not without compassion for the desperation that could motivate a person like Rezak. Yet she also tried to contain the irritation she felt toward the false accusations that had been made against the one she had chosen as her Most Special Friend. Still, the charge had been made, and it was the responsibility of the proper authorities to make a routine investigation of any serious accusation. Zhana made every effort to communicate to a skeptical Darrel Swift her confidence that he would be dealt with fairly.

The Enrisans followed patiently at Darrel's clumsy pace as they made their way over rocky bluffs or through thickets of foliage, past the rock-carved openings of burrowed-out dwellings. There were really no prominent structures to break up the rugged features of the landscape except the singular presence of Kerreih's Sanctuary.

The first indication that they were nearing the Sanctuary was the observation that the wild foliage was more trimmed and cultivated in a delicate beauty. There were gardens everywhere, with plants and gnarled branches blending with rock formations, and small ponds and waterfalls among the natural grottoes. Looming up from behind a wall was the massive granite Sanctuary. Perhaps in the outside world, mused Darrel, the Sanctuary would not seem so imposing. But here, in a land of rock and brush where architecture reached silently down into the Earth, the Sanctuary stood vast and alone upon the landscape.

Darrel and Zhana were led through a gate in the enclosing wall, which had been built through centuries of piling up the mud so it could dry to the hardness of stone. Through a garden walk passing between twin fountains, they came upon an outdoor forum, leading through a row of large pillars to an assembly hall left unendingly open to the outside. On the row of pillars was etched in metallic script the complete text of *Dazhan,* and at the front of the assembly hall, a small flame glowed from the center of a great stone altar, as in Nolak's Most High Sanctuary. A hall leading away from the assembly area was lined with small chambers in which the local Divines could conduct the business of their own jurisdictions, and there were other rooms and facilities whose purposes Darrel could not guess. A gentle melody of chimes and woodwinds, offered by unseen musicians, filtered through the halls. The strange Sanctuary ignited Darrel's curiosity, but he could not forget that his presence here was not by choice, and his wonderment was tempered by apprehension over his uncertain future.

Darrel's heart began to pound as he was led into the small chamber in which Kerreih's "court" would be held. Entering with confident strides that concealed his underlying insecurity, he was greeted by impressions foreign to his concept of a "court."

Squatting on the hard-Earth floor behind a low table of polished granite was a white-robed woman, much younger than Darrel would have expected. Seated around her were other local Divines, including Laros, but Kerreih was clearly in control.

As Darrel entered, she broke into a broad smile, and greeted him cheerfully. He was surprised. She did not seem to be serious and "judicial" in the management of her "courtroom." She studied Darrel with quiet thoroughness. Her strong, piercing eyes belied her slender, Enrisan frame. Darrel could see in her eyes not only the great strength that she radiated, but also the simultaneous expression of cheerful, tender compassion. She stood, walked over to Darrel, took one of his hands with both of hers, and greeted him warmly.

Squatting off to one side of the room was Rezak, uncharacteristically subdued in the presence of Authority. He would not look at Darrel directly, and seemed increasingly uncomfortable as Darrel and Zhana were welcomed briefly but warmly by Kerreih.

Watching Kerreih's pleasant but alert sense of firmness in controlling her "court," Darrel felt a momentary sense of cautious optimism. He felt she would really make a fair decision based on what had happened and what to do about it. Still, he kept a firm grip on the evidence he had prepared and the notes he had made, to enjoy every advantage in making sure that Kerreih's sense of fair play would be enhanced by exposure to his facts.

Squatting alongside Zhana into a place reserved for them, Darrel was fascinated by the layout of this "legal arena." It was so different from systems with which he was more familiar. There were no lawyers. There was no "prosecution." There was no "defense." The entire concept of an adversary legal proceeding, with two sides competing before an impartial magistrate, was non-existent. Here the Chief Divine provided leadership in working with the Council of Divines to gather whatever information was available from any source, to determine what had happened and what corrective action should be taken. There was no legal maneuvering, and no strategies for competing sides to "play" for a win. The whole proceeding consisted of a formal charge made by an accuser, and then an independent investigation made at the direction of the Divines. The possible presentation of any evidence by accusers or defendants would be at the direction of the "judges" rather than by those with an interest in the outcome.

Darrel's wandering thoughts were brought back to an abrupt sense of reality as Kerreih smiled and spoke. Zhana clasped Darrel's hand and squeezed a gentle reassurance of support, as the Chief Divine began: "Darrel Swift, the judgment of Enrisa is upon you as follows..."

A flash of anger and frustration swept through his consciousness as he realized that judgment was going to be made with no consideration of his account of the facts, and with no regard for the evidence he had accumulated or the defense he had so painstakingly prepared.

He shot to his feet in protest, but Zhana quickly restrained him. Darrel turned to his sweetheart with a pale, numbed expression. He felt betrayed. He started to speak but nothing came out. With quiet resignation, he slumped back into a squatting position, more ready to accept defeat than at any time since he had first entered the caves.

Kerreih began again. "Darrel Swift, the judgment of Enrisa is upon you as follows: this Council grants to you full rights, freedoms, and equal status as a contributing member of this community as though you had been born here. We have found only that you came to us as a stranger, and have begun to learn the values and feelings that we enjoy. There is no evidence that you have ever acted in any way contrary to the happiness of this community." Kerreih's smile radiated happiness as well as sincere tenderness. "This Council welcomes you to enjoy a happy life of compassionate joy with us, unrestrained, in our joyful community."

Darrel tried to formulate an appropriate response, but still could not speak. His head was spinning. He leaned on Zhana, overcome with relief. Zhana held him comfortingly. "I didn't mean for you to feel hurt when I held you back," she whispered. "But I knew that no judgment would be made against you if you had not been invited to make a defense. When Kerreih began to order a decision of judgment, I knew it meant she had arrived at a favorable decision without the need for a defense."

Regaining control of his senses, Darrel turned his attention toward Rezak. With mute objections of subdued anger, the metalworker glared in frustrated acceptance. A murmur buzzed through the chamber as all eyes turned toward the accuser. "White water-devil," he muttered quietly.

Kerreih, too, faced Rezak. She addressed her remarks to Rezak, gradually turning towards the full chamber. "There are many physical features by which we are distinguished," she announced. "Among our own people there are differences in hair color or eye color. But the essence of human value has nothing to do with the physical shell. Human experience is a function of the internal process of consciousness. The consciousness of this human being is no less real because he comes from a strange place or bears a different appearance. Differences in skin color or texture are no more important than hair or eye color, except that it may be more obvious, but still of *no greater significance..*"

Turning toward Rezak, Kerreih continued. "Rezak the Metalworker," she proclaimed, "the judgment of Enrisa is upon you as follows:" A hush swept across the chamber as the Chief Divine continued. "You have shown your inability to enjoy the spiritual practice of Dazhan. That is your right under our tradition of free individual choice. But you have allowed this social blindness to poison your behavior toward others and attempt to cause them harm. This Council has determined that you have sought to cause physical harm to Darrel Swift, and also that you have sought to have him falsely accused with serious offenses. Therefore, it is necessary that you no longer be permitted to share the benefits of a society in which you might again choose to cause suffering for others. Rezak the Metalworker, it is ordered that you be confined to long-term institutional treatment in the Isolation Zone. You will remain confined for the protection of this community through the time of six Watercycles. At that time, we will review your individual social growth to determine if you can then resume a productive role in this community."

The actual pronouncement of judgment was crisp and businesslike. Having completed "judicial" matters, Kerreih continued to speak, but with increased softness and gentleness. Darrel remained keenly aware of both the strength and warmth that flowed from her. "Rezak, you are talented and capable of enjoying freedom and of enjoying the deepest levels of spiritual joy offered by this community. We love you and hope to provide a nurturing environment in which you can seek to acquire these values. You will retain your freedom of choice to accept them or not. But we cannot permit you to interfere with the free choices of others in pursuing their own happiness."

White-clad officers led a stunned Rezak out of the room. The crowd slowly dissipated. Darrel was lightheaded with relief, his mind spinning with a thousand questions. How could Rezak, who was not on trial, be found guilty in this surprise judgment? What kind of "treatment"? What kind of "institution"? Where was this "Isolation Zone"?

Zhana tried to explain. Rezak, as the accuser, had already had a full opportunity to present his side of the story. As long as any potential defendant has had a chance to explain his story, the Chief Divine can make any judgment, at any time, without requiring a separate complaint, separate proceeding, or any other procedure which exists to aid Chief Divines in ordering fair judgments.

As to Rezak's future? Primarily to prevent a delinquent from causing future harm to others, he would be isolated from the community for *at least* the period of time ordered, and longer if necessary. While the isolation and loss of freedom might generate a certain degree of "punishment," there would not be any further attempt to cause suffering. In fact, he would be cared for under fairly comfortable conditions. As to the kind of "treatment" and the nature of the "institution"? Zhana deferred complex explanations for a time when more detail could be explored, but indicated that during the term of confinement an individualized plan of rehabilitation would be designed. While response to rehabilitation would not help to shorten the minimum term of confinement, the individual would at least be more likely to respond favorably in a normal social environment when the term was completed.

Zhana tried to explain that the system of corrections for adult delinquents was an extension of the overall system of general education.

Darrel seemed confused. He envisioned a "system of education" represented by innocent, cheerful schoolchildren, with all the joyfulness and spontaneity of the cave-people, in contrast with the worst criminal element from among the caves.

Furthermore, Darrel had known since the time of his arrival in the caves that somewhere, somehow, Zhana held a somewhat vague but unquestionably significant role in the Enrisan system of education — that she was somehow involved in working on special kinds of problems in education and communication. That's how she had gotten the assignment of tutoring Darrel when he had arrived as a helpless foreigner. Yet, beyond his own experience, he was not sure just exactly what she did. He expressed his uncertainties to Zhana.

Zhana gave her typical response, so cheerful, yet so knowing. "The essence of human value is in the process of conscious experience," she said, repeating a common theme from Darrel's earlier exposure to the Dazhan as they walked, climbed, and scrambled across the rocks and underbrush. "Because conscious experience is what makes life meaningful, we believe that *experience* is the key to learning information or values. When we develop plans for teaching children, our first effort is to provide actual experiences that are meaningful to the consciousness of each child. 'Teaching' is more than just 'telling'. We encourage children to learn through their natural inquisitiveness about the exciting world around them. This helps them develop enthusiasm for living, and an ability to reach outward in many creative directions.

"We start from each child's own interests and needs, allowing them to internalize facts or values in the course of actual experiences. To allow each child to develop positive feelings about human personal value, we make sure each child feels the real value and individual specialness each represents. We are constantly seeking to explore what is happening in each child's mind. What are they thinking? What are they feeling? We must make the child *feel* the internalization of facts or values rather than just ingest them intellectually."

"But you're not a teacher yourself," queried Darrel. "What do you do in this system?"

"When teachers or counselors who are actively involved in the process of experience-oriented education have compiled information about the interests, feelings, and past experiences of the child," she continued, "they meet with a Minister of Education such as myself, and we work out a specific strategy for motivating that individual, from *their* unique perspective of experience. The teacher or counselor will work with the individual from the plan we have designed to fit his specific personality and interests, and report to us on a regular basis what they are doing to make sure they have a personal relationship with each child."

Darrel stopped to rest on a small, flat rock, and Zhana snuggled up beside him. He couldn't help but reflect on how successfully this system seemed to operate. Here was a happy, productive, peaceful society, sharing a relaxed but prosperous community experience. He couldn't resist contrasting this with the distant memories of life in the outside world, where the social order was splintered into so many factions, fighting against each other to manipulate wealth. Crime was rampant, and individual greed was the common motivational factor. Darrel couldn't help but share his reflections with Zhana.

"Yes, we are a happy people," she responded. "But we are not perfect. I can assure you that we make every effort to reach the real needs of individuals entrusted to our care. We try to develop the most effective plan for each individual, and continually revise our plans to keep up with changing needs. This emphasis on *preventing* problems is our greatest tool in the fight against delinquent behavior. But we are not perfect. We can't help but make occasional errors of judgment, or fail to recognize quiet, hidden needs that go unmet. Or there may be factors in the family or peer group that we are not aware of or cannot control. Even if we see that they are not responding to our beautiful teachings, we cannot teach these children forever. Eventually they grow up. As long as their inability to share the spiritual practice of Dazhan does not interfere with the peaceful order of the community, then our tradition of free individual choice allows them to think or feel whatever they want, and we will leave them alone.

"However, if their behavior threatens mental or physical harm to others, then they must forfeit their right of individual freedom. For the protection of Enrisa, violent or dangerous delinquents are kept in the Isolation Zone, apart from the general community, for a minimum term."

Once again, Darrel was confused as Zhana's explanation started out with innocent children and ended up with adult delinquents.

Zhana smiled at his confusion. "It's really all part of the same problem," she said. "The adult delinquent is a failure of the educational system, and it is up to the educational system to correct the error. In the correctional system of the Isolation Zone, delinquents are again subject to the process of experience-oriented education, just like children. And, again, we as Ministers of Education are called to work out specific plans to determine what deficiencies must be reversed while they are back in our jurisdiction. These are our toughest cases, because we have to undo the previous failure, and reverse emotional habits reinforced over many Watercycles. Fortunately, because such occurrences are so rare in Enrisa, they can be given priority attention. And the circumstances of their delinquencies may give new clues that we can use in understanding the *causes* of their maladjustments."

Zhana tried to explain the basic concepts of Enrisan educational theory. She stressed the difference between *teaching* and *telling*. She described the Enrisan ideal of going beyond the mere intellectual understanding of concepts, to an emotional internalization of feelings that are consistent with good self-esteem and the ability to then develop good feelings toward others. At all levels of Enrisan education, the emphasis was on understanding the child or adult, and reaching those individuals from their own perspectives. And everything was to be kept at the highest possible level of enjoyment: the human mind *wants to learn* and *wants* to learn to be happy; there is a *natural enthusiasm and inquisitiveness* that can be developed into the understanding of both facts and values.

At this point Darrel had to interrupt. "Enjoyment? I can understand that for children, but delinquents?"

"Of course! Specific techniques may vary greatly between children or delinquents, but the same concepts of learning would apply."

Darrel was still confused. "Enjoyment for delinquents? What about punishment for what they've done?"

"Punishment?" responded Zhana quizzically. "The victims have already suffered. If we make them suffer we just increase the suffering in the world. 'Revenge' has nothing to do with it. We just want to solve problems."

Zhana could see that Darrel was still struggling to understand. It was too new, too foreign, to be assimilated all at once. "Why don't you see it for yourself!" suggested Zhana. "I can show you a children's learning center, and show you how we teach children, and then also show you the Isolation Zone, so you can see what we do if we need a second try."

Darrel expressed surprise at the invitations. "The Isolation Zone? Is it permissible for 'civilians' to tour such facilities?" wondered Darrel.

"Not really," Zhana smiled. "But we can work something out for you." Spotting a nearby pond, surrounded by the twisting branches of Enrisan cave-trees and some nearby rocky caves, Zhana had another suggestion. "Let's stop here and relax. Then I'll show you what I do here."

Zhana undressed and waded out into the pond. She beckoned Darrel to join her. He left his robe at the opening of a shallow cave, next to Zhana's, and followed her into the temperate pond. They splashed and frolicked in the gentle flow, feeling refreshed and relaxed after their lengthy wandering. When the two finally emerged from the water, Zhana spread herself across a smooth boulder to dry in the glistening rays of the kibihni, and Darrel gathered up some native fruit growing nearby. After eating, they snuggled up in the hollow of a small cave to rest.

Chapter Ten

School

Darrel looked around. It didn't look anything like his idea of a "school."

First, there was no classroom. Everyone was outdoors. But many of the cave people's activities were outdoors in the gentle environment of the caves, so that alone wasn't so unusual. But there didn't seem to be any learning going on! It was more like a recreational center at a public park. Everyone seemed to be playing.

He expressed his uncertainties to Zhana.

"Well of course they're having fun!" she said. "Learning is supposed to be fun. The human mind is naturally curious and *wants to learn*. We follow its natural course and help it along."

Darrel looked around again. Behind a clump of rocks, a teacher and some children were using wooden sticks, pieces of rock and scraps of metal to fashion some kind of craft. In a dug-out area of caves — the closest thing Darrel could see to a "classroom" — several teachers were using art projects to help students with fine-motor skills. From somewhere in the small cave area, gentle strains of music flowed out into the school area. In the trees, on rocks, and on ropes and vines that seemed to be hanging everywhere, children were climbing on anything around, outdone only by their teachers who were even more agile, more quick, and having more fun. Here and there, a teacher would be talking with one or more children, sometimes laughing playfully, sometimes in more seemingly serious conversation on some point of learning or discipline.

Darrel was still confused. Of course, these were fine activities for a summer camp, and every child should have some fun, but it somehow didn't seem like a school. He repeated his concerns to Zhana.

"Well, then, what *should* it be like?" she questioned. "What are schools like in your world?"

Darrel described the kind of schools he had grown up with. He described a classroom environment with essentially a single lesson plan for thirty students at a time, which each child had to follow at a more or less uniform pace. He recalled how, even as a small child, he had to sit quietly at a desk for hours at a time, struggling through reams of excruciatingly boring school *work*. He described a learning environment that definitely had not been *fun*.

"*Not fun!*" complained Zhana. "But children love to learn! Don't the children in your world love to learn? Don't they love to ask questions about every little thing?"

Dazhan

"Well, maybe when they're little," answered Darrel. "But they usually grow out of it...."

"Not too long after they've been in the kind of school you described?" interrupted Zhana, with uncharacteristic impatience.

"Uh, yeah," confirmed Darrel. He thought of little children, four or five years of age, making pests of themselves with so many questions about everything — with an *insatiable* appetite to learn of the world around them — and he could visualize it starting to fade not long after the age at which they entered into formal education. By the time kids were into their teenage years, the job was generally complete. Darrel considered that too few teenagers still cherished that same enthusiastic thirst for mental stimulation.

"No wonder!" exclaimed Zhana. "You snuff out their enthusiasm and creativity with demands for rigidity, conformity and drudgery, in place of natural, spontaneous learning."

"How do you do it here in Enrisa?" asked Darrel. "Children can't just play all the time!"

"Learning should be playful," insisted Zhana, "if you want to flow with the natural momentum of childhood enthusiasm and build on that natural curiosity and wonderment. But that doesn't mean it is either random or totally unstructured. We plan, very carefully, a program of intellectual and emotional learning for each child.

"First, we determine a personal profile of each child, which we continually monitor and update as the child grows and changes, or as we develop new insights into his needs. This profile is our best effort to understand where the child is *right now* — what his interests are, what he likes to do — and his level of sensitivity and emotional maturity. If we want to reach him, we have to understand where he is at. We don't ask the child to come to our level, or our program. We don't set up one uniform curriculum to which the child must conform We come to *him*. We 'talk his language'.

"Once we develop an initial profile of the child, we can develop an individualized curriculum that addresses his unique perspective, which we also monitor and update as needed. We can emphasize educational and emotional areas at a pace unique to his frame of reference. We can plan recreational activities that *he or she* likes to do, and teach emotional and educational skills within the context of those activities."

"But it still looks like everyone is just playing around," observed Darrel. "When do they learn basic skills, like reading, writing, and numeric computations? ...and, when do they learn *discipline?*"

"Reading, writing, numeric computation, social skills ... and discipline... are not learned in a vacuum," responded Zhana. "They are fundamental skills that are a part of everything we do. And, because of

102

that, they can be incorporated as a part of other activities instead of being taught as separate subjects. Let me show you what I mean...."

She led him under the low-hanging branch of a nearby tree, and they climbed up on one of the rocks near a small pond. "Look over there," she instructed, pointing to where an adult was working on some crafts with a small group of children. "That teacher is showing them how to make things. But, while some of our children love to read, and do well early, these children were having a harder time mastering the basics. So this teacher is working on crafts that these children were interested in. But, in order to enjoy this fun activity, they have to read some written instructions that have been prepared and make their own written plans, and use lettering on the project they are making. It's all fun. They are not 'learning to read'. They are making a project. They are happy and enthusiastic. And they will also learn to read."

Zhana pointed to another group of children. "Similarly, numeric computation is a natural part of many other activities. Children can learn to count items of value for exchange, calculate materials and measurements for making things, use geometric shapes and designs, and in many other ways use mathematics as a natural function of real life rather than as a separate, seemingly irrelevant abstraction of isolated skill. Learning is deeper and more thorough, and is retained longer — maybe forever — when it can be related as a meaningful part of real-life experience."

Darrel reflected on his own experience growing up. As a child he had found math to be difficult, and had especially struggled to learn long division. But he liked baseball, and quickly learned long division when trying to calculate batting averages and earned run averages. But he had never thought of that as educational until now.

Zhana directed Darrel's attention to the many children who were playing in the trees, on the rocks, and climbing and swinging on many other items of "playground" apparatus, as well as in other quiet activities, by themselves and with adult instructors. "Of course, education in any subject can be integrated in all the activities these children enjoy. What appears to be play is often part of a carefully-planned project. Learning is a part of the child's natural interaction with his environment. Children learn faster, with greater retention, by *doing* instead of lectures or theories. It's like learning a language. When you came to our world, you didn't know our language. Yet in a short time you have learned to speak fluently on a variety of subjects, by learning words and sentences in the course of real-life experience. But when you try to teach me your 'English', which I don't use in regular experience, I struggle to memorize vocabulary words and rules of grammar, which I promptly forget. It's the same with other subjects."

Darrel smiled.

Dazhan

"On the other hand, what appears to be play often is just that. Play. While we certainly want to teach our children basic educational skills, our first priority is to teach the values and feelings of Dazhan. We want to teach the spontaneous enjoyment of playful sharing as a natural part of interactions with others. Look, over there..." Zhana pointed to where a teacher and child were playing among the twisted branches and hanging vines of a nearby tree. The two had just climbed up one clump of vines, and swung over to a little perch where two branches came together. They were sitting, chatting casually.

"I love to climb and swing!" enthused the teacher.

"Me, too," agreed the child. "But I'm so much slower than you!"

"Well, you'll get faster and better as you grow bigger and get more practice. How does it make you *feel* when you seem to go slower, or can't climb as well as someone else?"

"It makes me feel bad," pouted the child. "I wish it was *me* who could do that well."

The teacher pointed to other children, and called the child's attention to other kids that were playing. The teacher helped the child explore his own feelings, and then to move through a simple practice of the steps of Dazhan at a childlike level. They explored the feelings of an even smaller child, who was having even more difficulty and more frustration than this child. The child could relate well to the smaller child, and could understand his feelings. They observed an older child, who could swing and climb with grace and ease. The child was able to vicariously enjoy the thrill of success and the feel of flying through the trees, which he would have loved to enjoy for himself, but which he could at least enjoy through the eyes of another. He was also able to identify and respond to feelings of envy, and also set goals for his own future achievement.

Zhana was able to point out to Darrel other similar exchanges, and to describe other ways in which children were encouraged to explore their own feelings, and to express their emotions. In the course of other activities, as with other subjects, children could learn to go through each of the steps. They learned self-value; they learned to recognize and enjoy the equal value in others; they shared the value in others' experiences and perspectives; and they found pleasure in doing something for someone else. There were no formal lessons in the underlying concepts — they just learned to *do it!*

"But aren't the children a little *young* to be learning behaviors based on issues of ethics from philosophy or psychology?" Darrel inquired.

"Too young to *start?*" answered Zhana. "We teach reading to small children, but they don't *start* with the Classics or advanced texts. We teach mathematical computation, but not at the highest levels of complexity. Don't your schools in the Outside teach basic values of compassion or sensitivity? What do children grow up like if they haven't been taught *values* in a practical, hands-on way?"

Darrel thought about children growing up without learning to experience the joy of compassion. How different would the Outside world be if business leaders, laborers, politicians and civil servants had grown up learning a *practical enjoyment* of compassionate values? ...if underprivileged children learned love and self-esteem instead of being inducted into lives of hopelessness and violence? ...if everyone learned to feel good about themselves and others, along with other academic subjects such as reading or math? Darrel considered the way in which educators are filled with concern for those who fail to learn academic subjects, while not even attempting to teach social skills and values. He had no answer for Zhana.

Darrel noticed a broad mixture of ages among the children, and that the kids mixed in constantly changing, seemingly informal groups rather than in formal classroom groups as in his own school days. He asked about classes, and how children were divided for purposes of grade-level work. He also wondered how, in a mostly timeless community, children were advanced from one grade level to the next. Was it by test scores? Grades on schoolwork? ...or what?

His questions only puzzled Zhana. To clarify, Darrel described the system with which he was familiar, of putting children into classes according to the right grade level — first grade, second grade, etc. — for each child's age. Along the way, children were given school work and tests for which they were given letter grades — *A, B, C, D, F* — to measure their progress and to confirm each child's ability in keeping up with the right grade level.

Zhana seemed shocked! "How can you give individual education for the needs of each child when they are herded through the system in a group?" she wondered. "And how can you teach them to produce quality work if you just give them a final grade on their first attempt and move on to the next assignment?" She described the Enrisan system in which children were given projects and assignments to do, with certain standards of expectation set by the teachers. It would be very rare if a child accomplished the project successfully on the first try. The child would, rather, turn in the project and get feedback from the teacher on how to improve it. Through repeated steps of redoing and refining work, children learned to stay with a task until it was completed to a minimum standard of performance. Only then would the child move on to the next project in that field. Darrel considered that perhaps such a system *would* be more realistic training for young minds. In the workplace of the adult world, projects would have to be re-worked until a desired level of quality was attained. If one purpose of school were to prepare young people for future careers, a similar approach to handling projects by school children might be worthwhile.

Similarly, there was no Enrisan equivalent to grade-level classroom groupings based on age. Rather, the children would work at their own pace, and progress at different speeds in different subject areas. One child might advance quickly in math, another more quickly in literary skills, another in mechanical abilities. A child may be working in one subject area with children much older, in another subject area with children much younger, and in another with those of his own age; and such differences might be more extreme as the years of schooling progress. And each would continue to advance in the various subject areas at their own pace.

Additionally, Darrel often noticed children working alone, as well as children teaching other children. He asked Zhana about this.

"Teachers *supervise* learning, and help to motivate ongoing interests and enthusiasm based on natural curiosity and energy. They even provide direct information or explanation when necessary. But as much as possible, we provide access to resources and encourage the children to find information on their own. This encourages independent thinking, the joy of discovery, and confidence in knowing that they are the ones who have determined their own course of learning — they *own* it!

"Also, by mixing children of different ages, older children can teach younger children. Of course, sometimes a younger child who is more advanced in a particular skill may beach an older one, but that's okay too. This accomplishes several things: First, children are often more receptive to what their older peers teach rather than from teachers or authority figures. Second, teaching by older children puts them 'on our side' and reduces the likelihood of rebelliousness, not to mention the reduction in teaching duties expected from teachers. Third, and most important, when a child has just recently learned something new, he is struggling to solidify that knowledge in his permanent experience. By explaining it to someone else, he presents it from the viewpoint of a new learner, which is most understandable to a fellow new learner, and the process of teaching someone else causes him to organize the information in his own mind in such a way that he learns it more thoroughly for his own long-term retention."

As Darrel and Zhana were talking, one of the smaller children got carried away with the enthusiasm of the moment, and started hitting another child. In seconds, a teacher leaped across a nearby boulder, stepped lightly across the lower branches of a nearby tree, and landed right in front of the children. The teacher was cheerful and enthusiastic, not harsh or scolding. To replace unpleasant feelings with happier feelings, the teacher attempted to divert the child's interest to another activity that would be a more constructive expression of his energies —

to divert his attention away from unpleasant self-preoccupation, to the enjoyment of outward-directed shared alternatives. In most situations, that would be enough to diffuse tensions and re-direct energies. But in this case, the child's immediate anger was too strong to be quickly diverted. Still maintaining a gentle and pleasant demeanor, but clearly becoming more firm and serious, the teacher asked the child to stop. In most cases, especially among older children who had been in the educational system longer, that would be enough to get an immediate response. But not in this case. The small child continued hitting the other one.

Quickly, the teacher's tone became more authoritative, but never departed from demonstrating caring warmth. The teacher, not allowing the child to continue harmful behavior, put a gentle arm around the child, warmly and firmly restraining the child from striking out at others, but without acting in an aggressive or dominant manner, while continuing to speak gently and supportively. The teacher gently but firmly guided the misbehaving child away from the others, and sat beside the child on a low branch. "Let's sit here quietly for a moment, so we can calm down. Then we'll talk about your feelings." The child, less consumed by anger but still feeling emotion, started to cry. "That's okay," assured the teacher. "Sit here and cry, and I'll sit here with you. When you finish crying, you'll feel better. Crying helps us get out the sad feelings so we can feel better."

Darrell watched with amazement at how the teacher interrupted harmful behavior without being overbearing, always remained comforting and supportive, while emphasizing the distinction between the problematic behavior and the child's intrinsic worth, which was always reinforced.

The teacher quietly reaffirmed loving support for the child, but that acceptance and love of the *child* didn't necessarily include acceptance of inappropriate *behavior*.

Zhana tried to explain. "We love our kids. The care and loving of our children is one of the highest priorities of our people. Therefore, we do whatever we can to teach them good feelings. We also do as much as we can to stop bad feelings, and redirect negative energies in positive ways. 'No,' expressed in positive affirmation, is an important word for children to learn as early as possible. But so is 'yes'. When we divert a child from an inappropriate behavior, we seek to redirect problematic behavior to more constructive alternatives, which will be more enjoyable in the long run to the child and to those around. And best of all is when you can say 'no' so gently the child hardly realizes they have been denied, while offering multiple options for alternatives so that the child is empowered to exercise free choice in selecting which 'yes' alternative is preferred."

"Sometimes the parents of our small children, in their great and gentle love, find it difficult to instill in their children the limitations that promote self-control and, ultimately, self-direction.

With very small children, we sometimes have to be quite firm, but that does not require us to be harsh or negative, and do so as early in life as possible. The time to teach children values is while they are still children, so they can grow up with behavioral habits that are positive and happy from the start. It is much easier than teaching adults, when we have to unlearn bad habits and re-learn new ones.

"Teaching values also requires approaching each individual child's unique feelings and personality. Some children are more active, or strong-willed than others and greater firmness, always still in love, may be required, with every 'no' limitations backed up by offering choices among multiple positive 'yes' alternatives. Others are more timid or passive and we must take extra care to be affirming and reassuring."

"Wow," responded Darrel. "You have an individualized, enjoyable curriculum individually tailored to each child's interests, feelings, and rate of learning. You teach the child to explore and express feelings constructively, and to become aware of others. And you provide a carefully balanced program with loving playfulness and disciplined structure. I can't see how that would ever fail! How does anyone ever end up in the Isolation Zone?"

Zhana smiled. "Yes, out of all the regions of Enrisa we have several hundred thousand people, yet maybe only thirty delinquents confined in the Isolation Zone involuntarily. In addition, there are maybe seventy to a hundred others who felt they were having difficulty following the values of *Dazhan* as well as they wanted to, who have gone there voluntarily, without waiting until they got to the point of committing a crime. Of course, they can leave any time they wish, but they usually stay long enough to follow through with an effective plan of adult education."

Darrel was surprised. "You mean, people *voluntarily* put themselves in 'jail' — as a 'self-improvement' program?"

Zhana laughed a little. "Crime and violence are rare here. The Isolation Zone is much more than just a place to 'warehouse' delinquents. It is not such an unpleasant place. It is really a part of our educational system, where people can learn important values isolated from the distractions of normal activities, either because they recognize the need to do so, or because inappropriate and harmful behavior requires us to protect others as well as themselves.

"Our initial programs are very successful in teaching values and skills to our children. But if we make an incorrect judgment in compiling or updating our initial profile, or if we develop a curriculum for the child that doesn't match that profile, or if we fail to implement that curriculum, or if we fail to recognize emotional needs that aren't being met, we could fail to get through to that child, and problems could remain hidden until they show up in adulthood as more serious aberrations. Then, if it is serious enough, the adult will have to be confined. We will try to pick up where we left off. We will try to re-educate the individual for as long as they remain in confinement."

"That's amazing," wondered Darrel. "But, where is the Isolation Zone? That's the one I really want to see — and the one I'm most afraid of."

"Come on!" laughed Zhana. "I'll show you!"

Zhana extended her arm toward a distant ridge, which marked the tribal limit of Kerreih's large central region. Above the ridge stretched another tribal region, and Zhana explained that the Isolation Zone was tucked behind the far side of that distant region.

As they walked, Darrel continued to express amazement that anyone would voluntarily place themselves in "jail." Still, Zhana's explanations made sense to him. Some people did need more help than others, and perhaps a specialized, isolated setting might provide the environment in which to be immersed in values and changes in lifestyle habits.

Darrel was hesitant to inquire about the questions that were going through his mind. Cautiously, noncommittally, he tried to formulate a vague exploration of other ideas: "When I first arrived in the Caves, my experience having grown up with no exposure to Dazhan, would be like a child who grows up and 'slips through the system'. The 'system' had failed me completely, since I was never exposed to it. I guess I probably needed complete immersion in an isolated, protected environment for learning values as much as anyone. Why didn't I go to the Isolation Zone? And, now that I'm learning the values, but struggling to actually make a regular practice of it, would it be beneficial for me to consider voluntarily placing myself in that environment until I master those values?"

Zhana was pleased with Darrel's questions, and smiled warmly. She knew he felt trust in her, and the inquiries reflected the degree to which mastering the practice of Dazhan had become a serious priority. "When you first came here," she answered, "we considered a variety of options as to how to share our values with you, including the Isolation Zone. But our system does not *require* that individuals live by the values we believe in. Unless someone is actually causing harm to others, we allow them the right of free choice. No matter how much they might need the Isolation Zone, they would have to *choose* it, unless there is a danger to others. So, that's the first reason we didn't send you there. However, if you had shown yourself to be harmful to others ..." she smiled as her voice trailed away. "The second reason is that your case was really unique. You didn't know our language, and even the most obvious aspects of cultural traditions were completely foreign to you. We thought it best to let you have your freedom, yet still provide a completely personalized program designed specifically for your situation."

As to whether he should choose to voluntarily spend some time in the Isolation Zone, Zhana didn't feel it would be necessary for now. "You are making good progress. Of course you are struggling with the transition from accepting the understanding of *ideas* and the *desire* to practice them, through the initial resistance to making them a habitual part of your lifestyle. That is normal. Considering your background, the progress is remarkable, and shows your determination to make it."

"But wouldn't I make it faster, smoother, totally immersed in a program designed to implement that transition?" queried Darrel.

"Hmmm, possibly," smiled Zhana. "But there is also a lot to be said for learning those values in the context of the real environment in which you live, if you can. And there are still a lot of opportunities available to learn those values using many of the same methods used in the Isolation Zone, without having to stay there."

"Such as… ?"

"There are various ongoing activities at the local Sanctuaries, to assist people not only in learning and understanding values, but also in their own practice of those values and in sharing them with others. We haven't exposed you to those kinds of activities yet, because you were still struggling to catch up with others. But maybe you're ready to join some good groups where your practice of Dazhan can really grow."

"But I think I'd still like to *see* the Isolation Zone."

Zhana led Darrel across the rocks, trees, and grottoes of the central cave, as they made their way upward, along the ridge that divided Kerreih's large central region from the smaller, peripheral tribal region administered by Chief Divine Namoro. As the ridge leveled off into a plateau that marked their entry into Namoro's region, Darrel noted a lessening in the lush greenery of the vast lower chamber, and noticed increasingly jagged formations in the dry, stony landscape.

Crawling through tunnels and hopping across rocky formations, they continued toward the upper edges of the Enrisan universe, toward the Isolation Zone. The distant walls eternally surrounding this little cave-world loomed ever closer as they pressed toward its outer fringes.

At length, they faced a deep chasm. Across the chasm, various levels of caves and tunnels were tucked into the mountainside. There, Darrel could see men and women wandering among the formations. Zhana pointed across the gulf.

"There," she announced, "is the Isolation Zone."

"But how do they get there?" wondered Darrel, noting the deadly canyon that separated this distinct little colony of caves.

Zhana led him further along the edge of the chasm, to where a suspension bridge spread across the gulf. As they approached, two guards, wearing the green robes of Nolak's central leadership, came defensively to life. Recognizing Zhana, they allowed the young Minister of Education to pass with her guest.

As they finished crossing the bridge, they passed two more guards stationed at the other side and entered the Isolation Zone.

A casual freedom among the residents and a scarcity of the green-clad guards made Darrel feel uneasy. Here he was mixing with the most dangerous criminal element in Enrisa, and supervision seemed unbelievably lax. He expressed this concern to Zhana, who just laughed.

"Only a few guards are uniformed, so the residents can quickly turn to them when they need to," she explained. "But remember, the number of actual residents is very small. Almost half the others are teachers or counselors who have volunteered for ongoing service in the Isolation Zone. The only thing is, you can't tell which half! Neither can the residents."

Darrel seemed confused.

"The Dazhan teaches behavior which is natural for human beings," smiled Zhana. "People who are unable to enjoy that experience suffer from deficiencies in their normal emotional needs. These deficiencies can be rooted deep within personal experiences, and cannot be corrected merely with formal lectures or explanations.

"Our approach to teaching values to delinquents is adapted from our approach to teaching children. First, we develop an initial profile of the individual. We use all the information that is available to us, including old records of childhood profiles, and information about the situations that led to their confinement. We develop projects and activities that allow them to develop enjoyable friendships with each other and with the unidentified teachers or counselors, and we use these activities and interactions to teach values.

"Additionally, we encourage these adults to explore their feelings together in groups, or individually through the writing of journals, to explore their thoughts and perceptions of themselves as a starting point from which they can then develop an awareness of other people. In groups, they can share their feelings with others and get feedback. When they write individual journals, they can reflect on past feelings and experiences and see how their present situation evolved.

"We care about the delinquent, and want to help solve his problems, and let all our people enjoy the full happiness of Dazhan. Yet it is still necessary to confine delinquents, to protect innocent citizens and provide a setting in which to help them. We make a distinction between the *person* and the *behavior:* we love the delinquent as a person, yet must still impose restrictions on his unacceptable behavior."

"So, when a person comes here and begins to make friends," mused Darrel, "he doesn't know which friendships are real and which are contrived." He had made a mental analogy to the use of undercover peace officers in the outside world, who feign friendships with ulterior motives.

Addressing Darrel's discomfort with the integrity of the system, Zhana continued. "Even the volunteers don't know who is whom, other than those who may be working together on a common project. Even I don't know, except for those whose plans I helped develop. The only ones who know for sure are the Zone administrators."

"But what happens when the residents find out that these friendships are a 'set-up'?" challenged Darrel. "Won't they feel even more insecure in social interactions? Can genuine human values be developed out of artificial relationships?"

Zhana seemed honestly baffled by Darrel's questioning. Some quick questions of her own revealed his comparison to Outside world systems, and a little about those undercover operations. "The problem in your world is that contrived friendships lead to subsequent betrayal," she responded. "Your 'professionals' maintain a deliberate detachment to avoid real involvement. But here it is the opposite. Volunteers choose to work here because they *do* care about those who have problems. In addition, those who come here for voluntary treatment — who *want* to improve themselves — also are very good about developing natural friendships with the delinquents that have been sent here. The voluntary residents and trained professional volunteers *are* seeking *genuine* relationships. Lasting friendships *are* developed. When their roles eventually become known, they are seen as close friends who came to help in a time of crisis. They did not betray others to get them *in* here; they came as friends to help them *out* of here. Relationships spawned in the bleak origins of the Isolation Zone often persist through lifetimes, long after confinement has been completed."

As issues of education, treatment, crime, and punishment were discussed, Darrel felt an increased understanding of Enrisan values and attitudes, from his exposure to the institutional formalities of its penal system, and with anticipation and curiosity about the "group activities" that Zhana and the local Divines might be planning for him at the local Sanctuary, to help in his own struggle to develop a real *practice* of Dazhan.

Chapter Eleven

Watercycle

Darrel gazed searchingly around the vast darkened chamber of the Most High Sanctuary. All of the kibihni lights had been removed from the main hall, leaving only an eerie flicker of light from the column of flame at the far end of the Hall. In a community dominated by continuous daylight, submission to prolonged darkness evoked a reverenced awe.

The selected gathering of all the local Divines from each tribe, Ministers of Education, special guests, and families, divided into seven regional tribal groups, waited in silence for the assembly of the Chief Divines to emerge from their seclusion with Nolak elsewhere in the Most High Sanctuary. With Darrel and Zhana stood Laros, their local Divine, and other men and women from their tribe, some of whom Darrel recognized, and others whom he did not.

It was the Time of the Watercycle. This was the only unit of Time in the subterranean universe of Enrisa — a symbolic regeneration of annual new life. Zhana had first noticed the rising waterflows while returning with Darrel from their tour of the Isolation Zone. Aware of the significance of the annual Watercycles, she had been quick to notice that the water levels in ponds and waterflows had risen significantly higher than what they had seen as they first passed by. By the time they returned to their dwelling on the main floor of the cavern, the community was already buzzing with the excitement of annual Watercycle rituals.

To the timeless Enrisans, such an event was the occasion for great celebration! A chapter in the historical record of Enrisa would be dated and closed, and a new record would begin. The Timeless Community would stop briefly to consider this moment in the ageless eternities, and then return to the timelessness of perpetual daylight, and interaction without schedules or appointments.

To Mr. Darrel Swift, whose roots grew out of a very different community, dominated by an almost neurotic addiction to clocks and calendars, such an event was of equal personal value. While he was adjusting as well as possible to the timeless nature of this strange realm, the conditioning of his past life was also an important part of his experience. It was a relief to be able to put things in some kind of seasonal perspective. He correctly figured that the rising waterflows would be triggered by melting snows on the Earth's surface far above.

It must be Springtime. "I entered the caves at the beginning of last June..." mused Darrel silently. Even allowing as much as two or three weeks for his wanderings in the dark peripheral caves of Timera, he could have found his way into Enrisa no later than the end of June or early July. While he had frequently been aware of the passing of long periods of unmeasured time, he now could estimate a calendar date. He figured it must now be late March or early April. He must have been in the caves at least nine months, perhaps as long as ten months, since he had last seen real daylight.

Darrel's thoughts were interrupted as the small crowd came to sudden attention.

As gentle Enrisan melodies floated through the vast chamber, a procession of the seven Chief Divines filed out from behind the pillar of flame, each dressed uniformly in spotless white robes, and each bearing an unlit torch. As they lined up along the row of granite tablets etched with the metallic script of *Dazhan,* Nolak emerged, clad in brilliant green, and stood in front of the symbolic flame. More than ever he radiated the intense compassionate cheerfulness that burned within him.

"Let Enrisa be alive with the new birth of the Watercycle!" he pronounced with vigor.

The seven Chief Divines, in unison with the gathering of local people, repeated, "Let Enrisa be alive with the new birth of the Watercycle!" Then, Nolak revealed a small pouch to those present.

"Watch this!" giggled Zhana in an excited whisper.

With several deft tosses, Nolak sprinkled the powdery contents of the pouch into the pillar of fire. The golden flames were quickly transformed into the brilliant green hue symbolic of the central Enrisan leadership. A hushed murmur raced among the selected spectators.

Nolak approached the first of the Chief Divines and gently lifted the unlit torch from her hand. Touching it to the central flame, it burst into a brilliant magenta flame. He returned it to the Divine and embraced her. Next stood Namoro, Chief Divine of that region through which Darrel and Zhana had passed en route to the Isolation Zone. Darrel had never seen this man, but had only heard of him by name. Nolak ignited his torch in a great flash of pastel yellow, and returned it to him with an affectionate embrace. Next was Kerreih, representing the large cavern region where Darrel and Zhana lived. Her torch was ignited in a bright flame of gentle blue. And so it continued until each of the Chief Divines stood holding a torch burning with a colored flame. All the colors of the rainbow were reflected in this display, except the bright green reserved for the central flame, which glowed brightly behind them all.

Those watching marveled at the strange magic of the colored flames. Even Darrel, who viewed this as an elementary display of fireworks, enjoyed the simple beauty of these colored lights.

Inside the Most High Sanctuary, Darrel recalled his first meager attempts to go through the steps of Dazhan that Nolak, this Old Man, had taught him. He was acutely aware of how little he was doing to develop a more regular, ongoing practice of the steps, and felt a desire to try and practice again in the Sanctuary. He looked around the room. No, this wasn't the time for a beginner. There was too much else going on to distract the attention of a curious foreigner from a concentrated effort at going through each of the steps. Darrel felt a flash of frustration. He would make a commitment to try all the harder to develop a serious practice until he could acquire that automatic, ongoing feeling of cheerful, compassionate joy.

While all attention was directed toward the Chief Divines presenting their colorful array of glowing flames, Nolak faded into the darkness behind them, and re-emerged on a high altar, above and behind the bright green flame of the central fire.

Gesturing toward the central flame, he addressed the seven Chief Divines in a booming voice that belied his frail stature and could be heard by all who were assembled, without the need for electronic amplification. "Behold the spiritual fire of Dazhan," he roared. "You Seven shall feed this Dazhan to our people. I have given you from the light of this Dazhan. You are my arms, my hands, my feet. Take this treasure to all the people of Enrisa. This is the new birth of the Watercycle! Go! And rekindle the spiritual fires within your Sanctuaries!" Nolak faded back from the altar and disappeared into the darkness.

The seven Chief Divines raised their colored torches high overhead and, to the gentle strains of background music, edged forward through the darkened hall. As they approached the waiting assembly of selected local leaders and guests, each of the Seven joined the group representing his or her region. Holding high her glowing blue torch with silent reverence, Kerreih entered the group that included Darrel, Zhana, Laros, and the others from her region. Like a Queen Bee gathering her hive, she assembled her people around her with unspoken majesty.

The massive stone gates of the Most High Sanctuary rumbled open as a flood of kibihni light filled the hall. The seven Chief Divines, with their respective followings, found their way out of the Hall, toward the various paths leading away from Nolak's templed palace, back to the various regions from whence they had come. Darrel and Zhana joined the others from Kerreih's region in a procession, following their leader down the face of the cliff, along the narrow switchbacked path that Darrel had traveled in his earlier visit with Nolak.

The lengthy trek down the face of the cliff to the main floor was completed in hushed silence. Darrel looked over the group. There was Kerreih, the Chief Divine whom he had met when she dismissed Rezak's false charges against him; there was Laros, the local Divine who was at his side when he first awakened in the Caves, and who would no doubt be helping Zhana implement a plan for his habituation of the practice of Dazhan; there were many others and, of course, there was Zhana.

As they descended along the trail, Darrel again looked over the crowd. Just slightly ahead and to the side of him was Zhana, preparing a way so he could keep up with the faster pace of the wiry, nimble cave people. Darrel focused his attention on his sweetheart with the thought of reaching outward toward the value of *her* consciousness in the pursuit of his elusive practice of Dazhan.

As Zhana's agile, feminine figure danced and swayed over the landscape, Darrel couldn't help but notice once again how cute she was and remember how much he was attracted to her. He considered how much he enjoyed being with her, and how much she contributed to his life. He really felt the strong desire of wanting to do things for her.

When Zhana turned back toward Darrel to check on him with her usual cheerful smile, Darrel leaned forward and kissed her cheek. She took his hand and squeezed it affectionately.

But as they continued downward, Darrel also considered that what he felt, though deep and wonderful and special, was not Dazhan. He remembered the difference between *expectation* and the unconditional outward expression of Dazhan. He loved Zhana not just for herself, but for the completeness of the relationship that they shared — for what she also added to *his* life. It was good and it was beautiful, but it was not Dazhan.

He remembered that Nolak had warned that positive relationships, while desirable, often complicated the separate practice of Dazhan because of the built-in factor of expectation. He also remembered that Nolak had suggested that the practice of Dazhan could also be added as a *separate addition* to such relationships.

Darrel thought about it for a moment as he continued to climb down the trail. In what ways was reciprocal expectation built into the relationship? In what ways could he by-pass such expectations and add the cheerful, outward feelings of Dazhan?

Did he really have expectations from Zhana? ... Yeah. He considered that romantic relationships, especially *exclusive* romantic relationships, always have certain expectations. You don't just fall in love with anybody or everybody. There are standards of attraction and of shared values and experiences and of the kind of relationship that is desired. The choice of a romantic partner is an important one, carefully made, and the basis of that choice revolves around mutual expectations. And the fulfillment of those expectations in each other was what made such relationships so precious.

So, how could he also incorporate the cheerful practice of Dazhan as a separate and additional element of the relationship? It would have to be something beyond those expectations, such as the kinds of things he might contribute to *any* other situation — truly based on a complete lack of expectation for anything in return.

Darrel wondered if Zhana ever added the practice of Dazhan in her feelings toward him. "She must," he thought. After all, Dazhan was a part of everything in her life. So, if Zhana might be doing it, then what would be some examples?

Darrel remembered that Zhana had been doing things for him completely apart from any expectation of return, long before their friendship had evolved into romance. And even afterward, there were many times that she expressed contributions of pure, unconditional outward concern completely apart from their romantic involvement. When she prepared little surprises, for no reason, she was reaching outward toward the enjoyment of *his* experience. And many times he would catch her gazing at him in a way that made him think that maybe she was going through the steps — reaching out to the value of *his* consciousness — apart from her own perspectives or expectations. Of course, in a relationship based on some degree of reciprocal expectation, he could not tell with absolute certainty. A person could appear to be reaching outward unconditionally, while actually just trying to enhance their position in the relationship. Still, if it was possible, then Zhana was probably doing it. And, if it was possible, then Darrel could learn to do it, too.

As they approached the end of the downward trek, Darrel considered that this might not be an appropriate time to struggle through the practice of each step in reaching outward toward Zhana. But he also considered that he could find the time and place to go through each step in appreciating her equal separate value, and reach out through *her* perspective to an appropriate behavioral contribution.

As they made the final descent into the main valley, a massive crowd from the tribal community thronged to greet them. Darrel estimated that the crowd must have included several thousand people who had all come to share in the Fire Rituals of the annual Watercycle.

Holding high the blue glowing flame, Kerreih marched forthright into the crowd as a band of white-robed aides protectively surrounded the party of those who had come with Kerreih from within the Most High Sanctuary. Isolated from the rest of the crowd, Kerreih and those with her marched boldly across the layered fractures of the cavern floor, toward the tribal Sanctuary. The surging crowd pulsated around the clustered body of its leaders as they were escorted by protective guards. The total community was stirred with the excitement of the Watercycles, in a scene that was being repeated elsewhere in each of the other six tribal regions.

The surging mass made its way across the terrain until, at length, they arrived at the Sanctuary. Kerreih and those in her party were led to an elevated area behind the stone altar at the front of the main hall. The remaining crowd quickly filled the assembly area, which opened up to the gentle outside air to allow for an almost unlimited overflow audience. Standing at the head of local leaders and guests, above the crowd, Kerreih still held the blue flame high, and still remained speechless. At Zhana's side, among those facing the crowd from the front, Darrel quickly observed that the small flame he had seen glowing in the center of the altar when he was here for his "trial," was now extinguished. He wanted to whisper all kinds of questions to Zhana, but discretion required that he maintain silent respect like the others, especially in his position up front.

As a hush finally settled over the vast audience, Kerreih finally stepped up to the altar and spoke: "At this time of the Watercycle, as the mightiest forces of Nature converge in a gentle new birth, let our Tribe be alive with this flame ignited in the spiritual fire of Dazhan by the hand of Nolak." Touching the torch gently to a wick in the center of the altar, it erupted into the steady flickering of a golden flame. Simultaneously, the twin fountains in the garden courtyard, left dry since the onset of the new Watercycle, gurgled to life as water splashed forth, symbolic of renewed life.

Unobtrusively dousing her torch and disposing of it behind the altar, Kerreih continued to speak from behind the pale glow of the flame which had been lit by Nolak's torch: "Through these past cycles of sleeping and waking since the rising of the waters, while those with me kept vigil in the main halls of the Most High Sanctuary, I have sat with Nolak within its deepest chambers...."

Darrel's thoughts wandered back to the visit he and Zhana had shared in the Chamber of Fire. Kerreih did not refer to the mystical Chamber by name, but Darrel's special experience added deeper understanding to her brief, passing reference.

Departing from the purely ritualistic aspects of the event, Kerreih elaborated on the meaning and practice of Dazhan, as Nolak had instructed. As she began to explore advanced aspects of feelings still new to him, Darrel began to have difficulty keeping up with ideas expressed largely in idiomatic colloquialisms for this audience of native Enrisans.

The Stranger's thoughts began to wander back toward his own experiences with Nolak, and his own understanding of the meaning and practice of Dazhan. He again recalled Nolak's explanation of the process by which an individual could reach outward to share the value of other consciousnesses, and Nolak's final urging to actually set up a regular practice by which to incorporate such a process into his automatic behavior rather than as just a lofty ideal. His lack of success so far in following Nolak's final emphasis still haunted him.

From his place at the front of the assembly hall, he looked out over the vast crowd that spread before him. He again considered Zhana's original analogy of the internal consciousness as a dot of light within the consuming darkness of the physical environment. Looking into the crowd, he envisioned thousands of lights combining into a powerful glow of spiritual value. With such a tremendous exposure to human value, he felt this might be a good time to again try to move forward in his own pursuit of Dazhan as a regular spiritual practice.

He looked up toward Kerreih, who was still speaking. He thought it might be interesting to extend his practice outward toward *her*. He reaffirmed his own Self value. He then directed his attention toward Kerreih and the equal value that she represented as an independent consciousness. He tried to visualize the world from the physical perspective of her present experience. He imagined himself to be looking at the world through her eyes. He tried to think about the little ways in which the crowd might appear different to her than to himself. She was standing in a slightly higher place; he imagined looking a little more downward. He visualized *her* perspective of the faces, the building, and the garden that blended off into the background. He tried to imagine the feeling within the physical space she occupied. She rested her forearms on the altar as she spoke; he imagined the cool roughness of the stone against her skin. A small gnat buzzed around her head; he imagined the annoying hum in her ears, and felt relief as she brushed it away. Like Kerreih, Darrel was standing, and probably in similarly comfortable air temperature; Darrel could easily relate to the perceptions of those sensations.

He tried to imagine the perspective of her *feelings*. The most immediate perception was an awareness of the crowd — thousands of faces united in attention. He imagined the feeling of "the crowd" as a mixed awareness of apprehension, of enjoying a key role of prominent leadership, and of living under the constant weight of public responsibility. He tried to imagine, from within Kerreih's consciousness, just what it should mean to be a Chief Divine in the Land of Enrisa. He thought of ultimate responsibility for all the affairs of the largest tribal region. She was widely thought of as a likely successor to Nolak — what kind of feelings or pressures would she feel from such a role? Darrel considered her meetings with Nolak and with other Chief Divines, to interpret consistently the practices and procedures of Dazhan. He tried to imagine Kerreih as a private person. How did she cope with personal feelings and her own exploration of relationships? What kind of individual tastes and personal habits did she find meaningful? Without knowing the answers to such questions, awareness of their existence suggested additional dimensions of special personal value.... Though awkward in his first attempts at such a practice, he found himself seeing the young Chief Divine through different eyes.

Darrel gazed out over the countless faces of strangers, spreading throughout the hall and beyond into the garden. Selecting a few faces at random from various parts of the crowd, he considered briefly the intense personal value of each one individually. One by one he imagined each person as a child, as the embryonic personality began to take form. He thought of how key events in each life may have shaped the developing character, and of how a unique chain of experiences and relationships combined to add a sense of continuity to the process of consciousness.

Looking through the eyes of each individual he had selected, he imagined how the world looked from their various perspectives, and then tried to imagine emotional perspectives as well. While he could only speculate as to actual present experience — never really intruding into another consciousness — he began to understand a whole new depth of real personal value in each strange face. But he also knew it would be necessary to go beyond those aspects of *awareness,* to *action!*

Darrel brought his attention back to Kerreih, who was still speaking. She was tying the various themes of her Watercycle message into a conclusion. She spoke of the rising and receding of the seasonal Watercycles in terms of life, death, and rebirth, made meaningful through the concurrent spiritual interactions of Dazhan. As Kerreih finished, the crowd slowly broke up.

Darrel and Zhana chatted briefly with both Kerreih and Laros, expressing eagerness at participating with groups in the Sanctuary, and then faded off into the garden area. As they walked out, Darrel looked around, wondering what could be in other rooms and halls, and curious as to what activities he would be joining. Zhana, meanwhile, expressed satisfaction with the Watercycle observances. "Wasn't that exciting!" she squealed with cheerful enthusiasm, moved by the powerful messages of her leaders.

Darrel nodded in silent approval, moved by a different Watercycle experience.

Zhana studied him closely for a moment. She became silently content as she pondered the intensity of his expression, and gave a quiet, knowing smile as they made their way back toward their cave-dwellings, to join family and friends in the feasting, decorations, and exchanging of written or artistic tributes to the appreciation of each other and the renewal of relationships, in the spirit of this season — the timeless Enrisans' only observation of a "calendar" holiday.

Chapter Twelve

Sharing

By now, the local Sanctuary was becoming a familiar sight to Darrel. As he made his way with Zhana toward the Sanctuary area, the outlying gardens nestled among the ponds and waterfalls, the surrounding wall, and the granite building rising up from the floor of the main cave were still intriguing, but no longer so foreign.

Darrel and Zhana passed through the gate and walked through the inside gardens between the twin fountains, to the outdoor forum that led into the open-air assembly hall. The local Divine, Laros, and the regional Chief Divine, Kerreih, appeared from the shadows of the assembly hall and approached them.

Laros took Darrel by one hand while Kerreih gently clasped the other. "Hi, Darrel," she exclaimed. "It's so good to see you here! I think you'll have a great time!"

"Yeah," agreed Laros. "We hope you'll enjoy sharing and growing and, most important, having a good time relaxing and enjoying pleasant interactions in this beautiful place."

Darrel smiled and relaxed. But he was still curious as to what he was getting himself into. "What will we be doing here?" he inquired. "Or, is that something I have to wait and find out?"

Laros smiled. "It's no big mystery. All we want to do is give people who are trying to improve their ongoing, habitual practice of Dazhan a chance to help each other through the obstacles."

"What do we do? Sit around and discuss Dazhan?"

Glancing first toward Kerreih, Laros again answered. "We try to keep our visits as casual and informal as possible. We want them to be pleasant and enjoyable. We may try to help each other with the *concepts* of Dazhan, but our intent is mostly to go beyond the *understanding,* to the habituation of an ongoing *practice* of Dazhan. The emphasis is on action — what we can *do.*

"To do that, we assemble a group of people who are all trying to improve their *practice* of Dazhan. We try to select a diverse group — people who are at different levels, from beginner to advanced, with different *kinds* of problems and different experiences and points of view. This blend of widely varying viewpoints can then be stirred together, with a sharing of resources, so that each one can gain new insights from the others. We try to bridge the transition from *theory* to *practice.* But we also want it to be pleasant and enjoyable. The *spirit* is most receptive to learning and growth in the enjoyment of positive feelings. You have nothing to be worried about!"

Darrel smiled. He was both relieved and intrigued. He was beginning to look forward to this new adventure.

The little group turned and headed through the open-air assembly hall, deeper into the Sanctuary, stopping in front of a small curtained archway. With one hand, Kerreih pulled back the drape, and with the other hand she beckoned the others to enter. Extending her sincerest expressions of optimism to each as they passed, Kerreih then turned and departed, returning to the other business in the Sanctuary.

Passing into this new "room," Darrel looked around. He wasn't sure if he was still in the Sanctuary or if the group would be meeting outside. The granite walls of the Sanctuary enclosed only two sides of the "room"; the ceiling was only a partial overhang extending from the main building; there was a short, narrow trail leading down through rocks and plants to a garden area with a small waterfall spilling into a shallow pond. A gnarled old cave-tree was at the side of the pond, with its branches twisting over and away from the water. Several thick vines hung from the middle and upper branches of the tree, and from an overhanging rocky bluff behind the pond. Steam rising from the surface of the pond suggested to Darrel that this was another one of the natural hot springs in the cave, which were often used for bathing, and which Darrel also enjoyed as a natural "hot tub."

Several other people were already down in the pond area. Two female figures were squatting in the lower branches of the tree overhanging the water, a male was squatting on a rock between the pond and the tree, and a man and woman were relaxing in the warmth of the shallow hot springs. None of them were individuals who Darrel recognized.

Laros led Zhana and Darrel down to the hot springs area.

At the base of the short trail, several steep steps led them past a stone ridge about four feet in height. As they approached the pond, Darrel turned and could see a series of stone slabs along the inside face of the ridge, on which was inscribed the text of *Dazhan* as seen from the viewpoint of the pond area.

"Hi, everyone," announced Laros. "You all know Zhana, and this is Darrel, who most of you have seen before."

The man squatting on the ground, who was upper-middle aged and very slender, smiled cheerfully and looked up. "Hi, Zhana. Hi, Darrel. I'm Zhikahr."

The woman sitting in the steamy pond also faced the new arrivals with a cheerful smile. She was about the same age and build as the first man, and identified herself as his wife, Wakemah. Laros commented to Darrel that Zhikahr and Wakemah were very experienced in the understanding and practice of Dazhan and had joined the group to fine-tune their skills and overcome minor annoying distractions. Laros indicated that Zhikahr and Wakemah would likely be able to contribute a great deal — not only in polishing their own practice, but also in helping other participants.

One of the women perched in the tree spoke next. She was very young, very tiny (even for the Enrisans), and appeared to be strong and athletic. Darrel mused to himself that she might have been a great gymnast in the outside world. "I'm Tijah," she said with a pleasant smile. She, too, seemed friendly and cheerful, but Darrel also noticed that she seemed high-strung and fast-paced — attributes not usually seen among the casual cave people.

The other woman in the tree was older, maybe young middle-aged, and quite plump. Darrel had not seen many Enrisans who were overweight. She seemed pleasant, and smiled as she identified herself as Nierren.

The other man sitting in the warm pond gave his name as Hanahkalo. He was strong and robust, muscular but not overweight, with thinning hair. He appeared to be about the same age as Zhikahr and Wakemah, and seemed to be friends with them. He appeared to have been in conversation with them when Darrel and Zhana had arrived with Laros.

Laros looked over the group. "Hmmm. Everyone seems to be here except Larehnk. He should be here soon." Darrel couldn't help but reflect on the difficulties in arranging group activities in a society that had no standard for keeping track of time.

Darrel noticed that there was a small table behind the pond area, which held some wafer snacks, and what appeared to be some kind of juice or fruit drink. Nierren, the heavy-set woman in the tree, noticed Darrel glancing toward the refreshments. Quickly, she reached out to a nearby vine, and swung down across and behind the pond. At the right moment, she let go of the vine and landed gracefully and lightly in front of the table. A few extra pounds had not caused her to lose any of the quickness and agility so noticeable among the cave-people.

Darrel also noticed that, even among this group of people seeking help in improving their ongoing *practice* of Dazhan, these people still seemed to be so cheerful and thoughtful. It made him feel self-conscious — he was *really* a beginner, while these people reflected a lifetime of exposure to Dazhan and were just looking for a bit of a motivational push.

As Nierren brought some wafers and drink over to Darrel and Zhana, Darrel accepted the offering with a pleasant nod. Zhana did the same.

The remaining member of the group, Larehnk, soon arrived. There was no apology nor acknowledgement of lateness. In this timeless land, promptness and tardiness were non-existent. Darrel considered that, while it could complicate the planning of activities, it also made for a slower-paced, more relaxed lifestyle.

After mutual introductions were completed, Darrel readied himself for the start of the meeting. But the timeless cave-people were in no hurry. They chatted casually, enjoyed refreshments, and got better acquainted with informal, pleasant visiting. They were also active and playful. Without hesitation, they scampered over the grottoed rock formations, scurried up the tree, up and down and across the hanging vines — moving around nimbly and effortlessly as conversations moved from one center of attention to another. Neither age nor body structure seemed to impede their mobility. Darrel couldn't help but notice that the same playfulness he had observed in the children's learning center had not been lost as the cave people matured into adulthood and even the senior years. In the course of casual visiting, each participant made sure that everyone else in the group not only got to know his or her name, but also something of their personality, activities and interests, and how to find their cave residence so they could build stronger social contacts between gatherings, and also be accessible to help each other in problem situations that might arise.

At length, the group moved back around the hot springs area. Again, some slipped into the warm pond, others found perches in the lower branches of the tree, and others sat or squatted on the rocks. Darrel and Zhana found places in the "hot tub," and melted into the soothing water. Darrel noticed that the water was clearly warm, but not quite as hot as he would have normally set the spa back in his old condo. Like the others, he set aside his outer robe, and let the warm water soak into his inner garments. He rested his arms on the rim of the "pool" and relaxed. He decided that the cave people had a much better approach to "meetings" than what he was used to in the Outside.

Because it was a newly-formed group, Laros took a moment to introduce the nature and purpose of the group, and to describe the "agenda." After a few simple preliminaries, the meeting would be opened up for a discussion of problems and solutions in habituating an ongoing practice of the steps of Dazhan in normal activities. At that point, there would no longer be a "leader," other than to keep the focus of the group on the *practice* of Dazhan rather than theoretical aspects, or from drifting into unrelated topics. Everyone had room for improvement in their practice of Dazhan and could benefit from the suggestions of others, and anyone was capable of offering creative insights for someone else. Even Laros or Zhana, clearly advanced in practicing the steps, could always improve further, and the newest beginner might observe some small idea that even Nolak might have overlooked.

"We have all taken a few moments to get acquainted, and that is good," began Laros. "We might also take a moment to re-acquaint ourselves with what *Dazhan,* the source of our practice, actually says." He asked for a volunteer to read from the large text of *Dazhan* that was etched in the stone tablets near the steps behind them.

Wakemah, the thin older woman, who had now moved from the hot spring into the tree, volunteered to do it. Slowly, carefully, she read through each of the twenty-seven short paragraphs that made up the complete text of *Dazhan,* adjusting her inflection and emphasis as necessary to stress each detail of the Enrisans' spiritual practice.

When she was done, Laros thanked her pleasantly. "At this point, we should take a few minutes to answer any questions about the ideas or concepts of Dazhan. While that is not to be the focus of our discussion, we know that sometimes people do have questions, and this is a good time to take care of that, then move on to a focus on the *practice* of Dazhan. I will try to answer any questions, and we are fortunate to have Zhana with us who is advanced in her understanding of Dazhan, and anyone else may also provide further enlightenment."

Tiny Tijah, moving and speaking quickly, had a question about the psychology of reaching outward, away from self concerns, and its effect on creating positive emotional processes such as "happiness." Laros responded briefly, and Zhikahr also provided some additional comment. Darrel was impressed with Zhikahr's articulate speech and his understanding of the intricacies of detail in the *theory* of Dazhan. Nierren then had several simple questions relating to aspects of expectation, reciprocation, and cooperation in various types of relationships. Laros solicited assistance from Zhana, who provided some commentary on the subject. With no additional questions about the *theory* of Dazhan, Laros opened the discussion up for problems and solutions in the *practice* of Dazhan — expressing the *spirit* of compassionate joy through *action.*

Zhikahr spoke first. Darrel's attention immediately perked up, as he was curious as to what kind of problems could be bothering Zhikahr, who seemed so articulate, intelligent, and the epitome of Dazhan.

"At this stage of my life," began the older man, "I really feel some confidence in my understanding of Dazhan, and pretty much in the way I practice it in my regular lifestyle. I am able to go through the steps thoroughly and completely, and I do it in most situations. But I'm involved in a variety of projects and activities, which are also valuable expressions of outward attention away from myself, but which some-times distract me from remembering the practice of Dazhan. Especially at such times I tend to fall back on my *understanding* of Dazhan as a substitute for *practicing* it. Another problem is that there are times when it is necessary to confront negative situations, and even to do so with some firmness. At such times, especially, I feel I am too impatient. Or I react with more negativity than firmness." He looked up at his wife, Wakemah, perched in the tree. "She knows what I mean."

Wakemah hadn't planned to speak quite yet, but also knew her husband was soliciting input that would help him. "For example," she said, "recently our neighbor was outside her cave banging on raw metallic tablets to make some writing plates. It was noisy, while Zhikahr was trying to concentrate on the fine details of an art project."

Zhikahr gave a short laugh and picked up the story. "I went over my neighbor to see if she could work with less noise. Wakemah knows I get impatient, and she tried to stop me from going over. But it was a reasonable request. And our neighbor is a good person; she would cooperate. But when I went there I was already annoyed because of the noise, and I spoke in an angry tone of voice. The neighbor was still willing to cooperate, but the encounter was unpleasant. I still think the request was all right. I just need to remember the feeling and practice of Dazhan, even in unpleasant situations, *before* I go confront someone."

Just talking through it made him sheepishly aware of his impatience, and in the relaxed atmosphere of the group setting, the expression on his face made it clear that he was already thinking of how he could have responded better.

"How did you feel when Wakemah tried to dissuade you from going over there?" inquired Hanahkalo.

"That annoyed me, too, because I thought my request was reasonable. And it was. I just handled it poorly — without the steps of Dazhan."

"So you were already annoyed by the noise, and then Wakemah made you even more impatient, so Dazhan didn't have a chance?" continued Hanahkalo.

"Yeah, I guess so," agreed Zhikahr. "What I need is some way to remember Dazhan *before* I get into the situation. If I can just remind myself first, I know I can go through the steps smoothly."

Darrel, who had been listening intently, now spoke. "At a different level, it is similar to *my* situation. The steps are easy, but I need to actually *go through* the process of applying the steps."

There was a brief silence. Then Nierren spoke. "You are both fortunate to be in close romantic relationships. Let your partners help you." She faced Wakemah. "It is good for you to try to help your husband avoid an unpleasant confrontation. But when you try to get him to stop completely from expressing something he feels is right to express, then it just becomes more unpleasant. Maybe … instead of trying to prevent him from saying anything, help him find a constructive way to express himself. He wants to remember to go through the steps; he is a good person and wants a constructive alternative. He just needs a reminder to do the steps first, and maybe suggestions on how to express a constructive request to a cooperative neighbor." She turned toward Zhana. "Similarly, Zhana, you can help Darrel find ways in which to add the practice of Dazhan into his regular flow of activities, and help him find opportunities instead of letting them slip by."

Darrel noticed how quickly the conversation always moved to specific suggestions for *action*, focusing particularly on ideas for improving behavioral responses in specific situations.

Hanahkalo, friend of Zhikahr and Wakemah, also made an observation. "Yes, Nierren, you are right," he said. "Close, special relationships hold special opportunities for us to help each other in improving our practice of Dazhan. But I detect in your voice that you are dissatisfied with the state of 'relationships' in your life. Are you involved in that kind of close, special relationship right now?" Darrel was taken aback somewhat at how candid Hanahkalo's comments were, but also noticed that he spoke with warmth and tenderness as he looked deep into her eyes and put her at ease.

Still, Nierren's previously cheerful expression grew more serious. "No," she answered slowly. "I don't have that kind of relationship right now. I've been feeling self-conscious because I am overweight. I want a romantic relationship, or just to have other friends, but I feel unattractive. And the more I feel self-conscious about my attractiveness, the more I am focused inward, unable to get out and feel comfortable about meeting people. It's a vicious cycle."

Tijah, sitting near Nierren, responded. As usual her movements and speech were quick and restless. "And Dazhan is the key to breaking that 'vicious cycle'...."

"That's easy for you to say, because you are tiny and attractive. Any man would want to be with you," responded Nierren.

"There is more to relationships than being attractive," answered Tijah. "It is the personality, the spirit, the contribution that you share with another person, in romance or any other kind of relationship."

"Yes," agreed Wakemah. "Any relationship is more than just a first impression of attractiveness, which varies with each person's preferences. The real problem is your self-consciousness, looking inward toward yourself, that distracts you from feeling comfortable and enjoying interpersonal happiness. Tijah is right. The way to break that vicious cycle is through Dazhan. If you can break out of that self-preoccupation and go through each step of the practice, then you will draw yourself outward and feel happy and relaxed. If you focus your attention on what you can contribute to others, instead of introspective preoccupations, then you will cheerfully brighten the lives of those around you. People will enjoy being with you and you will suddenly realize that you no longer have a problem with relationships, friendships — anything."

"Relationships require special caution," added Tijah. "They are so wonderful when they work out, and there is so much pain when they don't. Because they are based on *expectation*, it is easy to forget that they are separate from Dazhan, and how easily they distract us from the steps. But if we add the steps as a *separate and additional practice,* they not only contribute to the closeness of the relationship, but provide the means for getting through the difficult times ...."

And so it went on. Each person identified the problems or distractions that were interfering with their implementation of a smooth, ongoing practice of Dazhan in the regular process of their normal activities. Tijah was looking for guidance in becoming more relaxed and casual in her practice of the cheerful steps. Hanahkalo was coming through a death in the family and, in addition to special counseling to help him deal with his grief, he needed help in breaking through the loneliness and self-preoccupation that accompanied his sense of loss. Larehnk had noticed that in the course of his activities and projects, among friends and family and elsewhere in his general lifestyle, that when other people made requests for his assistance he found it to be distracting, as though they were intruding into his personal space — yet he noticed that other Enrisans, in extending themselves outward, often saw such requests as *opportunities* to extend themselves happily outward, and he sought assistance in re-directing his attitude in that direction.

The "problem" that Darrel presented, of course, was not in the way he was *practicing* Dazhan, but rather in getting *started* with a practice at all — overcoming his initial resistance to acquiring new habits and finding *regular* opportunities to practice the steps. He described to the group his initial attempts at practicing the steps. When they heard how his first attempts had usually come to the conclusion that the appropriate behavioral response was for "no action," the group cautioned him to practice in situations that would lead him to make an active contribution to those with whom he interacted. While there were certainly times when "no action" would be most appropriate, the real power of Dazhan should be to create increased happiness in the world and share in the enjoyment of that happiness.

And so it went. As problems were presented, the group united its collective spirit in search of solutions, emphasizing specific *actions* that could be taken, rather than just feelings or attitudes. Not every solution was easy or immediate. On the other hand, sometimes an obvious solution would emerge from the process of verbalizing the difficulty.

Darrel was deeply impressed. It gave him a chance to see how other people applied the practice in real life situations, and helped him perceive Dazhan as something real and practical, not just vague and idealistic.

At length, Darrel sensed that the session was getting ready to break up. The discussion tapered off, and the group became more informal, like a social gathering. But the participants did not drift apart. In addition to exchanging personal information and making arrangements to keep in contact until their next gathering, the emphasis of their conversations was on what they would *do*. Members of the group agreed to get together and develop plans for specific projects to identify and handle situations involving positive, negative or neutral interactions. They would help each other come up with creative ideas for pleasant ways in which to *enjoy* contributing to others.

The group made plans to meet again several more times, and Darrel expressed to both Laros and Zhana his enthusiastic anticipation for future meetings.

Laros was quick to agree that the get-togethers were a valuable resource. But he also cautioned Darrel to keep in mind that the gatherings are not a substitute for Dazhan; Dazhan is something that goes on in real life activities, while the meetings are just an optional aid for helping to implement the process more smoothly.

"As you have questions or difficulties, feel free to talk with me," offered Laros. "Also, you live with Zhana (as Wakemah pointed out), and she is a valuable resource. And there are other group members who live near you and would be glad to be available between gatherings. Let them share with you creative and enjoyable ideas for putting Dazhan into *action*. But mostly, remember that it is *you* who needs to develop the practice of Dazhan. *You* are the one who must find the occasions when you can go through the steps — all the way to *action*."

He rested his arm on Darrel's shoulder. "You'll make it!"

Chapter Thirteen

Breakthrough

Darrel stood on a stone "table" so he could reach a little higher on the cave wall. Additional months had passed unmeasured, and to become more functional as a member of the community, Darrel had taken up a trade. Because of the Enrisan interest in Darrel's "exotic" cultural tastes from the outside world, and their interpretation of what "providing housing" in his erstwhile real estate business might have included, Zhana had encouraged him to assist Enrisans in decorating and finishing their burrowed-out tunnel-dwellings. Now, he was stretching up the side of an Enrisan residence, working with several of the natives, helping to "Americanize" it. He had come to love and enjoy the Enrisan culture, but was also pleased to see that cultural sharing could flow in two directions.

As he was straining to fine-tune some adjustments in a shelf arrangement, Zhana burst into the room, flanked by Kerreih, Laros, Rimani, and three green-clad guards from the palace of Nolak. Zhana's face was white as a sheet. "Darrel!" she exclaimed. "Come with us. Hurry!"

Darrel's thoughts were flooded with frantic questions. He leaped down to Zhana's side. "What's going on?" he asked breathlessly. He wondered if maybe someone from Zhana's family or his Dazhan group had gotten hurt or was in some kind of trouble.

"Just come on," she insisted, pulling him toward the outside.

The group raced across the fractured surface of the landscape as fast as Darrel's clumsy pace would allow, toward the governing fortress of Kerreih's Sanctuary. They hurried inside and down through a tunnel of narrow steps into a cloistered stone dungeon. In the pale light of scattered kibihni, Darrel saw additional guards, some in local white outfits and others in the green colors of the central leadership, poised defensively with sticks and clubs. Looking into the shadows of the far wall, Darrel was stunned to see huddled together the sweaty, unshaven faces of American visitors.

"Darrel," shouted one of the strangers in the beautiful English so long absent from Darrel's ears, "you're really alive!"

"Then you know them?" confirmed Kerreih in the Enrisan language, as Darrel squinted into the shadows with disbelief, and moved in to where he could see the newcomers more closely.

Recognizing old companions, Darrel broke freely into English as though he had never stopped using it. "Alan!" he exclaimed, easing past the guards, "What are you doing here?"

Cautiously approaching Darrel and the Americans, Kerreih and Zhana explained that the group of strangers had been surprised by a lone Enrisan wandering in the brush just as they entered the central cavern of Enrisa. Recognizing the tall stature and pale complexion and the resemblance of these men to the well-known Darrel, the native rushed toward the strangers with an enthusiastic greeting. Caught off guard by a native rushing toward them and yelling, one of the Americans had responded with fear and had knocked the Enrisan down with his lantern and kicked him away. A crowd of Enrisans, attracted by the commotion, quickly gathered to subdue the intruders and bring them hastily to Kerreih.

"Who was hurt?" asked Darrel, reverting to the Enrisan language.

Kerreih and Zhana responded with a name unknown to Darrel.

"How bad was he hurt?" continued Darrel.

He learned that the man was conscious and responding well to treatment, but the intruders would have to be tried for their violent behavior. Possible consequences might include treatment in the Isolation Zone.

Darrel turned back to the Americans and spoke in English.

"Hey, you're pretty good with that stuff," blurted Alan, surprised to hear his little cousin babbling strange tongues so effortlessly. "What have they done to you?"

"I'm fine," started Darrel, "but what did you guys do?"

Alan responded, and Darrel relayed his message into Enrisan words for Kerreih and Zhana. After searching for Darrel at great length following his disappearance so long ago, Alan, Lee, and the rest of the rescue party had finally stumbled into the vast lighted caverns of Enrisa. Already concerned as to the fate of their long-lost companion, and not knowing whether strange beings might be friendly or hostile, they were suddenly rushed by a screaming native. One of the men reflexively attacked the Enrisan in self-defense.

Darrel backed off from his friends and took up their cause in his own Enrisan words. "They were just scared." He appealed to their outward-oriented compassion of Dazhan. "Try to understand how they *felt*. They were in a strange place. They didn't expect to find human life way down here in the caves and, when they did, they didn't know what these people would do to them. They were caught off guard. They just reacted with fear. I know these people. This kind of thing would never have happened in a normal situation."

Kerreih discussed the matter briefly with Zhana, and paused hesitantly. She wanted to be fair in considering special circumstances and unique perspectives of foreign feelings, but also felt the need to make sure her community was protected. "You know these people?" she repeated.

"Sure," answered Darrel. "This is Alan, my cousin. This is his friend, Lee — my friend, too. I don't know the others, but they came to help on a rescue mission. I'm sure they're all good people." Darrel was silently thankful that no one had been carrying a gun.

Determining that Alan and Lee were the only outsiders actually known to Darrel personally, and that it was one of the *other* men who had committed the violent act, Kerreih decided to release Alan and Lee under Darrel's supervision and based on his assurances. She would continue to detain the others until a further determination of facts and solutions could be made. Kerreih was satisfied with this as a fair, temporary compromise. Darrel obtained promises of good behavior from the men in exchange for Kerreih's assurance of generous comfort for those detained. Then Darrel and Zhana led Alan and Lee out of the Sanctuary toward their burrowed-out residence.

Zhana sensed that Darrel might have a lot of catching up to do with his old companions. Realizing that she would probably be left out of their foreign conversations, she excused herself to take care of other business.

"Hey, you're really somethin' else, Darrel!" exclaimed Alan. "How'd you ever get to be such a big wheel down here?"

"Hold it," answered Darrel. "First things first. How'd you guys ever find me?"

"Hey, you left wrappers, trash, used-up equipment, even torn pieces of clothing all over the caves," teased Alan. "Gawd, you're a slob! It wasn't easy after the cave-in, but we went back to the nearest town and got together a rescue team. The tough part was getting all them men and machines up the mountain to dig through that rockslide. We never thought we'd find you alive. When we finally broke through and began to find your trail of litter, we had a little hope. But we couldn't imagine how you would ever be able to stay alive so long in the caves. We were just lookin' for a body. We found you, ol' buddy, but it sure took us a long enough time!"

Time. *Time*. **TIME!**

Gripped with a sudden obsession, Darrel looked outward toward the unending brightness of the kibihni, and glanced at the watches on Alan's and Lee's wrists. Time! "What time is it?" he gasped. "What day is it?"

Alan looked at the calendar on his watch and chuckled. "Hey, it's July 4," he announced. "Independence Day! We can celebrate by liberating you from these Gawd-awful caves."

Actually, Darrel had come to love the caves as his new home among real friends. He felt no pressing desire to find "liberation" from the land of Sanctuaries, Divines and underground mysteries. But that would be a subject for later discussion. "July 4," mused Darrel. It had been more than a full year since he had last seen real daylight. This was the first real opportunity in all these months to get any accurate perspective of actual time. "What time is it?" he asked.

Lee glanced at his watch. "6:15," he replied.

"AM or PM?" wondered Darrel.

Lee responded with a funny stare. "It is 6:15 in the afternoon," he explained. "Should be getting dark pretty soon."

Darrel just laughed.

Alan and Lee spent hours listening to Darrel describe the subtle mysteries of the hidden world they had stumbled into. They wanted to know all about the strange lighted caves and about the history and development of the cave people. What kind of treatment could they expect from the natives? What special customs should they quickly adopt? In particular, they were concerned about what Darrel thought might be done to their companions detained back at the Sanctuary.

Likewise, Darrel wanted to catch up on all the news that he had missed during a year of absence. He was interested in the most current political developments, economic trends and social fads. It was mid-July, so he wanted to know how the Dodgers were doing, and how they had finished up the previous season.

Relaxing into casual English dialogue, "shooting the bull" with old companions from the past, and hearing the latest reports from the outside world drew a strange response from deep within Darrel. It made him really *feel* like an American again. He loved Enrisa. Only here had he come to feel like a complete person. But he also felt a strong sense of identity with his personal and cultural roots, and a desire to see old people and places again. He asked about some of his old friends.

Alan gave as much detail as he could about who was doing what and with whom, and volunteered some extra news — mentioning the name of Linda Ferret, the ex-girlfriend Darrel had left behind.

"That's one I don't need," responded Darrel with mock gagging.

Alan went on without interruption: "Boy, did she take it hard when you disappeared! She kinda blamed herself for what happened. I guess she felt personally responsible — kinda guilty — what with the timing an' all. Ya know, she put up a lot of the money for this effort...."

Just then Zhana appeared.

"Cool it," warned Lee. "One o' them chicks just came back. The cute one. What the hell is this, Darrel? This place run by women?"

"If it is, no wonder Darrel's been gettin' along so well!" cracked Alan.

Darrel quickly realized that there had been no indication to Alan or Lee of his personal relationship with Zhana. All they had seen of Zhana was that she had taken an active role with Kerreih in deciding how they and their friends would be dealt with. Beyond that, she had walked with Darrel back to this burrowed-out residence and then left. For all they could tell, Zhana was escorting "prisoners" in transfer to Darrel's custody. They couldn't understand what the two lovers might have been talking about. Darrel quickly filled them in on the kind of relationship that had emerged during the past year.

"You mean she lives here? With you?" exclaimed Lee with a leering wink. "Not bad! Now you gotta find an extra one for me!"

Darrel felt a flash of resentment, but he didn't know what to do. Zhana was the most special element of his life. She had taken him through difficult cultural adjustments to help him become a contributing member of this exotic community. She had led him to a new spiritual awareness, and brought into harmony the splintered fragments of the wasted life she had found. It bothered him that close friends could talk about her so flippantly. But what could he say? A year ago he would have been leading the way. Could he really have changed so much in just one year?

Zhana helped Darrel set up bedding materials for the visitors, and then followed Darrel into their own private retreat in the next room.

As he was loosening his robe, Darrel was startled by the sudden crash of clanging metal. He rushed back to see if Alan and Lee were all right, with Zhana right behind him. He found Lee quickly gathering together the metallic pages of a *Dazhan,* which he had dropped all over the floor. "Can't you guys stay out of trouble for a minute!?" snapped Darrel, half kidding, trying to conceal his irritation.

"Hey, Darrel — sorry!" answered Lee, throwing up his hands with a shrug. "I was just looking at some of the crazy junk you got here, and this just fell out. Hey, can you read this stuff, too?"

"That's *Dazhan,*" explained Darrel, racing over to help put it back together. He couldn't quite get the binding assembly into place. "That's the 'Holy Book' here...," he explained, fondling the plates gently.

"Holy Book!?" whooped Lee. "You mean the local mumbo-jumbo for the natives? Don't tell me that's what you're into these days!"

Darrel felt sheepish, almost apologetic. How could he explain the brief but powerful text of *Dazhan,* and his experiences over long months of gradual development, in the ten-minute summary he knew they would be expecting? He looked at his erstwhile companions. Had he really changed so much in a year's time? He recalled his own early skepticism about Dazhan, and his initial intent to become familiar with it only as a way of understanding the Enrisans so he could "get ahead" in his new surroundings. He recalled how he had grown from an arrogant outsider to really hungering to understand the simple steps that added so much happiness to the lives of the cave-people, and then from *understanding* to his primitive attempts at putting those ideas into *practice.*

Zhana adjusted the metallic binder and snapped the pages into place, taking hold of Darrel's hand as they returned to their quarters. Darrel climbed into the bedding and snuggled up very close to Zhana. He lay very silently, holding her in thoughtful tenderness.

After more than a year of separation, he was miraculously reunited with his cousin and friend. But what should have been a happy, joyous celebration was tempered by the extent to which his values had grown different from theirs. He had only been with them a few hours and the relationship was already feeling strained. Choking back a lump in his throat, he expressed his apprehensions to Zhana.

"It was clear that something was wrong," she whispered after a long pause. "I don't know what you were talking about, but I could tell when I came back that you were upset." She squeezed his hand.

"What am I going to do?" he wondered, feeling the knot of emotion tightening. "Alan's my cousin. I've known him all my life. We used to play ... uh ..." he realized he had no Enrisan word for *baseball* "...outdoor games together when we were kids."

Zhana rolled over and propped herself up in front of Darrel. "You're the one that's changed, Darrel," she reminded him. "Alan is still your cousin and Lee is still your friend. You can't expect them to understand what Dazhan means to you. This hasn't been easy on them, either, and they did come here for *you.* So, what are you going to do about it?"

"I'm not sure," he answered. "I just don't know."

"You know how Dazhan works," insisted Zhana. "Relate to them through their own consciousness. Accept them the way they are. Darrel, you're the only one who can! You know where they're at. You've been there. You don't have to agree with them or expect them to be perfect. But the only thing that makes you any different than them is Dazhan, and that's what Dazhan means."

Long after Zhana had been taken by sleep, Darrel lay awake in silent thought. He reflected on his own life, and he related that to the current experience of his companions. He focused his spiritual energies toward really understanding the perspectives through which meaningful experience was now processing through their consciousnesses. It was no longer just a matter of routine practice.

As he lay in pensive silence, he heard mumbling through the cavern walls. He drew himself up to the side of the wall and could hear Lee whispering excitedly on the other side: "...artifacts, fluorescent stones, Gawd! We could even set up a chain of food places selling Enrisan cuisine! The possibilities are endless. And this place must be crawling with all kinds of minerals and resources. We're gonna be rich!"

"Yeah," whispered Alan. "But Darrel's the key to it. You've seen how they do for him. Hell, he must be sleepin' with half of 'em."

"You think he's game?" wondered Lee.

"Darrel? Sure!" insisted Alan. "He's a natural. He's sharp. You saw how he ran them land deals before he left. Not only that, but he's got an 'in' with the locals...."

"I dunno," continued Lee. "He's been kinda weird lately."

"Naw," finished Alan. "He's okay. He's just been through a lot. Once we get him outta here he'll snap out of it."

Darrel pulled back away from the wall. At a time when he was trying to bring his feelings into closer harmony, he was afraid of what else he might hear. He looked at Zhana, nestled so peacefully into her dreams. How could she possibly understand the kinds of apprehensions that plagued him? Yet she was right. If he couldn't make Dazhan work in his closest personal relationships, how much had he really learned?

He thought of the steps in the practice. He could understand and appreciate his own self-value and understand the unique that had led him from where Alan and Lee were. He could direct himself outward to the equal value of his companions. He could intensify the specific sharing of their physical and spiritual perspectives, and find the right behavioral response with which to contribute to their experience. In fact, that would be his main challenge: not only to find the right *feelings*, but to let those feelings guide him in his *action* toward them, as the Enrisans had suggested. Alan and Lee might have some values that were shallow and inadequate — even truly malicious. But he also thought of all the old values and feelings he had had to unlearn, and the new spirit of compassionate joy that he was still struggling to practice. He could still love them and extend himself outward toward them without having to be a part of misguided perspectives that he had outgrown. He could feel compassion for them even if he had to actively take action against any efforts that might hurt others.

He also thought of Nolak and the grand social community that was threatened by the whispered schemes of two helpless visitors. He thought of the other Americans who had been detained, but about them he worried least of all. He knew that they would be treated with kind and generous hospitality.

His head was spinning as he finally joined his sweetheart in the refuge of sleep.

Chapter Fourteen

Excursion

"Darrel, wake up!" whispered Zhana, shaking him firmly.

Darrel continued to toss and kick in his sleep. A stray fist pounded the bedding. "Don't touch it," he sputtered in sleep-governed English words, meaningless to Zhana. "No, no ... dirty ... hurts to touch it...."

She continued to shake him. "Wake up, Sweetie...."

He gasped, sputtered, and stopped thrashing. An eye fluttered open. "What..." he saw Zhana propped up in front of him and shifted mental gears, returning to a flow of Enrisan vocabulary: "What's going on?"

"Darrel, you were dreaming!" announced Zhana. Never having seen such restlessness in him before, she had become alarmed.

Glancing around the familiar stone chamber, his tensed body relaxed. Caught in the middle of his dream, the procession of subconscious images was still vivid in his mind. "Yeah, it was just a bad dream," he assured her. "I'm okay." In his sleeping mind, he had been haunted by a recurring vision in which Lee had dropped the *Dazhan* and was trying to gather up its scattered metal pages. In the dream, Darrel tried to get it back together, but couldn't. Only Zhana could do it. But when she had all the pieces in place and gave it back to Lee, it had become soft and papery and green, like sheets of dollar bills. How could he explain such a dream to Zhana?

Darrel and Zhana quickly dressed and joined their guests in the other room. Darrel was determined to mend any rift that might threaten the relationship with his companions. He was equally determined to protect the cultural integrity of his adopted Enrisan home.

A short while later, the three Americans were lounging around on the rocky edges of the garden ponds, dripping wet after a refreshing swim. Zhana had gone to take care of other business, allowing Darrel some time to show Alan and Lee the wonderland formations of the exotic garden grottoes.

Through the course of otherwise casual chit-chat, Alan and Lee frequently dropped subtle references to life on the outside, trying to revive a nostalgic feeling for his old lifestyle and snap him out of the "trauma" of his cave-bound isolation.

Darrel, too, was doing some heavy thinking of his own. He had decided that his most fulfilling experiences had been in the caves and was determined not only to remain here, but also to resist any influence that would threaten the beauty of this place as he had found it.

On the other hand, life in the Outside had been a major part of his recent life. He could enjoy the pleasant memories and the best aspects of his former experience without giving up the new directions of his life.

He really did want to return for a *visit* to California, as long as he could return home to Enrisa later. Depending on how Zhana felt, he hoped she would join him with Alan and Lee and the other Americans in returning to wide open spaces and real daylight. While coming from very different intentions, they all had no difficulty in agreeing on plans for a return to the outside as soon as possible.

As the three Americans continued to swim and relax in the pleasant environment of the exotic gardens, Alan and Lee felt their rescue mission was beginning to seem more like a vacation in the subterranean paradise, and Darrel felt more at ease with his old buddies. After several hours, they were still enjoying the beauty of the ponds. Lee was spread out on a smooth boulder basking in the temperate cavern brightness, Alan was diving from various rock formations, and Darrel was exploring hidden features concealed among the underwater fractures of the pools' depths.

After a while, Zhana completed her other business and came to join Darrel and become better acquainted with his companions. She danced nimbly over the ridge of flowering brush and small, rocky cliffs, slipped between the crystalline formations and rainbows down the side of a small waterfall, descending with catlike agility to the pond area where she had enjoyed so many pleasant hours alone with Darrel.

She was greeted by Lee, who pointed to the water to indicate where Darrel was swimming down among the underwater formations, as he often liked to do. Zhana smiled appreciatively back, and slipped off her outer robes and stepped into the shallow area of the ponds.

Many months had passed since the first time Darrel had helped her swim those first awkward strokes, and she had since become skilled enough to swim with confidence in all areas of the ponds.

She waited until she saw Darrel shooting upward, and swam out to meet him with a kiss as he broke through the surface and drank in great swallows of air. He was surprised and pleased to see her, and followed her back to shallow water. After all these hours alone with his cousin and friend, it was nice to see the person who had become his closest confidant. At any rate, he did have a lot to talk about with her. Hand in hand, they excused themselves and retreated to a secluded grotto area.

"How's everything going?" queried Zhana, with a brief but very affectionate embrace. She was hoping that Darrel had been able to smooth over the earlier rough edges, and was very pleased to hear that they were getting along so pleasantly.

"They want me to return with them to the Outside," announced Darrel. "I can't wait to see all the old places again!" Zhana's suddenly troubled expression prompted Darrel to make clear that he only intended to be gone for a short visit, and that he wanted to bring her with him, to show her the world he had come from.

Zhana was ecstatic! Always filled with zest, and eager for new challenges, she was especially enthusiastic about the Outside. During the long months of tutoring Darrel as a helpless stranger in the caves, she had often put herself in his place and wondered how she would have reacted if *she* had to wrestle with the baffling uncertainties of strange places, unknown cultural habits, and foreign words. Later, as communication was established and he could describe the strangeness of his Outside world, she was always confused trying to make sense of the diverse wonders so different from the quiet beauty of the caves. She wanted to see it for herself!

Zhana and the three Americans quickly agreed that an excursion to the Outside would be arranged as soon as the remaining members of the rescue party could be released from Kerreih's Sanctuary. Darrel and Zhana would approach Kerreih to work out the details.

A little later, Darrel and Zhana waited briefly outside Kerreih's chamber as the Chief Divine completed other business, until a white-clad official escorted them in to where they were greeted cheerfully by Kerreih. The young Chief Divine quickly guessed the nature of their business, and advised them that Nolak, the Most High Divine, had assumed personal jurisdiction over the matter due to the unique circumstances involved and the potential ramifications for all of Enrisa. Darrel and Zhana quickly left and made their way toward the Most High Sanctuary.

They scrambled across the terraced layers of fractured stone, forging through the underbrush as quickly as possible. When they reached the base of the great cliffs whose majestic peaks were crowned with Nolak's massive Sanctuary, Darrel paused to catch his breath.

"Come on!" urged Zhana. "We're almost there!"

Darrel's gaze drifted upward across the face of the cliffs, following the winding trail of switchbacks to the top. He was no longer a stranger to the cryptic fortress, and he fully realized the grueling hours of travel still ahead for one already tired from a full day's activity. But with encouragement from Zhana and a brief rest, they continued upward.

Pausing at intervals to rest, they pressed upward along the narrow stone switchbacks. The steep pace of the barren stone trail caused Darrel to feel tired and sweaty, but Zhana encouraged him on, and the two of them eventually rounded the final turn and came across the solid granite gates of the Most High Sanctuary. The massive stones loomed ominously silent, sealed tightly shut.

Darrel marched up to the closed gates and hollered. Nothing happened. He knocked against the stones and quickly realized the futility of that.

"What do we do now?" he asked, turning back to Zhana.

"I guess they're not expecting anyone right now," she shrugged. Previous visits had been arranged in advance, generally by invitation of Nolak himself. Darrel hollered again. The stones remained silent and motionless. Darrel and Zhana sat down together on the narrow trail, as Darrel tried to figure out what to do and Zhana just resigned herself to waiting patiently. "Nolak won't let us die out here," she assured Darrel.

Before long, a green-clad officer emerged seemingly from nowhere. He was pleasant, but firm. "What are you doing here?" he asked.

"We have come to see Nolak," answered Zhana.

"I wasn't advised that he is expecting you," answered the guard, with a puzzled expression, recognizing both Darrel and Zhana as past visitors. "Can I let Nolak know the nature of your visit?"

"We must talk with him regarding the Outsiders who are being detained in Kerreih's Sanctuary," explained Zhana. "It is important that we see him immediately."

The aide promised to relay the message, and scampered deftly up the face of the cliffs and disappeared into an unseen opening.

Darrel and Zhana only had to wait a short time before the massive stone gates creaked open, and Darrel followed Zhana into the Most High Sanctuary with a sense of relief.

They were led through the lush greenery of the main hall, past the gently flowing waters that spilled over carefully-arranged stone ridges, toward the central flame that glowed from the massive inscribed pillars. Sitting poised and alert was Nolak, who dismissed Darrel's awkward apology and welcomed his returning visitors and beckoned them closer.

Exhausted from physical and emotional exertion, Darrel squatted into a place at Zhana's side and began to discuss the recent developments that had suddenly caused so much turmoil in Enrisa. He could sense that while the Most High Divine was still enthusiastic and pleasant, the Old Man gave his full attention to the current matters of State.

The immediate question was what to do about the Americans. Darrel recalled from his own experience at trial in Enrisa that Nolak was not considering a final judgment against the Americans yet, as they had not been brought in to present a defense. He just wanted to see if he could resolve the matter without requiring a formal hearing.

Nolak had sent messengers to question the Enrisan who had been injured, and shared with Darrel and Zhana the responses that had been received. The man had not been badly hurt, and had recovered pretty well except for a few superficial markings that remained. He was not bitter about what had happened. If anything, he was sorry to have misjudged the "culture-shock" factor and to have frightened the Americans, and he still hoped they would be made welcome in the caves.

Nolak had also received messages from Kerreih assuring him that the visitors in her custody were being well treated, and that they were well behaved and had caused no problems at the Sanctuary.

Nolak questioned Darrel about the feelings and intentions of the Americans. Not only was he the single person who could communicate with them, but also the only one who would be able to understand how cultural backgrounds might influence the current situation. Darrel tried to describe, as briefly as possible, that there were many nations and cultures in the Outside, and they had different values and social systems, some friendly and some not. It would be normal for the Americans to be cautiously defensive in meeting strange peoples for the first time. Darrel further assured the Enrisan leader that, having become aware of the high social values and friendliness of the cave-people, the Americans would respond accordingly, and should represent no further threat. They just wanted to be free so they could go back to where they had come from.

"They just want to leave?" confirmed Nolak. At this point he was already inclined to dismiss the whole thing as an unfortunate intercultural misunderstanding. Especially since they just wanted to leave anyway, he could see no reason to detain them. Even if he had thought them guilty, it was not the function of Enrisan system to *punish* delinquents, but to protect the community by removing them while trying to rehabilitate them. As long as their intent was to voluntarily remove themselves, Nolak could not justify any official involvement.

His only concern was that, to avoid additional misunderstandings, they be released under Darrel's supervision, like Alan and Lee.

Sending a message to Kerreih that she release the remaining men to Darrel as soon as Darrel could come for them, Nolak invited Darrel and Zhana to stay briefly for additional counseling.

"So ... you also wish to leave with the Outsiders," he said. "Have you fully considered what that would mean?"

Facing blank, silent stares, Nolak elaborated. He drew close and rested a hand on each of his guests. Maintaining his characteristic cheerfulness, he also spoke with firmness. He felt that the other Outsiders, who would probably never adjust to Enrisan ways as long as they could stick together and depend on a go-between like Darrel, should be free to return to their homes. But he was reluctant to see Enrisans go out and face the harsh outside existence that Darrel had so often described. He predicted tragic consequences to the simple lifestyle of the easy-going Enrisan social order if cave-people should be emotionally damaged in the Outside, and then return to bring those scars back into the sheltered Enrisan community.

Nevertheless, in dismissing them, he reminded them of the Enrisan tradition of free choice, and left the decision to them with this warning: "After you leave here, you will never return to the same Enrisa."

Zhana and Darrel re-evaluated their plans for leaving as they wandered slowly down the winding path. Zhana still wanted to experience the sights and sounds of the Outside, but was deeply troubled by Nolak's warning. She was torn between the excitement of new challenges, and obedience to the highest spiritual authority in her life.

Darrel was less concerned about Nolak's strong reservations about their leaving, and was still determined to go if Zhana would join him. He respected and loved the wise old Enrisan leader, but felt Nolak was dealing with complex issues of intercultural communication that were new to him, and which he could not possibly understand.

He felt it was necessary to protect the cultural integrity of Enrisa by leading Alan, Lee, and the others out of the caves, and going with them so they could leave with the satisfaction of a successful rescue operation. Furthermore, it had been more than a year since he had seen the Outside, and he wanted to return for a visit he could share with Zhana. And he dreamed of sharing the "compassionate joy" of Dazhan with the American culture that needed it so badly. These were not all things that could be easily understood by any leader who only had the experience of a single cultural perspective. Darrel explained his point of view to Zhana.

"Yes, I agree with you," conceded Zhana, "that you have the advantage of looking from both sides. But sometimes Nolak just feels things intuitively, and he may sense danger in ways that you can't anticipate, or even he can't pinpoint. If Nolak felt strongly enough to warn us like that, I'm not sure I like going against it." They continued to discuss the issues back and forth at great length all the way down.

Zhana maintained the highest reverence for Nolak's spiritual leadership, but she had also developed great confidence in Darrel. She was torn between competing loyalties and trusts. Her own enthusiasm for exploring new adventures was the deciding factor. By the time they had arrived back to the main floor of the caverns, she had decided to accept the unknown risks, and join Darrel and his friends in the Outside.

The rest was just a matter of taking care of details. Alan and Lee went with Darrel to obtain the release of those detained in Kerreih's Sanctuary, while Zhana replenished supplies and equipment for the long return trip to the Outside.

Returning with all the Americans to his living area, Darrel retrieved his tattered old hiking jeans, along with the wallet and other personal effects he had saved as his last mementoes of the Outside. In the wallet was some money, several credit cards that had all expired, and all his identification. He was glad to have saved it.

Darrel changed into his American clothes, along with the old pair of shoes he had since located and stored with his other belongings. He put on the shoes and walked around a little. The sensation seemed very different after walking on only bare feet for over a year.

When Zhana joined him after finishing her preparations, he noted that none of the rescue party had any extra female clothing, or even any other clothing, which she could use in the right size. But, she looked at American clothing as tight and restrictive, and seemed to feel it would be quite uncomfortable. In particular, she noted the Americans' tight, rigid footwear and felt she could never walk or scamper across the rocks in such restraints.

The entire party assembled at Darrel's and Zhana's underground residence for final arrangements. Rimani and Lena, Zhana's parents, came with Jamak to help. They were very apprehensive about seeing their daughter off to the uncertainties of a strange universe, but could only trust her judgment and hope the future would bring a speedy, happy reunion.

Darrel and the rest of the group made a final review of their travel arrangements. Food, supplies, and equipment carried by each of them should be more than adequate. They would go back the same way they had come in. By now, the trail was well marked, and ropes and materials had been placed at strategic points along the way to facilitate a speedy return. Conditions would be as favorable as possible. This time there would be no hunger, no darkness, and no isolation. Apart from the long, grueling ascent itself, Darrel anticipated an experience very different from his previous struggle alone in the darkness of Timera's outer caves.

The little party gathered its stuff together, and climbed up to the outer fringes of the Enrisan universe. A small crowd of curious well wishers, led by Rimani, Lena, Laros, and a few other close family friends, followed them up to where the cavern walls opened into the narrow tunnels of Timera.

Alan and Lee led the rest of the rescue team through the narrow fracture, and waited for Darrel and Zhana. Rimani and Lena choked back feelings of apprehension as they embraced Darrel and their daughter and sent them off into the darkness. Holding Zhana's hand and responding to the affection of the small crowd's good-byes, Darrel stepped nervously into the dusky shadows as painful memories of his earlier trauma haunted him. With encouragement from Alan ahead and Zhana behind, he stepped through the rocky fractures into caves dimly lit by scattered kibihni.

Zhana followed with nervous excitement, and they headed upward toward new adventures.

Chapter Fifteen

Outside

Darrel looked up with awe and gently squeezed Zhana's hand. "There it is!" he whispered, pointing up to a tiny break in the rocks far above, where a flood of brightness poured into the caves.

They had been trudging upward for nine full days and nights through the grimy, miserable darkness of the cave's labyrinthed tunnels. Especially in the final trying days, confined within the parallel granite walls of the narrow, slanting passage, patience had often worn thin and tempers had flared. It had been a difficult ordeal for all. Even Zhana, after a lifetime sheltered in the quiet beauty of Enrisa, was filled with a new appreciation for the intensity of the initial trauma Darrel had survived alone and in darkness, with insufficient food and supplies. While Zhana was able to maintain her cheerful nature better than the others, she still needed Darrel's frequent reassurances that this was not a prelude to the harsh nature of the Outside.

It was with great relief that they finally emerged from the confining passage walls, through the escape route carved out of the original landslide's granite debris, and into the main chamber of the little cave Darrel had been so eager to explore that fateful June day so long ago.

A gentle ray of sunlight filtered down from the tiny, jagged opening, and stirred each person with renewed enthusiasm.

Darrel trembled with excitement.

Zhana was also excited. But her curious anticipation of new adventures was tempered with apprehension. But the sight of gentle sunbeams sparked a curious enthusiasm to look outside and see Darrel's strange universe and the strange light coming from beyond Timera.

Ropes were secured and tested. One by one each person climbed up to the rim and stepped out onto the mountainside. As Darrel took his turn on the rope, Zhana scampered easily up the rocks, gripping them with bare hands and feet, and met him at the top. Darrel rested his hand in Zhana's, and they turned together to face the Outside World.

Flinching quickly away to shield their eyes from the awesome brightness, they huddled together on a rocky perch. The gentle kibihni of the Enrisan caverns could never compare with the massive brilliance of the summer sun on a July afternoon. The contrast was further heightened by their recent days and nights of total darkness.

After a few moments, Darrel's eyes had adjusted enough to allow him to gaze out into raw daylight. But Zhana, after a lifetime — after generations of lifetimes — in the kibihni-lit caves, required a much longer adjustment, and in the long run could only look outside cupping her hands to shade her eyes, and squinting narrowly. But what she could see was very impressive.

"It's amazing!" confessed Zhana.

As their eyes adjusted further to the afternoon sun, Darrel and Zhana stepped forward together into the Outside World. Zhana peered out over the wide expanses of the panoramic Canadian horizon through the protective shading of her fingertips. She could see the vast and wide panorama, but was still too blinded by the sudden and overwhelming brightness to see specific details of the landscape.

For the first time in her life, the protective security of the surrounding cave walls was gone. Not only was the universe suddenly larger, but the firm stone boundaries that had defined its limits so precisely had were gone. Even with Darrel at her side, she stood on the mountainside, dwarfed by the vastness of the Earth. She felt small and exposed.

The rest of the party was already part way down the mountain. "Come on!" yelled one of the men. "You're holding us up!" With a few nimble leaps, Zhana quickly caught up, and Darrel was not too far behind.

Zhana's steps were quick as well as careful. She stepped lightly, and with great agility, yet getting a feel for the textures of rock and brush beneath her feet, and how they differed from that of the caves.

Just as they blended into the group, Zhana glanced upward and was seized with sudden panic. As her eyes continued to slowly adjust to the light, she was able to perceive things that were previously overlooked. "What is it?" she gasped, clinging to Darrel in terror. She was pointing up at a massive ball of fire, hanging motionless in the sky with no visible means of support. "Will it fall on us? Will it burn everything?"

Darrel's first impulse was to laugh. But he remembered his own long months struggling to adjust to confusing realities, which must have seemed equally simple to the Enrisans.

"That's the 'sun'," he answered, gently trying to explain the source of light, warmth and energy for the Outside. He assured her that it would remain securely in its place.

The man who had complained earlier erupted in outrage. "Goddammit," he stormed. "What is it this time!?"

"Take it easy, Ralph," warned Darrel. "Zhana needs a few moments to adjust, and we'll take as long as she needs."

"Fer cryin' out loud," yelled Ralph. "We've got enough to worry about without some whinin' broad...."

Darrel straightened up defensively. "We'll get back okay," he answered firmly, as his own voice began to rise with anger. "But I said we'll take as long as she needs...."

Furiously, the other man stormed over to confront Darrel directly, but Alan stepped in to break things up.

Zhana was bewildered by all the new sights and sounds, and caught off guard by the Americans' eagerness to explode in anger. She couldn't tell what they were saying, but she knew it wasn't pleasant. She wondered if maybe Kerreih and Nolak had acted too quickly in releasing all of these volatile strangers from confinement.

As Zhana's eyes continued to adjust and she was able to see more detail in the landscape, she also noticed additional differences from the cave environment with which she was familiar. Here were no kibihni lights. There were cliffs and mountain rocks, but they were either plain or covered with skimpy brush — no lush garden of tropical trees, foliage and flowers covering the fractured layers; there were no scattered ponds fed by bubbling waterfalls; there were no grottoed cavelets and crystal formations acting in concert with the watersprays as prisms to form the many rainbows that added so much color and beauty to the caves. Still, it was something new.

Zhana felt small and helpless in the vastness of this open land; she was still unsure about the huge flame suspended without support in the sky; she was concerned about facing life in a community of Americans of uncertain temperament; and now, the air itself was beginning to move, as a gentle breeze drifted across the mountainside. Zhana, always adventuresome and enthusiastic, felt frightened and lonely. She remembered Nolak's warning, and wondered if she would regret having ventured outward. She turned to Darrel for reassurance.

As she drew close to him, she thought about the first time she had seen him, carried barely alive into her care. His first experience in a strange place must have been no less traumatic, she considered, yet he had adjusted happily, even with no one he could talk to for answering those first frightening questions. With Darrel to help her, Zhana quickly decided she could explore this new environment fully, and seek positive experiences. No one else seemed bothered by the wind. It must be normal here. In fact, the cool breeze was somewhat refreshing. As they continued downward, Zhana's initial apprehension grew into an enjoyment of the breezy open-air sunshine.

They climbed downward. Hours passed. The air was filled with strange and exotic noises as the chirping and screeching of distant birds blended into the tireless rustling of the wind-blown mountain brush. A chorus of squeaking crickets lay hidden in the shrubs, and tiny summer insects buzzed endlessly around.

After months in the quiet beauty of Enrisa, Darrel had almost forgotten the constant presence of Sound in the world. Each sensation caused long-forgotten thoughts to become instantly familiar.

But for Zhana there was nothing to recall. It was all new. As long as Darrel and the others seemed to be at ease, she just soaked in the new world with acceptance. She continued to probe Darrel for new information as they walked, but she didn't want to delay the others or cause additional tension. If she just followed along, she could move over the rocks and brush faster than any of the men, even while talking. Darrel soon learned, though, not to make any sudden moves, lest Zhana, who was watching him for guidance, imagine something to be wrong.

At length, Zhana could no longer contain herself. She was trying to be patient, and no one else seemed to be concerned, but it was just too much. She tugged on Darrel's arm, and continued to advance as she spoke. She pointed to the sun, which Darrel had promised would be secure in its celestial place. "When we came out of the caves, it was way up in the sky," she observed. "Now it's way down there, almost to the ground. I'm sure it's going to fall down."

Keeping pace with the others, Darrel tried to explain the workings of the strange Outside. He explained that the sun was not like the Enrisan kibihni, permanently fixed into place on the cavern ceiling. The sun, as seen from the Earth, moved through celestial cycles in patterns so regular that the people of the Outside could depend on it very precisely. He tried to explain about daily time schedules, and how Time was measured in increments based on the movements of the sun, but this just confused Zhana.

Even as they were speaking, the Sun eased gently down past the horizon. Zhana could see that the brightness of the sunlit sky was quickly fading. Even Darrel's reassurances of normalcy were of little comfort to one who had been raised to adulthood without ever having seen the "normal world" change from light to dark. Had it not been for the conditioning of her days and nights in the darkness of Timera's labyrinth, it might have been beyond her ability to cope. Even so, she was turning more and more to Darrel for reassurance.

As darkness fell, it became necessary to make camp. Freed from the confining stuffiness of the dark, narrow caves, sleep could be enjoyed in greater comfort.

On the other hand, the small party was now exposed to the fiercest wilds of the Canadian Rockies. In this untamed back country, the darkness of night could conceal more real dangers than even Zhana's imagination could invent.

Zhana and the men cleared a wide circle of all brush and rocks that might shelter snakes or other crawling things. Into the cleared area was piled an arrangement of twigs and small branches, stuffed with dry brush and paper waste that had accumulated. One of the men ignited the brush and paper with his lighter, and soon a fire was safely blazing to provide light, warmth, and to frighten away dangerous beasts. Each person was assigned a two-hour shift to stand watch during the night, as further guard against intrusion, and to keep the fire alive.

Beginning the first shift, which he would share with Zhana, Darrel was relieved to see a blanket of clouds gathering across the darkened sky. The moon, which other romantics might enjoy but which would just mean more questions from Zhana, would not be seen tonight. That could be a discussion for another evening.

After a while, they were relieved by one of the other men, and they found the spot reserved for them to spend the night. Zhana snuggled up close to Darrel. She was still nervously apprehensive about the strange wonders of the Outside, but she was also excited by the curious sense of adventure. She wanted to tell the people back in Enrisa about the mysteries of this vast dimension that so completely dwarfed the caverns that comprised their entire known universe. Her mind was racing with anticipation and worries. She shouldn't expect to feel sleepy with so much going on. But it had been a long, grueling day of physical and emotional exertion. She needed rest. She pulled herself closer against Darrel's protective body and slept.

By the time Darrel awoke, Zhana was squatting cheerily at his side, perusing the metallic text of a small Dazhan she had insisted on bringing out with her. For all her initial apprehensions, she had survived a day and a night in the Outside. Now rested, she was eager to see more of Darrel's strange universe.

An early-morning haze settled lightly on the mountainside in a gentle mist. By the time the others in the group had each awakened and completed a morning meal, the mist had settled upward into an overcast sky. Zhana and the men gathered up their things, extinguished their fire, and continued trekking down toward the remote Canadian village, which would represent their return to the civilization of the Outside.

Keeping pace with the others, Zhana continued to inquire about each strange perception, no longer with the same apprehensive insecurity as at first, but with a curious sense of intrigue.

As soon as they were back on the trail, her first real concern was, again, the sun. The day before, Darrel had finally explained to her initial satisfaction the endless regularity of the day-night cycles governed by the sun. She had overcome her strong early fears to accept this on Darrel's word. Now, this cycle, which was explained as being so regular and predictable, had come back to "daylight" as Darrel had promised, but there was no sun!

Darrel could see she was thrown off by something as elementary as a cloudy day. He tried to explain clouds, and weather, and new ideas about the workings of the Outside. But each new explanation only generated all the more questions, and she was only becoming more confused.

As they continued to explore new ideas and experiences, the cloudy skies grew heavily darker. A brilliant flash streaked across the summer sky, followed by a thundering roar. Zhana froze in sudden panic. Darrel, too, was startled by the sudden burst of brightness and sound, and a reaction from him intensified Zhana's sudden terror. As he reached to comfort her, he was startled again by a second clap of lightning and thunder.

Before he could explain anything to his terrified sweetheart, the Earth was suddenly pelted by great drops of water. A gentle summer rain fell upon the mountainside, but to Zhana this was the most terrifying exhibition yet of the universe gone crazy. She clung to Darrel, trembling with fearful sobs, as the group sought refuge under a rocky bluff.

For the first time, Zhana did not respond readily to Darrel's reassurances. Not only had the brightness been fast and blinding, and the thundering roar sudden and deafening for one accustomed to the quiet of Enrisa, but even the Outsiders had been startled by its unexpected electrical fury.

Darrel held her close. The lightning ended as quickly as it had appeared, and only the gentle rainfall continued. He watched as the raindrops rolled together, drawn to each other as they found their way down to gullies and valleys.

"Zhana," whispered Darrel tenderly. "Look around you. This is the origin of the Watercycles."

"Huh?" Zhana looked up, surprised at Darrel's reference to the sacred Enrisan Watercycles here in the harsh Outside. And, she was puzzled. "The time of this Watercycle is still new; do you mean a new Watercycle will start again?"

Darrel laughed and pointed to the scattered raindrops running together into little streamlets. He explained how water was condensed out of the Outside air in little droplets, which ran together to form creeks, streams, and rivers. Some of these flows seeped down through the surface layers of the Earth to provide the subterranean waters of the Enrisan gardens. The process continued throughout the year, but during the melting snows and heavy rainfalls of springtime, flows were particularly heavy, causing the rising of the waterflows for the annual Watercycles celebrated by the Enrisans.

Zhana looked around. So this was how it happened! This was the embryonic conception of the sacred Watercycles! She looked up at the rain with great awe, wondering how water could be condensed out of air. So, it wasn't such a frightful thing, this "rain." The brightness and the noise were great and powerful — worthy of profound reverence — but not so terrible. Darrel had linked the experiences of her past to the moment of present experience in an important way, and Zhana was no longer afraid. She looked up again at the beautiful rain, with an understanding of sacred mysteries not known to the rest of her people.

In a little while, the rain stopped and the journey resumed. Gradually, the cloudy skies began to clear, and by afternoon the brightness of the sun shone amid a deep blue sky laced with fluffy white clouds. Zhana marveled at the beauty. She was further amazed as they walked and walked with no end to the sprawling panorama before them. In Enrisa, the walled limits of the known universe could be seen in all directions from any point within the caverns.

They trekked all afternoon and into the evening. At nightfall they again made camp, and were back on the trail in the morning. By the third day, Zhana was feeling more at home in the Outside, enjoying each puzzling challenge and turning to Darrel for explanations. Zhana was fascinated by the vastness of Darrel's strange world, but could not understand that this was only a very small part of it, and very different from the urban environment to which they were going.

By noon of the fourth day, Alan and one of the other men in front paused to look out over a small ridge, and called excitedly to the others. Darrel and Zhana hurried over. Off in the distance was the little town to which they were headed. It was near enough that they could expect to arrive before evening. The men cheered with noisy excitement, and Zhana embraced Darrel enthusiastically. To Darrel, the town was just a tiny rural outpost. But to Zhana, the arrangement of so many structures clustered together above the ground was an impressive architectural wonder, dwarfing even the majesty of the Sanctuaries.

The descent became steeper, and the pace quickened as the travelers eagerly covered the remaining miles. They climbed down across rocky formations, scrambled down sloping fields, and made their way through wooded thickets. As they saw the distant village drawing nearer and nearer, they pressed on with renewed energy. Zhana was especially excited about the mysteries of this strange thing Darrel called a "town."

By late afternoon, they met up with the main highway going into town, and hiked the brief remaining distance. Zhana was just studying the odd nature of this "highway" when a station wagon filled with passengers roared past. Zhana was startled, but by now had come to expect such surprises. Darrel had already described the fantastic machines and vehicles of the Outside, and Zhana could quickly see that, in a world spread out over such great distances, foot travel would not be practical for journeys of any significance. Still, she was fascinated by the awesome machine, and wanted to see more.

The town wasn't exactly overrun with space for travelers. There was one small, weathered hotel and diner. The sun was just starting to set as the weary party stepped into the lobby. Darrel hoped that there would be room enough for all of them.

They entered the building. Immediately, Zhana was puzzled. There was the sound of music, coming from somewhere. She was used to music in the Sanctuaries, and in the background for many situations in Enrisa. But this music was so different. It was just a simple *Muzak* melody, playing in the background of the hotel. But the tone and instrumentation was very different from the simple chimes and woodwinds of the cave peoples' music. It really made her *feel* that she was in a strange and foreign place.

As they walked up to the desk, the manager rushed frantically over to Zhana. "Mister, somethin's terribly wrong with your wife," he said to Darrel, noting her strange complexion and features. Her bare feet and strange robe didn't make her look any *less* unusual. "Take her in where she can lie down and I'll call a doctor...."

"It's just a skin condition," answered Darrel, not wanting a big scene and not feeling up to a long explanation. "She's okay. Really. We just need a room, and she'll be fine."

Even in the middle of summer, the isolated mountain town attracted few guests, and there were several rooms available. Darrel checked into a room with Zhana, Alan and Lee shared a room with one of the others, and the remaining trio took a third room.

Finding their room, Darrel surprised Zhana by scooping her into his arms and carrying her across the threshold in a gesture that would be meaningful only to him. While Zhana looked around the room with curious awe, Darrel called downstairs for something from the diner.

After hunger had been satisfied, they were still annoyed by the gritty unpleasantness of sweat and grime that had accumulated during their days and nights in caves and on the mountainside. They undressed, and Darrel led Zhana into the bathroom. She was astonished when he turned a few knobs and a waterfall suddenly appeared right on the wall! The temperature could even be adjusted! They stepped into the pleasant spray of water and scrubbed each other tenderly, and afterwards dried each other in the fluffy softness of terrycloth. Clean and refreshed, if somewhat tired, they found their way over to the bed.

Darrel crawled into the cool freshness of tightly-fitted sheets, and Zhana snuggled close at his side. While Zhana squirmed and wriggled, seeking comfort in the strange tangle of foreign bedding, Darrel just drew her close and enjoyed the comfort of a real bed.

Chapter Sixteen

Journey

As the first bright rays of morning sunlight poured into the room, Zhana stirred awake and sat up. While bright days and dark nights were still a novelty to the cave-woman, she was getting used to the strange cycles that governed the Outside. She looked around. It wasn't a dream. She was still in the same strange place that Darrel had brought her to. She was alert and fully awake, filled with curiosity and eager to see more of the fascinating mysteries so foreign to her experience.

Feeling the movement of the bed as Zhana sat up and moved around, Darrel awoke and smiled. Although Zhana was ready to seek new adventures, it was still very early on a summer morning and Darrel wanted a little more sleep. He sat up just long enough to explain that he was still sleepy, drew her close for a little kiss, and turned to the other side to sleep as Zhana quietly stepped out of bed to explore the surroundings.

Pulling the delicate, toga-like Enrisan robe around her, she studied the bare, weathered chamber. Slipping over to the window, she parted the sheer curtain fabric and gazed toward the mountain slopes from which she had come. Her eye caught the jagged face of a distant stone cliff, whose uneven vertical markings signaled the entrance to the little cave that led down into the homeland she had left. She felt a yearning for the safety and familiarity of the caves, but at the same time was excited about new challenges in Darrel's world. She let the curtains fall back into place and turned away from the window. There was too much here to see and do. She would find her way home soon enough.

She scurried quietly over to the big door leading to the outside. She turned the knob as she had seen Darrel do. The knob turned easily enough, but nothing happened. She pulled the door, pushed it and shook it. It wouldn't open. Not understanding that Darrel had bolted it for the night, she turned away to let Darrel figure it out later. She decided she shouldn't go out alone anyway, as there were still too many surprises that she didn't want to discover alone.

She headed for the bathroom. She flashed the lights, flushed the toilet and marveled as sink and tub filled with rushing water at the touch of a knob. The Outside was full of fun and exciting discoveries.

Finally, Darrel again sat up. With doors banging, lights flashing, and all the other noises, sleep was simply not possible. His first thought was to be annoyed with the distractions. But there was much to look forward to this day, and he was also excited. He watched Zhana playing in the bathroom and smiled knowingly. He thought back to his own first experiences in the caves of Enrisa and couldn't feel angry. He knew what it meant to puzzle over the impossible uncertainties of a strange new place. He tried to imagine how these simple, everyday objects would be perceived through *Zhana's* senses, and was surprised that feelings of Dazhan were beginning to pop up spontaneously.

Noticing that Darrel had awakened again, Zhana rushed over to him.

"I'm sorry to wake you up!"

Darrel pulled her close again. "Oh, I'm really too excited to sleep," he answered. "We have so much to do today!"

Dressing in a spare outfit that Alan had let him take instead of the tattered old clothes he had saved from the caves, he led Zhana around the room, providing the secrets to each mystery that had baffled her.

They had been up only a short time when there was a knock at the door. Darrel figured it must be Alan or one of the others in the group.

He opened the door without any particular thought, and was greeted with a flash of light that caught him off guard. Zhana whimpered softly and drew back, afraid. Darrel stood facing two men, both dressed in suits and ties. The thin one in front held a narrow briefcase, and the swarthy fellow behind him wielded a camera.

"Henry Waxford. UPI," announced the man in front matter-of-factly, extending an open palm and a business card in a single motion as he stepped quickly into the room, followed by the man with the camera who closed the door behind them.

Alan had already called interested parties in California, as well as local peace officers, to confirm that the rescue effort had been unexpectedly successful; Darrel Swift had survived more than a year isolated in subterranean caverns; a civilization of cave-people lived beneath the Earth's surface; one of the cave-people had been brought out with the rescue party. The manager of the hotel and several patrons of the diner had confirmed sightings of the strange cave-woman. The word was out.

"Do you have just a minute for a couple o' quick questions?" pushed Mr. Waxford, as the other man continued snapping photos of Darrel and the terrified cave-girl.

Drawing Zhana protectively toward him, he reassured her of no harm.

In the past, Darrel would have just brushed the news people aside, unless he thought he could them to his promotional advantage. But now, he thought for a moment. The men were just doing their jobs. The public had a "right to know" about a newsworthy occurrence. It would only take a minute. "Uh, I guess so," he answered.

He told about his struggle for survival in the darkness of the caves after the original rockslide, and how he had found water, then light, and finally the vast cavern filled with life and activity. He told about his life among the Enrisans, and gave the man a small luminous *kibih* he had saved. He talked and answered questions for almost an hour.

Finally there was another knock on the door, and he heard Alan shouting from the other side. "Come on, Darrel," called his cousin, "let's go down and get some breakfast." The reporters thanked Darrel and hastily excused themselves. Darrel took Zhana's hand and led her out into the hall.

Entering the diner for breakfast, another flock of newsmen swarmed past the manager, asking a dozen questions at the same time to an optical chorus of popping flashcubes. Darrel wanted to do his civic duty and help each one of them, but he was completely overwhelmed. And he was still hungry. He glanced toward Alan for support.

Alan faced the reporters. "Mr. Swift will hold a press conference at 10:30 this morning," he announced with authority as he cleared a path toward breakfast for Darrel and Zhana. As the newsmen checked their watches and scurried away, Alan whispered to Darrel with a grin, "You have to handle these things 'just so'...."

"Well, we've got a celebrity!" quipped Lee as Darrel found a place at Zhana's side across the table from his old friend.

As the men bantered back and forth through the meal, Darrel tried to help Zhana keep up with the dialogue by whispering periodic updates in Enrisan. But it was really impossible for him to join in with his friends and keep up with Zhana at the same time.

Zhana's feeling of isolation — of being out of place — had begun to set in during dinner the previous evening, but she had dismissed it. Now the feeling was becoming more intense. She was sitting in front of strange food, surrounded by tables of people gawking at her foreign features, listening to lengthy ramblings of unintelligible chatter punctuated with laughter and expressions, all summarized at uncertain intervals by a single brief comment of translation from Darrel. She tried to imagine Darrel's experience of facing odd food preparations, or his own feeling of being conspicuous, or of his isolation, but it didn't make the breakfast in front of her any more appetizing or make her feel any less out of place.

She began to feel tense and uncomfortable. She felt like she needed to breathe. Darrel sensed her discomfort and turned to her. He rested his hand around hers and patted it gently.

"Darrel, I've got to get out of here," she whispered, as unobtrusively as possible. "I just need a few moments to myself to get everything back together in my mind."

"I understand," answered Darrel as she excused herself and headed quickly back to their room amid a flurry of flashbulbs. He looked at her longingly as she disappeared up the stairs. More than anyone else on

Earth, he really did understand, and he felt like kicking himself for not being sufficiently alert to intercept those feelings before they got out of hand. He fought back an urge to follow her. She did need time alone to regain control of her feelings, and he remained downstairs to share breakfast with his companions.

After the meal, and after completing the brief news conference Alan had promised to the assemblage of reporters, Darrel returned to his room to look for Zhana. As he eased the door open, he could see her clutching the metallic pages of a *Dazhan* and sitting by the window, gazing toward the distant peaks. She turned to face him as he entered.

"How ya doin'?" he asked, taking hold of both her hands.

"I'm okay," she assured him. This had not been her first difficult moment and she suspected there would yet be others. But she had no regrets. She would have to deal with feelings as they came up, and make necessary adjustments. But she would do it. And Dazhan would be the tool that would help her in focusing her concerns away from self-preoccupation. It was a skill that she was good at. As long as she could direct herself *outward*, away from those concerns about herself that enabled fears and insecurities to fester, she could overcome those unpleasant feelings. She was not ready to call it "quits" yet!

Darrel explained the schedule that had been worked out with Alan and Lee. They would spend the afternoon driving to Calgary, Alberta, where their plane was tied down, and the following day flying back to Santa Barbara, California. It was impossible for Zhana to relate to activities in terms of timed schedules, but once again she put her faith in Darrel.

Before they could leave, however, Darrel needed to handle one more issue in hopes of minimizing unpleasant feelings in the future. He presented a change of clothes that had been selected for her by a female reporter. Darrel explained that, just as he had learned to use Enrisan robes and go barefoot in the caves, she would feel less out of place using clothes similar to other people in the Outside. He presented a pair of ladies' jeans, outdoor shirt, some undergarments — and a pair of *shoes*.

Zhana looked over the odd assortment of fabric. Reluctantly, she agreed that it might be more appropriate to adopt the Outsiders' apparel to some extent while in their world. With Darrel, who was not exactly an expert himself in putting on women's' clothing, she struggled awkwardly into the strange garments. Except the shoes.

"I'm not going to put my feet in those tiny things," she insisted.

"Just try them out," suggested Darrel. "You don't have to wear them all the time, but in the Outside there are just some times when you *need* to wear shoes."

"I think that's silly," she complained. But she tried them on. The shoes were just a pair of casual ladies' tennis shoes, light and springy. But, after Darrel helped her tie the strange tangle of laces, she stood up and almost fell over. Zhana was not one to complain easily, but she clearly did not like confining her nimble feet and toes in these little prisons. "Darrel, I can't even walk in these things."

Still, with her natural agility and coordination, and a few moments of practice, she was soon able to walk around awkwardly. "No wonder the Outsiders are so awkward in climbing in our rocks and trees," she mumbled to herself. Darrel didn't look forward to explaining occasions when more formal wear would be appropriate and was just glad that she wouldn't have to tie a necktie around her neck.

When they were finally ready, they went out to where Alan and Lee were waiting in a rented car. Zhana squealed with delight, looking forward to trying out one of these speeding metallic vehicles that she had seen on the road as they trekked the last portion of the way from the mouth of the cave. They climbed into the back seat, as Lee got in behind the wheel and Alan joined him in the front passenger seat.

Lee turned the ignition. The engine roared to life, causing Zhana to jump slightly, but more from excitement than from apprehension. Along with the roar of the engine, the stereo system also roared to life. This was no longer the same shallow *Muzak* coming from the background of a hotel. This was deep, rich stereo, orchestrated with full instrumentation and blending of harmonies and rhythms. And, in the small space of this little vehicle, there was no place in the background to conceal musicians. Zhana was amazed and puzzled. How did such music exist? Who produced such tones and harmonies? What kind of instruments created such sounds? And where was it coming from? She pumped Darrel with questions, and he tried to answer as much as he could. He wondered what would happen if he took her to a live concert — rock or classical — once they were back in California.

Soon, Zhana was speeding across the Canadian countryside next to Darrel in the back seat. With a sigh of relief, she slipped off her shoes and let her feet relax in comfort during the long drive. The other Americans had made their own arrangements for returning home.

Zhana was thrilled at the idea of racing across a land whose vastness she still couldn't comprehend, at speeds she still couldn't fully appreciate. Winding through the open spaces of the mountainous terrain, they periodically passed through whole villages at such a pace that the town was left behind in a matter of moments, underscoring the distances traveled over the hours in between. Even as the afternoon wore on, Zhana remained ecstatic with the fascination of the new discoveries that were rushing upon her. Of all the amazing new wonders, so far she liked this "automobile" the best. She wanted to go faster and faster!

As daylight began to fade and the dusk settled into nightfall, the highway wandered down into Calgary, and the city lights glittered from afar. Zhana stared with awe and disbelief. She had been fascinated hour by hour with the vastnesses of occasional mountain towns, as well as by the intriguing newness of the different kinds of outdoor environments in between. It had been an exciting and wondrous journey for the cave-girl. But here before her now stretched a single city of colors and lights that was individually greater than all of Enrisa combined! How small the underground Sanctuaries now seemed.

It was night and they needed to rest and unwind before tomorrow's long flight home in their small rented aircraft. Lee guided the car into a motel that looked invitingly sanitary but not overly luxurious, and they went up to the front office to register.

Passing a collection of newsstands, Darrel called the attention of his friends to the headlines. Splashed across the front of each paper, accented generously with photographs, were banner titles proclaiming, *"American Found Alive After Year in Caves";* and *"Californian Discovers Race of Cave-People — Returns with Specimen."*

Darrel and Zhana waited outside while Alan and Lee went in and quietly registered them under assumed names. As before, Alan and Lee roomed together and Darrel stayed with Zhana, remaining in their room to avoid possible crowds who might recognize their widely-published faces, as Alan and Lee went out to pick up some dinner.

They soon returned with something to eat and several newspapers. They all ate together in Darrel and Zhana's room and read about themselves. Darrel was amazed that the shockwaves had already carried so far. Revived interest in a long abandoned manhunt, the thrill of a successful survival story and the discovery of new civilizations underground combined to generate excitement throughout North America and beyond. Darrel was an instant celebrity and Zhana an object of public interest, as her existence drew curious inquiry from society in general and the scientific communities in particular. After eating and reading, Alan and Lee went off to their own room and everyone retired early.

As dawn broke the following morning, the foursome gathered around their rented Cessna. By now, Zhana had seen many cars on the mountain roads and in city traffic and was still fascinated by them. But this "car" looked different. Even in the early morning hours, air traffic was beginning to build, and Zhana could see similar "cars" running quickly and gliding up into the air. Zhana was amazed! People flying like bats! Machines capable of speeding in *seconds* across areas equal to the entire known world of Enrisa!

Under other circumstances, Zhana would have been terrified of such a venture. She had no way of realizing that, even among the Outsiders, there were many who harbored fears of such machines. But by now she was so used to accepting strange novelties that she also just took this one in stride. Besides, she had enjoyed the "car" so much, this "plane" might be even better!

They loaded their things into the plane and, while it was being serviced and refueled, Lee turned in the rental car and Alan filed his flight plan and called interested parties in California to inform them of an approximate schedule.

Darrel climbed into the rear of the plane and helped Zhana into the seat beside him. Alan took command of the pilot's seat, with Lee up front to assist. They closed the hatch and taxied to the head of the runway to await radioed instructions for takeoff. Darrel took Zhana's hand and smiled as the plane rolled forward and gathered speed. As velocity increased, the wheels eased up from the runway and the little plane soared up into the open sky. Zhana squealed with delight. It *was* more fun than a car!

She stared in amazement as the sprawling metropolitan landscape grew tinier and tinier. Huge structures began to look like toys as the plane gained altitude, and the cars in traffic looked like little ants creeping across the face of a great stone ball.

As they drifted out over the countryside, away from Calgary, Zhana could get an even greater perspective of the Earth's vastness. She had already come to think of the Outside as a place without limits. But after a lifetime in a place where physical limits existed as a constant presence, she was still struggling to comprehend this endlessness.

Alan guided them on a course over and through the Rocky Mountains, across a panorama of beautifully rugged wilderness. Within an hour or so, they had crossed into United States airspace and by noon they were approaching Boise, Idaho, to rest, refuel and have lunch.

While on the ground they checked the local stateside papers. Darrel and Zhana were still making big waves in all the headlines. They had lunch, serviced the plane and were soon back in the air with a couple of papers, which the Americans could read, while Zhana enjoyed the fascination of photoengraved images.

South from Boise, they flew over terrain that was significantly less treacherous. The land leveled off into arid desert country and continued like that for several hours until they were well into California. By late afternoon, Alan spotted the shoreline of the vast Pacific Ocean off in the distance and, soon after that, some of the most prominent landmarks from the town of Santa Barbara could be identified. Lee caught sight of the rising bell tower of the University campus and just ahead of that was the airstrip where they would touch down.

Alan made a pass over the shoreline, circling over the university, and headed down for a landing. They eased onto the runway, taxied to where the rental plane could be returned, and climbed out of the cabin.

As they made their way back to the flight lounge, Alan quickly reminded Darrel that during the past year, his business had been neglected, his car had been repossessed, his management company had rented out his condominium to someone else, and his credit cards had all expired. "Why don't you and the girl stay with me for a while 'til you get back on your feet," offered the elder cousin.

Darrel may have suffered some losses while away, but he also had been incurring no expenses. He had immediate access to bank savings, negotiable securities, other assets that could be quickly liquidated, plus some commercial accounts receivables that had not been paid to him since his disappearance. He only intended to stay for a short visit in California before taking Zhana back home to Enrisa, so he felt he could survive adequately until then. He thanked Alan, but declined the offer.

Entering the flight lounge, they were besieged by a mob of hungry reporters, representatives from the scientific communities, and some friends and business people who had turned out to welcome Darrel after his lengthy absence.

Darrel stood on a chair so he could be seen by everyone. "We will have a press conference at eight o'clock tonight in the conference room of my office," he announced. "First, I want to get a motel room, get cleaned up and get some dinner. And I want to thank you all for this warm reception. After the meeting tonight, my appearances will be limited to brief visits with the scientific people at the campus here and limited media participation by appointment, and a complete exclusive interview will be sold to the most favorable journalistic offer." He winked at Alan. "Since you've all been so gracious and waited so long," he continued, "I will present the two most significant aspects of my experience underground these past thirteen months." He pulled Zhana up to his side. "This is the woman who saved my life and allowed me to survive a year in the caves." There was a round of applause and flashcubes popped like crazy. He then held up the small, metallic *Dazhan* that Zhana had brought. "And this is what she did it with." A buzz murmured across the room. More flashcubes. No one could figure out exactly what he was holding. He promised to share it more fully in due time.

He dismissed the gathering and made his way with Zhana through the crowd to where they could pick up a rental car. He stopped a couple of times to say "Hi" to friends who were there, but kept such exchanges painfully brief. Finally, they were able to secure the rental of a car and stepped outside.

As he escorted Zhana into the car and blended off into the traffic, he thought he recognized a familiar figure following them out of the flight lounge.

It was Linda Ferret.

Chapter Seventeen

Anticipation

Standing at Darrel's side in the ebbing wash of the Pacific shoreline, Zhana felt herself losing balance as the wavelets quickly receded. She fell against Darrel and leaned on him for support. Of all the wonders of the Outside, which continued to surprise her many times each day, the Ocean was the most awesome discovery since thunder and rain. She couldn't imagine how so much funny-tasting water could be gathered in a single place, especially when Darrel tried to explain that even the vast miles they had traveled over land on foot, by auto and in flight, represented only a fraction of the Earth's land surface. And there was twice as much ocean surface as land!

Darrel enjoyed swimming out beyond where the nearest waves were forming and gliding into shore when he was lucky enough to catch a wave just right with his body. But Zhana, after venturing in up to her chest, found the water too cold and impossible to swim in. She remained in the gentlest traces of expired breakers. Still, she enjoyed the beach. It was so relaxed and casual, and the first time she saw so many people in the Outside all barefooted at the same time!

Between intervals of water fun, Frisbee, sand play and other enjoyment of the beach, they returned to the spot between two brackish slabs of stone where Darrel had spread a beach blanket. The protective shadows would keep Zhana's sensitive complexion, evolved from generations of her peoples' existence underground, out of sunlight and away from public view. They also consumed generous supplies of sunscreen. Huddled together, they worked on the project Darrel felt would be his most immediate contribution to the outside world: translation of *Dazhan* into English.

Through each line of the Ancient Text, he would question Zhana as to the most subtle inferences of each word and phrase and seek her explanation as to how the particular segment was understood and interpreted in common Enrisan practice. Then, he would try to understand each concept as a whole, and rephrase its meaning in the English words that Zhana or Nolak might use if they knew the language. At that point, it would be expressed in written words.

Zhana was fascinated by the pencils, paper and erasers that made spontaneous written expression so much more accessible to Outsiders than to the cave-people with their cumbersome metallic paraphernalia.

Dazhan

Titling the work *"Compassionate Joy"* as his translation of the Enrisan contraction "Dazhan," Darrel struggled tediously through line after line, pausing at intervals to enjoy the beach with Zhana. The pleasant ocean surroundings and Zhana's casual nature allowed him to adopt a relaxed work routine, providing an effective balance for his natural drive and thorough work habits.

Darrel and Zhana spent several long but satisfying days at the beach until a rough draft was complete. Additional time was necessary to make corrections and polish up the final wording for style and clarity. By the time they were finished, Darrel was surprised that the brief metallic volume of Enrisan text seemed even more abbreviated in English words and on paper pages. It was just a few scant pages when written out by hand. Darrel was hoping to present a *Classic* to the Outside world, and all he had was a fleeting pamphlet.

Back at their apartment, Darrel made final refinements and planned his strategy for maximum public exposure.

After their first days in a local hotel, Darrel and Zhana had found a furnished apartment to stay in. At first, Darrel just planned to stay in the apartment long enough to recover occupancy of his own condominium, then reconsidered. He would be back in Enrisa before the "wheels of justice" could re-secure his home and, anyway, felt uncomfortable with the thought of displacing the current occupants and then moving out right away to return to Enrisa.

Zhana was still fascinated by the continuing onslaught of wonders from the Twentieth Century.

Just within her American home, she was surrounded with marvelous creations, accessible at the touch of a finger. Television was a miracle beyond what she could possibly comprehend. At first, she couldn't see how so many fast-changing scenes, with complex settings and vast castings of characterizations, could fit in a single small box. Even after she learned that it was just a visual reproduction of images, sounds and colors originating from far away, she had difficulty understanding that most of the material was fictional to begin with — a presentation of events and characters which didn't really exist. She could never keep straight which strange creatures were real animals from zoos and distant lands, or which were just fanciful imaginations from the writers of science-fiction scripts. She could never tell if strange landscapes were the exotic horizons of real jungles, deserts, mountains, or polar tundra, or if they were imaginary scenes from distant galaxies, make-believe continents, or contrived civilizations. It was all very baffling, but she loved it.

Equally intriguing was that odd little colored box Darrel called a "telephone." Periodically it would emit a strange ringing loudness and Darrel could use it to talk with unseen persons far away. How exciting!

Because she could not speak English and was unable to talk with anyone but Darrel, Zhana avoided using the phone herself, or even answering for Darrel when he was out. But they did work out a one-ring-hangup-call-back routine so she would know to answer when he was out and was calling for her. He made a point of calling her on occasions when he was out alone, so she could enjoy the funny talking box without being fearful of it. He even taught her how to use a pay phone to call *him* at home for those occasions when *she* was the one who had gone out. This helped her to develop increasing confidence in going out into the strange society around her, as Darrel encouraged her to seek greater personal independence in his world, as she had done for him in hers.

The strange and beautiful mechanical wonders were everywhere. Instant fire for cooking. Instant cool for storage, or instant cold for freezing. Lights, water, power — all at the flick of a switch. Home computers for drawing, writing, organizing and calculating! Even such simple objects as a hair dryer or a toaster were bold new innovations to the Enrisan.

* * * * *

Late one Friday evening, after Darrel and Zhana had gone to bed, they were awakened by the ringing of the telephone. Darrel groped for the light, stumbled into the living room and answered the phone.

It was Linda Ferret.

Darrel was instantly wide awake. His first impulse was to hang up and call it a wrong number. But that would run counter to everything Dazhan had come to mean. Linda Ferret also represented an individual consciousness of unique personal value. And even though past romantic love had faded, personal concern and at least some residue of reflective curiosity, remained.

"This is Linda." Alan had given her the number.

Darrel politely expressed appreciation for her concern and for the effort she had put forward for his rescue, while hedging toward as brief a conversation as possible.

"We haven't seen each other for over a year. We should get together just for 'ol' times' sake." She had been drinking. "We can at least still be friends...."

Darrel wanted to be pleasant, and he wanted to be reasonable, but he didn't want to encourage any awkward situations. With some people, "just friendship" might be possible, if it was really based on common goals and values. But Darrel knew too well the possessive side of Linda's nature and could not accept any kind of contact that might cause disappointment and frustration for Linda, and unpleasantness for Zhana and himself.

Still, Darrel wanted to act in a manner consistent with his developing practice of Dazhan, and find the right expression of behavior that would be firm, yet as constructive as possible.

Meanwhile, Linda talked about herself, her feelings and her needs, pushing Darrel for his sympathy and taking advantage of his efforts to be understanding. Darrel tried to encourage Linda to reach outward — to find enjoyment in activities in which she could divert her attention away from self-preoccupation and perhaps meet other people with similar interests. Linda resisted any attempts by Darrel to give her any advice different from what she wanted to hear. Darrel quickly understood that what Linda felt for him was not love, but possession — the desire to *control* another human being. She had no interest in *his* feelings, but was consumed entirely with her own expectations. Darrel realized he could not be the one to help her break out of that self-directed obsession. Linda cautiously probed Darrel about his relationship with the strange cave woman and learned that it was a strong one. She began to sob and the conversation deteriorated as Darrel's efforts to comfort her without compromising collapsed in failure.

Zhana could see that Darrel was distressed as he returned to bed with her. He explained who the caller was and about her role in his personal history. Zhana's reaction was positive, but not entirely uncritical. She was pleased with Darrel's desire to be understanding toward another human being. She felt concern for Linda as a person. But she was also disturbed by the intended threat to their special relationship. Not sure exactly how to handle the situation, and not wanting to deal with it in the late-night moment, the issue was temporarily set aside. Darrel returned to sleep, while Zhana tossed and turned briefly until she could resist the concerns of self-preoccupation long enough to also become lost in sleep.

While Darrel enthusiastically continued his project of trying to bring Enrisan spiritual wealth to the American people, Alan and Lee were just as excited about the prospects of developing economic relations with the cave-people and share Twentieth Century wonders with the Enrisans — for a price, of course.

They hoped to capitalize on the richness of the subterranean mineral wealth, importing luminous kibihni stones and other exotic substances, and the promotion of cultural novelties for sale topside. In exchange, the two hoped to distribute as little of the fascinating technical gadgetry as the natives below would be satisfied with. Had they been around when Manhattan Island was purchased for twenty-four dollars worth of baubles, the Dutch wouldn't have had a chance. Naturally, they wanted Darrel to help. His knowledge of the language and customs, and the natives' confidence in him, would be invaluable commercial assets.

Alan and Lee were puzzled by Darrel's very cool reception of their proposals. Not only was Darrel no longer impressed by visions of great wealth, but his first concern was with the cultural integrity of Enrisan society. Darrel tried to be as positive and as pleasant as possible, while remaining firm about his role in their schemes.

Darrel was surprised to find Zhana, of all people, in disagreement with him. To her, each new discovery was a fascinating wonder. Confused by what she felt was Darrel's unexpected lack of cooperation in sharing the Outsiders' wealth with her people, she thought she detected for the first time a glimmer of cultural chauvinism now that he was safely back in his own element. After all, she was perfectly willing to help him translate *Dazhan* and appear in silly news presentations, which she couldn't even understand, in an effort to share her culture with the Americans. Why shouldn't it work both ways? To Zhana, Alan and Lee seemed to be offering the technical wealth of the Outside as a fair exchange for the spiritual wealth of Enrisa. With a few proper safeguards, what harm could there be?

In her naïveté as to the realities of human nature and the historical cruelties of Western civilizations, Zhana could not possibly understand Darrel's sincerity in defense of his adopted homeland. Darrel was haunted by visions of Native Americans driven from their ancestral tribal lands; or of Western invaders subjugating venerable and ancient civilizations of the Orient; or of dark-skinned human beings seized without warning and taken from loved ones, carried in the dark stench of ships' holds to live as slaves in strange new lands; or of tropical island paradises filled with happy, contented people, transformed into bastions of the commercial tourist trade as "heathen islanders" were willingly sacrificed — first on an altar of Christian conversion and then in homage to the almighty dollar. Darrel did not want to wait two hundred years to find out what kind of *Roots* saga might be offered in memory of the simple and compassionate Enrisan lifestyle.

Darrel clearly hoped to share the benefits of technology and science that he personally used and appreciated, but wanted to make sure that such benefits would be introduced in a manner that would reflect mutual, equal cultural respect. It would have to be a slow process of educational training rather than quick commercial exploitation.

Still, Zhana's interpretation of his caution as chauvinism was eventually more than he could resist. Perhaps his position was too extreme. With proper safeguards, perhaps some early commercial ventures could be worked out.

Darrel conceded the possibility that more Enrisans could explore the Outside and assume direct Enrisan control over any economic exchange, on Enrisan terms. Darrel and Zhana both expressed hopes that they could work together to serve the best interests of Enrisa. Meanwhile, Alan and Lee grew increasingly impatient and Darrel also had to realize the possibility that they might just go ahead and do something without him.

At least by working with them, Darrel could retain some measure of influence.

But Darrel's first concern remained in further promotion of Dazhan. At least in this effort Zhana could lend total support. With his translation of the Enrisan text into English now completed, Darrel could direct more attention to promotional efforts. Picking up on the early popular interest in his adventures in the caves, it was not difficult to secure good media exposure.

As soon as it was released, the Enrisan text was brief enough that it could be printed in its entirety as a news item in many newspapers. In addition, Darrel had it printed up as a pamphlet for further distribution. With Zhana, he began to accept invitations for public appearances, to satisfy popular curiosity while promoting Enrisan social values. As the message was delivered in national magazines and on network talk shows, Dazhan drew increased comment in the national dialogue.

In the beginning, there was a generally favorable reception. There was still a growing popular interest in the new cave-culture, and serious critical analysis took a back seat to the latest novelty. As they traveled, Darrel and Zhana began to see Dazhan T-shirts, Dazhan posters, and lyrics about Dazhan in popular music. Darrel was pleased with the early positive reaction, and naïve enough to believe that the Outside world was heading toward acceptance of Dazhan and the development of a new social consciousness.

Helping Darrel with his translation of *Dazhan,* Zhana had become fascinated with his use of paper and pencils. Such simple devices made it so much easier to write than the metallic equipment used in her homeland. And, by simply rubbing a little "eraser" on something that had been written, mistakes could be undone. For now, word processing skills on the computer were beyond what she could comprehend.

Zhana loved to use paper and pencils to write in her native Enrisan and, as she had often done in Enrisa, she liked to surprise Darrel with pleasant little notes hidden around their apartment, to be unexpectedly discovered from time to time. Zhana even dabbled in learning a few more English words. She could already write and recognize her own name, Darrel's name, and a few other words, but as long as she could depend on Darrel, and planned to return to her own home culture soon, progress in English as a mere novelty was predictably slow.

As she enjoyed writing little notes and letters for Darrel, Zhana also became more aware of the massive amount of paper communication that was so important in the Outside. Newspapers were delivered to the apartment. Memos were scribbled onto paper. Records and documents were made and kept. Bills, advertisements, or other communications were delivered by mail.

Zhana was particularly fascinated by the system that allowed senders isolated in their various remote locations to channel paper messages into a network of messengers who would sort and deliver them as a link between the many senders and receivers. Though she could not understand most of it, Zhana enjoyed bringing in the mail and looking through it with fond curiosity before Darrel got to it. Occasionally, he would play her own little game and invest the price of a postage stamp so she could pull out something with her own name on it as she looked through the mail.

Quickly, Zhana began to recognize the difference between business correspondence, junk mail and personal letters. Personal mail was the least common but the most enjoyed. It represented thoughts, feelings and personal messages from individual human beings.

One afternoon, however, Zhana found a note that was less than pleasing. She was getting ready to go out with Darrel for a drive into the Los Angeles area to tape an interview at one of the studios, when the mail came. She pulled a cute friendship card out of the mail. As she always enjoyed this kind of mail, she opened it first and waited expectantly to hear who it was from.

Anticipation turned to dismay as Darrel announced that it was a card from Linda Ferret and translated its suggestive content. Wouldn't she ever give up? Abandoning unpleasant confrontations, Linda was trying to rekindle in Darrel a nostalgic desire for their old romance. Darrel was more annoyed than anything else, and concerned with how Zhana might feel, as he disposed of the card.

Zhana did feel a quick flash of resentment, but quickly put it in perspective. Darrel had been good to her and gave her a great deal in exchange for the spiritual values he had gotten from her and her people. He had never given her any reason to doubt the integrity of their special closeness and was not responsible for the actions of someone else. She also tried to keep in mind the feelings and experiences of Linda Ferret — trying to understand the motivations that would drive a rejected lover to unpleasant extremes. How could she blame Linda for feeling the same kind of love for a wonderful and special person? She was just sorry it was the same person.

Darrel glanced over at Zhana and could see that she was lost in thought. Was she going through the steps of Dazhan to redirect difficult feelings into constructive ones? He wondered what thoughts would go through the spirit of a truly skilled practitioner in a difficult situation. How would she direct her thoughts from appreciation of self-value, to acceptance of the equal, general value of another person, to the intimate merging of physical and spiritual perspectives, to finding an appropriate behavioral response, when that other person was trying to undermine her most special relationship? What kind of constructive, happy behavioral response could someone like Zhana extend toward someone like Linda Ferret?

Zhana noticed that Darrel was watching her, and smiled. She slipped her little hand into Darrel's, and they went out to the car for their trip to the television studio.

As they drove toward Los Angeles, Darrel looked around and tried to enjoy the value represented in the many strangers that surrounded them on the freeway. Darrel's growing success in practicing the steps allowed him to relax and enjoy a situation that, in the past, had been one of his most frustrating. Previously, he had always driven protectively and defensively, perceiving each other driver as a competitor for precious freeway space. Now, he looked on them differently. Sure, he still had to drive "defensively" in the sense of watching out for those few drivers who may be reckless, unskilled, or drunk. But now, he also saw in every driver a fellow traveler, sharing a common goal of arriving safely at their respective destinations. Behind each steering wheel was a unique story and chain of events leading to the sharing of this same small space of concrete.

Darrel thought how much more pleasant driving could be just by adding the steps of Dazhan. He went through the practice of each step, to draw himself away from the unpleasantness of traffic and into the value of those around him. He let himself relax and feel good about his own self; he directed the value that he perceived in himself as being equally valuable in those around him; he tried to visualize the physical perspective of freeway and traffic as it might appear from the viewpoints of others around him and evolved into a sharing of their *feelings;* he tried to consider what might be an appropriate behavioral response toward these anonymous strangers passing in and out of his life in brief moments at 60 miles an hour.

He was tempted to conclude that the appropriate behavioral response in these random, anonymous encounters was "no response," as he had done in other early practices. But he remembered that Zhana, as well as the members in his Enrisan discussion group, had suggested he make more effort to find ways to contribute to the moments of interaction that came along as he practiced. He wondered what kind of behavioral contributions he could make in a situation like this. With very little effort, many ideas for expressing cheerful friendliness to others and helping them complete maneuvers began pouring into his consciousness. In fact, he found that the process of looking for ways to help those around (instead of competing with them) transformed the drudgery of driving into a much more pleasant experience.

As they entered the San Fernando Valley, however, Darrel noticed a large truck following very closely behind his small sports car. Darrel was not in the fast lane, and was keeping up with the flow of traffic, so there was no point in changing lanes, as the truck would still have nowhere to go. In the past, his first reaction would have been an angry one. Now, his concern was with the inherent danger of what that big truck could do to his small car if a sudden slowing or stopping were required. He thought about the other driver. It was easy to get complacent and carelessly drift too close to the traffic ahead. Darrel had been guilty of the same impatient offense many times. He felt no anger, only understanding toward the truck driver. He only wished to find the most constructive expression with which to communicate the need for solving a problem.

Darrel lightly tapped the brake lights several times, as a gentle reminder not to tailgate. There was no response from the truck. Darrel repeated the gesture with the same lack of response. He reached through the sunroof with a gesture to back off, still with no success.

At that point, Darrel fell out of his practice of Dazhan and got angry. Obviously, a gentle reminder wasn't enough. Darrel hit the brakes hard, forcing the truck driver to slam on his brakes and swerve, then accelerated to get out of the way of the truck. This made the truck driver angry, too, resulting in a mutual exchange of unpleasantness as they drove.

Zhana was quiet.

Darrel apologized for "losing it," but also expressed his concern that he did not know what else to do. "I was doing so well in the steps," he said. "I wasn't trying to be malicious — I just wanted to protect our safety. I ran out of constructive behavioral ideas, and didn't know what to do."

Zhana was careful not to lecture, but to respond to the question of what he could have done. She recognized the difficult spot he was in. "But, don't lose sight of the difference between the *person* and the *behavior*. It is okay — it is *necessary* — to stop dangerous or violent or malicious behavior. But recognize the value of the consciousness from which that wrong behavior originates. Maybe the person is frustrated or uneducated or just not as skilled as you in the art of driving. Or maybe there is something else, beyond what you can understand. If you can just hold onto that appreciation for his unique value and perspective, you can at least avoid letting it turn into an unpleasant exchange. Find a way to address the wrong *behavior* with communication that is creatively cheerful and upbeat. What if that truck driver had been a close friend? Or your brother? Or a customer? You would find a way to stop them from putting you in danger— perhaps very firmly—yet as constructively as possible, without causing damage to the relationship. I don't know what other alternatives you may have had for a more constructive response. Maybe just get out of his way, even if there was nowhere else he could go. I don't know. We'll think about it. It's the kind of thing we would want to bring up in our discussion group back home so that other members of the group could offer suggestions." She laughed. "How would we explain to them about traffic and freeways!?"

As they continued driving, Darrel noticed that Zhana was unusually quiet. He wasn't sure if she was still upset about Linda Ferret or the incident with the truck, or what. But it was neither of those. Zhana had satisfactorily moved beyond each of those events, directing her feelings outward. She was in control of her own emotional destiny.

At length, Zhana took hold of Darrel's hand and rested it on her thigh. She scooted over as close to Darrel as bucket seats would comfortably allow and moved his hand firmly into place on her tummy.

"Darrel," she whispered softly, nervously, "you're going to be a father."

Darrel was so stunned by the suddenness of this announcement that he almost crashed the car.

"I'm going to have a baby," she repeated, still looking for a more specific response from Darrel.

Darrel thought about it for a long, silent moment. It would mean a lot of new responsibility. Complete freedom to enjoy spontaneous pleasures or to pack up and go places at a moment's notice would be restricted. Yet the experience itself could be an exciting challenge! Darrel was just coming to appreciate the value of human consciousness and individual personality. Now he could share with Zhana the task of providing an infant consciousness — a personality in embryo — with day-to-day exposure to experiences that would mold raw potentials into a happy, productive human being. He thought of the helpless infant, confronted by the need to sort out meaningful perceptions from the many stimuli rushing in from the surrounding environment. What impressions would get through? The new child would be like a blank sheet of paper. Not good or bad — just a blank sheet waiting to be written on. He and Zhana would write good things. The child would enjoy the greatest treasures of Outside technology and learn the precious teachings of Dazhan. It would glean the best from two great heritages. Yes! He wanted to be a good father. And this new Person could further cement his lifelong commitment of love for Zhana. He expressed these impressions to Zhana, who seemed pleased and relieved.

Zhana pressed Darrel's hand closer against her tummy and squeezed it firmly. "There's just one thing I really want," she whispered. "I want you to return with me to Enrisa before the baby comes." It was an easy promise for Darrel to make. He was already counting his time in the Outside in weeks rather than months.

Driving around the Hollywood-Los Angeles area as they went for their talk-show interview, out to dinner and other errands brought Zhana into contact with the central business district of a major urban area for the first time. She was amazed by the gleaming skyscrapers, brilliant neon colors that seemed to be everywhere (even in daylight, but especially as darkness fell), and the tremendous crush of people crowding together everywhere. It made her feel that the caves of Enrisa from which she had come were so tiny by comparison.

Yet, it was not *all* beauty and splendor. Many of the buildings were old and rundown. Many of the areas appeared to be dirty and strewn with litter. And as she looked into the faces of the many people crowded so closely together, she did not get the impression that it was all warmth or sharing. In fact, she perceived a certain coldness, emptiness, in many of the faces, even some well-polished, "successful"-looking faces. She yearned to share something of value with them. Particularly troublesome were occasional specters of haggard, dirty, pathetic-looking men and women hunched with desperation behind overflowing shopping carts or tattered bedrolls. She asked Darrel about them.

Darrel explained that these were the "homeless." "Bums. Tramps. Real eyesores that obstruct businesses and drive property values down."

"You mean they have no home to sleep in? In the harsh Outside? What do they do on cold nights? Or when it rains?" She was in Los Angeles in the closing days of summer. She hadn't been exposed to any really cold weather yet — she hadn't even heard of *snow.* "How could that be? In the Outside, with all the wealth and buildings and technology, how could people live with no place to go home to?" She was truly incredulous. And taken aback by Darrel's seeming apathy, almost disgust, toward these wretched beings.

Zhana was startled by the filth and suffering, but felt no revulsion toward the individuals, only sympathetic concern. She asked all about them. Where did they come from? How did they get that way? As she sought from Darrel more information to help her understand the feelings and perspectives of these people, she inadvertently led Darrel with her through the first steps of Dazhan. In very little time, he found himself no longer feeling disgust or revulsion, but rather sharing Zhana's disbelief that a wealthy, technological land could allow people's lives to collapse into such conditions of desperation and then abandon them to the streets. The homeless peoples' *condition* of desperate suffering was revolting and disgusting, but not the individuals themselves. As Darrel explained how people could be troubled by mental or emotional problems, or lack employment skills or opportunities, or other routes into homelessness, he felt a compassion toward them that he had not felt before.

As they came to the last step — appropriate behavioral response — Darrel's first inclination was to say that these were anonymous, brief encounters with strangers trapped in social conditions beyond his control. The appropriate response was understanding and sympathy, but there was nothing he could really do.

Zhana was not so quick to rule out the possibility of *action.* "What if we started a conversation with one of them? Get to know them? Maybe invite one of them for coffee, or out to dinner with us? Maybe we could brighten their experience just a little. Or maybe we could find ways to identify the problems in their lives and help them find solutions, so they can become productive and happy — really make a *permanent* contribution to their well-being..."

Darrel was intrigued by the possibility that they could really *do* something to add sunshine into the depths of such despair. Yet he was also concerned about safety, hygiene and convenience in dealing with people that he still felt might be emotionally unstable or even potentially violent, since he and Zhana had no training or knowledge for such work.

Zhana acknowledged that such obstacles would have to be dealt with, but that it could be done. They could do something if they really wanted to. Still, she noted how quickly Darrel had redirected his initial revulsion from the homeless *persons* to the *conditions,* and didn't want to push him too much while he was making some progress. Especially when she learned that there were also plenty of homeless in and around Santa Barbara, she would wait for an appropriate time and place to find a creative, cheerful contribution that they could make together.

During the next few weeks, Darrel and Zhana continued their promotion of Dazhan, continued exploring the wonders of the Outside, and attempted to work out their differences over how to introduce the technological wealth of the Outside to the cave-people without violating Enrisan cultural integrity. But mostly it was a time dominated by excitement about the coming birth. Zhana wished she could tell her mother and her friends back home.

There remained the continuing annoyance of periodic love notes and cutesy friendship cards from Linda Ferret. But each item was routinely disposed of and eventually drew minimal attention.

The night their talk-show interview was shown on TV, Darrel and Zhana stayed up into the wee hours of the morning to watch it. As usual, they again enjoyed watching as Darrel fielded questions and helped Zhana through the language barrier to do the same. As the program ended, the phone quickly rang. It was Linda Ferret again.

Continual media publicity made it impossible to forget her ex-lover, and she just "needed" to talk with him. Darrel ignored an impulsive flash of anger and did not tell her off or hang up. He was polite but firm.

"I need to see you," she pleaded. "I can't live without you." She felt if she could just talk with him face to face everything would be all right.

Despite his real concern, Darrel remained firm through her pleading and sobbing.

She called him a hypocrite. She said he was so busy going around the country talking about how to make other people happy that he had no time to concern himself with the feelings of real people, such as herself. Darrel remained quiet and firm.

"Oh, if you don't care any more, I might as well just die," she stormed, elaborating on a threat to end her own life.

Darrel was quiet for a moment. He did not want to be responsible for a Human Life. Then the thought of Zhana, and of the baby, and of his own life. He could not jeopardize the *value* of three human lives, either.

"You are a special human individual and I do care about you," Darrel responded. "I don't want you to die. I hope you can enjoy a good life. But you are the only one responsible for your own life. *You* must choose to live."

Darrel gently hung up the phone, unplugged it from the wall socket, turned on the phone answering machine and climbed back into bed with Zhana.

Chapter Eighteen

Reality

As Zhana danced breezily into the apartment, she noticed Darrel huddled closely with Alan and Lee watching something on TV. When she had stepped out a little earlier, they had been discussing economic aspects of commercial interaction with Enrisa. Now they were drawn attentively to the amazing little tube that was still so fascinating to Zhana. She moved in closer to see what they were watching. All she could see were a bunch of men taking turns swinging a stick at a little white ball that another guy was throwing at them. She couldn't make any sense out of it. She asked Darrel what it was.

"Baseball!" answered Darrel. He explained that it was a game in which two teams competed in a contest of physical skill and mental alertness, trying to outmaneuver each other to win.

Zhana was confused. It was difficult for Darrel to explain, as there was no similar organized competition in the Enrisan culture. Zhana couldn't understand how "play" could be so structured, or why it was necessary to have winners and losers. Especially perplexing was how so many thousands of people could pay good money to sit around and watch a few men on the field having all the fun. How could so much attention be focused by so many people on something that had so little effect on real life situations?

Drawing away from the TV and talking in whispers so as not to distract Alan and Lee, Darrel tried to explain, using the backdrop of TV action to illustrate his points. He sketched on paper a diagram of the playing field and explained in simplified form how each team took turns trying to hit the ball, move safely around from base to base, trying to return "home." He explained all about "strikes," "outs" and counting the runs scored to determine a winner. It was an exciting game filled with strategy, intrigue and raw physical skill. Zhana herself was active and alert and Darrel was certain that if she had grown up in the sports-conscious culture of America she would have been a fine competitor herself.

Zhana quickly caught on to the basics of the game and, while she still couldn't understand why so much attention was given to "just a game," she became interested in the development of play-by-play activity.

Between innings, and with more complete attention after the game was finished, Darrel continued his discussions with Alan and Lee about the issues of cultural and economic trade with Enrisa, intermittently translating the dialogue into Enrisan so Zhana could also participate.

Dazhan

"Darrel, look at all the jewels, minerals, oil, everything they have down there," insisted Alan enthusiastically. "Even that 'Dazhan' of yours is dripping with cash! Look at the way they write about you in the press; the way people flock to your lectures. People plus devotion equals big bucks. You could even be some kind of a guru or something — teach Dazhan to *lots* of people! You'd have it made..."

Darrel's quickly translated the suggestion to Zhana.

Zhana's reaction was not positive. "Dazhan brings people together. If you set yourself up as a 'guru' — better than others — you cut yourself off from them. Think of how Nolak teaches. He *shares* with people; he doesn't distance himself from them. He includes them."

With just a brief moment of reflection, Darrel quickly realized she was right. He thought of other teachers from the past, such as Jesus or Buddha and wondered how they would react if they could come back and see the elaborate institutions that had grown out of their simple teachings, and the acts of cruelty or violence often committed in their names. He shuddered.

In other matters of economic exchange, Darrel accepted the idea of trade with Enrisa as long as it would be based on mutual benefit to both societies, and only with adequate restraints and safeguards to protect the Enrisans from being taken advantage of.

Once it became clear to Alan and Lee that Darrel was serious about safeguarding the interests of the cave-people, they were willing to accept any protective restraints that would be "economically feasible." They still felt Darrel's understanding of Enrisan ways and the cave-peoples' trust in him, coupled with his proven record of business skill, would be worth more than the few concessions they anticipated.

Still, Alan and Lee were displeased with the slow pace of Darrel's cooperation. Already they had staked a claim under an old Canadian mining law, and had assumed control over the part of the mountain that included the entrance to the cave. Materials were being transported there and workers were already in Canada to install supplies and equipment inside the cave and make modifications to improve accessibility of the route to Enrisa.

They were investing a lot of time and money in this venture and were hopeful of great rewards. But they could not continue to put up with delays from Darrel.

Already hoping for an early return to Enrisa, Darrel promised Alan and Lee that as soon as travel and trade arrangements were operational, he and Zhana would return to the caves. Back in Enrisa he promised to assist in trade arrangements and supervise the protection of Enrisan interests. For the present, this was all they could agree on. Darrel interpreted this as an assurance of a prompt return "home" and a commitment to give him control over protecting the caves, while Alan and Lee saw this as approval to increase their pace of economic planning.

As he made plans to take Zhana back to the caves, Darrel continued to use his remaining time on the outside to promote Dazhan and expose Zhana to the wonders of his foreign world. As much as possible he tried to combine the two efforts. They traveled a lot.

As they ventured from city to city and state to state to meet curious fans, answer questions and try to teach Dazhan, Darrel would also make time to see scenic wonders, natural and man-made landmarks, historical and cultural centers, museums and other points of interest.

Between traveling, promoting social objectives and trying to fit a thorough exploration of the vast nation into a small calendar, they enjoyed continuous activity. It was a tall order for the cave-girl, long sheltered in Enrisa, but she found the Outside beautiful and exciting and could enjoy a more relaxed pace after she returned home.

Meanwhile, Darrel was becoming disenchanted with the positive reception with which the American pop culture embraced *Dazhan* and all things Enrisan. Sure, the crowds were still positive and enthusiastic. But he didn't feel the response was quite what he had been hoping for. There were still the T-shirts, posters and other novelties. There were even some who hailed it as "the Truth," while others enjoyed a new fad, and most people simply saw it as an important news event.

For all the hubbub, there was no real rise in social consciousness. Darrel was getting a lot of attention, but he felt discouraged at how his attempts to publicize his spiritual treasure deteriorated into a media circus. Even his growing cult of "true believers" professed love of the Enrisan text, but did not seem to grasp its real meaning in *action*. Certainly they did not seem to carefully follow through with each step of its spiritual practice. His most loyal followers often caused him more embarrassment than encouragement; their behavior was so out of tune with the practice of compassionate joy he was trying to teach. On more than one occasion when he was speaking to large crowds of them, they would fight for the best seating, shoving their way through crowds or lines, with ruthless competition through parking lots as they arrived and departed.

Darrel quickly became convinced that mere "loyalty" to Dazhan, or labeling oneself as a "follower" of Dazhan, or claiming "membership" in *any* organization or cause, could never be a substitute for actually *learning* and *practicing* the simple steps; he also considered that the dangers of cultism, extremism, or any form of fanaticism should never be allowed to divert people from the actual practice of Dazhan in the mainstream of general activity. Adherence to the message of Dazhan would have to be reflected in changes of behavior and deep-seated feelings, not in the mere espousal of Dazhan as a theoretical concept.

Dazhan

Not only was Darrel discouraged by the lack of real social response to all the effort he and Zhana had spent, he was also somewhat perplexed. He felt in his own life a new spiritual awareness since stumbling into Enrisa and learning about Dazhan. He felt an added appreciation and enjoyment of other people, which added a new dimension to all his feelings and behavior. But he was an American, too. He had developed from the same cultural milieu as everyone else; if anything, he had been less sensitive and more opportunistic than other people he had known. So, he was confused by the superficial acceptance of Dazhan.

As he expressed to Zhana aboard one commercial flight, "Am I so different from everyone else out here that I can learn this and they can't?" Zhana did not share Darrel's confusion. First of all, she pointed out that a much different time factor was involved. Without regard by Zhana for the calendar, which still baffled her, they were just entering the first days of September. They had not even been out of the caves two full months. He would simply have to allow more time than that for massive social change! Darrel himself had enjoyed more than a year in Enrisa in which to learn it and, while comfortable with the concepts, was still struggling himself to put it into action. And he had gone through a very different process of experience. "You can't just give someone a book, or say a few words in a speech and expect them to change deeply-rooted behavior patterns. *Teaching* is more than just *telling*," she explained, repeating an old theme from the programs of experience-based learning he had seen in the caves.

"Learning is a function of *experience*," she stressed. "New concepts, new understandings and real changes of feelings must be internalized through *action* and *experience*. Darrel, you went through extreme processes of experience over a long period of time in Enrisa. Even so, you understood Dazhan intellectually long before you began to practice the steps. If Alan or Lee were exposed to Dazhan in the same intense way, they might now have very different feelings about a lot of things. If all the rest of those people out there had gone through what you did, step-by-step, they might see the practical aspects of this Dazhan in a very different way."

By the first week in September, the hectic pace had begun to catch up with Darrel. He needed a little rest back home in Santa Barbara. He used the excuse that the little "mother-to-be" should take it easier. But Zhana was enjoying the action, and gently chided Darrel about using her "condition" as an excuse for anything. She wasn't even showing yet and could keep up a very active pace for yet a long time. So, for Darrel's benefit, they came back to spend some time in California.

Back home on the West Coast, it was soon apparent that Linda Ferret's threatened suicide had not materialized. While the frequency of her hopeful love-notes had eased somewhat after the pain of her latest defeat, she emphasized a new theme in her correspondence. It was the face-to-face visit. It had been just a hint in the last phone call, but now it took on a dimension of fanciful desperation.

She had invested a year of agonized patience and tremendous financial expense to help bring Darrel back from the caves, and now he was just beyond her reach. He had come back a hero, and his new media popularity made it impossible for Miss Ferret to relinquish her emotional hold. Everywhere she turned was His Face. She became obsessed with the hope that if he could only see her in person, the old chemistry would work on him again, and she would take him in her arms and blink away the painful nightmare.

She began to include photos in her letters, sending everything from a prim, attractive facial portrait, to provocative figure shots suggestively presented in various stages of undress.

The first time that happened, Darrel started to throw away the notes and letters out of respect and loyalty for Zhana. Zhana stopped him. "Maybe we don't need to save these, and maybe the trash is the best place for them," she said. "But before you get rid of them, you should read them and take a moment to understand and feel compassion for a troubled human being who is unable to let go of past dreams and reach outward to a future that she *can* enjoy. We must not allow her misguided behavior to prevent us from enjoying the tenderness and depth of compassion."

Zhana continued to bring in the mail each day — faithfully delivering *all* of it. When it included items from Linda, Darrel and Zhana would share it, sometimes with a laugh, but never with cruelty, and reflect on the shared values that Linda could not take from them.

Still, with Zhana's natural curiosity about the "other woman" having quickly been satisfied, she still disliked Linda's unilateral intrusion into romantic feelings from which Darrel had long since dismissed her. He had gone to the caves to get away from her in the first place, and now that she had spent so much of herself to find him and bring him back, he didn't want to stay here anyway! Zhana couldn't blame Linda's feelings of admiration for the man she also loved, but she did resent the intrusion. Miss Ferret should at least allow him the simple option of consent. *Consent.* An important little word in relationships, but a concept unknown to the possessive nature of Linda Ferret. Even so, Zhana never lost sight of her concern for a fellow human sister, whose behavior she may not appreciate but in whom she still recognized special and precious value. In enjoying and appreciating the special value of Linda Ferret, Zhana was able to minimize Linda's ability to undermine her own cheerful celebration of life and relationships.

Dazhan

When Darrel returned home one mid-September afternoon from one of his semi-regular visits with those at the local University studying his experience in the caves, he found that Zhana was not alone. As he opened the apartment door, he was immediately aware of Linda Ferret. His ex-lover was sitting on the sofa, and Zhana was crouched on the floor across the coffee table from her, turning the pages of a scrapbook she and Darrel had compiled of newspaper clippings, photos and other mementoes of their newfound celebrity status. They were sipping coffee that Zhana had come to enjoy with American friends, and laughing through their language-barrier to communicate with spontaneous gestures and Zhana's few English words.

Something didn't seem quite right to Darrel. The two women should have been fighting like cats, but here they were getting along like old school chums, except that they couldn't talk to each other. Even in spite of that, they seemed to be doing okay.

The two women grew suddenly silent as they became aware of Darrel's arrival. Zhana eased the scrapbook shut and set it on the table. Linda Ferret was the first to speak.

"Hi, Darrel," she said. "You really look good."

Darrel just stared in a furiously silent response. "Why did you come here?" he said at length, slowly moving to Zhana's side and taking gentle hold of one hand.

Linda did not speak for a moment.

Darrel took his cue from Zhana's quiet, pleasant demeanor. "Linda," he said. "We never really had a good relationship. I'm sorry. But right now I have everything I ever really wanted. It's not right for you to come here and try to take it away from me. I'm really sorry, Linda, but you must leave us alone."

Linda stood up and reached for her purse. She had completed the face-to-face encounter that had encouraged her final, desperate hopes. "I'm the one that's sorry," she said. She was struggling to hold back her emotions. She showed no bitterness and made no more threats of drastic action. "But I'm glad I came here," she continued. "I think I understand better now. I won't bother you anymore." She gently touched Darrel's face, then reached out to Zhana in a complete embrace as a splash of tears escaped. Easing away, she turned quickly and left.

As the door slipped firmly shut, Darrel turned to face Zhana.

"What happened in here?" he puzzled. He wanted to know how Zhana had received the "fury beyond what hell hath" and turned it away like a gentle lamb. Zhana gave an innocent grin.

"When she got here, I didn't know what to do," confessed Zhana, who had quickly recognized Linda from the pictures. "At first, I was a little scared. But I knew she wanted to see you and she would probably keep coming back 'til she did, so I let her in. Besides, I would never turn a stranger away. I looked into her eyes. I could see the pain she caused herself with this destructive jealousy. I knew she was wrong but, through her eyes, I could at least understand her."

"Even though she has tried so hard to hurt us?" Darrel questioned.

"That's just it," Zhana explained. "By focusing *away from my self,* I no longer felt hurt or angry. She no longer had the power to hurt us. When I was able to understand her background — her feelings — I just let myself respond automatically to *her* perspective of unique value. I didn't have to think of what to do or say. I just let it flow with what was right for *her.*" She continued to describe how, in the way she had conditioned herself through the years, she looked toward Linda Ferret to find the positive experience she could create out of this awkward encounter. "It's funny, it made me think of Rezak. He had the same problem — unable to accept another person's free choice to love someone else. While disappointment is normal, this possessive obsession is an emotional sickness. But, Darrel, I remembered how you responded when a vicious Rezak attacked you. When he fell in the water, you saved his life. When I thought about that, and looked at this troubled young girl, I just wanted to save her, too.

"So I fixed some coffee and showed her around the apartment. We had a funny time trying to communicate. I showed her the kibihni and let her take one stone as a souvenir, and I showed her our *Dazhan* in the original Enrisan and gave her one of your translations. She seemed to come out of her shell and warm up a little. She tried to explain about herself, but it was hard to understand in English. But I didn't do so bad. I could understand a lot of what was in her mind. I expressed our concern and our caring; I tried to encourage confidence in finding her own way to build a constructive, hopeful life ... I dunno ... I just did the best I could. By the time you got here, I think she understood a little more about 'love', and I think she began to see how much she wanted to take away from the person she 'loves'."

Darrel was amazed. He still wasn't sure exactly what had happened. But he knew that if anyone could find the right behavioral response, even in that extreme situation, Zhana was the one who could do it. But he was still amazed.

"This is good for her," concluded Zhana. "Now she can finally accept the way things are. She has her whole life ahead of her. She can go out now and find someone of her own."

It was still only mid-afternoon, so Darrel and Zhana decided it would be nice to walk to a nearby public park before going out later in the evening for another public appearance in town. They walked hand-in-hand through the landscaped grounds and snuggled together on a park bench. After a few moments, Zhana's head, resting on Darrel's shoulder, suddenly popped up. Her eye had caught a group of kids playing over on one of the fields. "What's that?" she puzzled, noting that it looked familiar.

"That's baseball!" answered Darrel. "Just like we saw on TV."

Well, it wasn't *exactly* like they had seen on TV. They wandered over to the playing field and found a seat in the empty bleachers. It was a bunch of Little Leaguers practicing together, at a very different level of performance than the smooth professionalism of the major leagues. But they were laughing, hitting the ball and having fun.

Zhana enjoyed just watching them have such a good time. "That really looks like fun," she mused. It was something she had never had a chance to try herself.

But as they watched, they also noticed that it wasn't *all* fun. There was a coach, stern and hardened, barking orders in military style. The kids enjoyed their turns at bat, or their turns at fielding practice, but in between there was a lot of standing around and waiting. It was too sterile and organized *too* carefully.

Zhana couldn't help but notice the difference between this structured, organized form of competitive play and the kind of recreation enjoyed by children in Enrisa. In her homeland, there were no similarly organized competitive sports. Children would play with casual spontaneity, running and climbing among the trees and caves, keeping busy and enjoying each others' company in free and unstructured playfulness.

Still, they also did not have this "baseball." And Zhana still thought it would be a fun game to play ... if it didn't have to be so formally structured.

Moments later they were down at the sporting goods section of a nearby store, looking over bats, balls and gloves. Darrel had always kept his old mitt and some baseball stuff around, but like everything else it had gotten lost during the last year. Darrel paused between the baseballs and the softballs. Zhana picked up one of each. "I know what these are," she said. "The little one is for the kids and the big one is what the men on TV use!"

Darrel laughed and explained, and they bought both balls, a bat, a couple of gloves, and hurried back to the playground while there was still some daylight left.

They found an empty diamond. Darrel showed Zhana how to stand, how to hold the bat, how to swing and made his way to the pitching rubber. He lobbed a gentle toss toward the plate and hoped she wouldn't be too disappointed on her first try. She socked it back at him within an inch of his life, and stood grinning at the plate as he chased down the ball. "Hey, I like this 'baseball'!" she announced. All the "help" from Darrel, or watching how others played, was not as important as her own native eye-hand coordination, refined through years of physical agility in the caves. Still, it was her first time at the plate and she didn't hit the ball every time, but she did get a few more solid shots and quickly decided this was a game she could get along with.

As the afternoon wore on and they had to meet other commitments, they packed up their gear and headed homeward. Zhana was still excited with this new discovery. She rushed to the TV to see more of how the "pro's" played the game, but there was no game on TV at that moment.

Darrel put his arms around Zhana and snuggled against her neck.

"How would you like to see the pro's play? In person!" he whispered.

"You mean it!?" shrieked Zhana.

There were still a few games left in the baseball season. It would be no trouble to get tickets for a mid-week night game at Dodger Stadium and then stay over to enjoy other activities in the Los Angeles area.

Chapter Nineteen

Competition

At that all-gray time of evening, when it is not yet night nor any longer afternoon and shadows blend in a colorless mix of dusk, Darrel helped Zhana out into the vast acreage of Dodger Stadium parking. Never before had she seen such a sprawling mass of automobiles assembled in a single location, nor felt so closely the press of vast crowds. And they weren't even in the stadium yet.

This was to be another reenactment of the traditional Dodgers-Giants rivalry, with both teams still nurturing pennant hopes in the final days of season play. It promised to be a sizable crowd. Zhana had seen large crowds before. Several times she had been the main attraction. Now she would see what it meant to know a crowd this size from the inside.

They made their way through the gray September dusk, through the facelessness of the pressing crowds, into the massive steel and concrete Temple of Sport. The Sanctuaries back home in Enrisa now seemed so insignificant.

Darrel and Zhana pushed toward the first tier of reserved seats between third base and Home. As they made their way from the gray outside surrounding walkway into the interior of the Stadium, they were dazzled by the massive brilliance that lit up the night.

In contrast to the dreary grays of the outside evening, the world inside Dodger Stadium was alive with color. Pale billows of light filtered down from towering lampposts and bathed the interior of the Stadium in a gentle mist of color. The grass shone with pastel green illumination. The crowd was no longer a faceless gray mass, but a moving kaleidoscope of color. The white of the chalk lines was a shining white. Even the infield dirt was not just plain brown dirt — it was *glowing* brown dirt. There was a feeling of lightheaded magic in the electric-lit air as they found their seats in the reserved level, overlooking the third base line and one layer above the ground-level fans below. Darrel and Zhana were near enough to the front to have a commanding view of all the action.

There were pre-game ceremonies. There was the announcing of the lineups. Then the national anthem trumpeted over the crowd. Zhana was amazed. As in Enrisa, music seemed to be everywhere. But in the Outside, the music always seemed to come from somewhere different. There was so much *variety,* both as to kinds of music and the tone and richness of the instruments used to produce it. And there was the *reverence* with which this anthem was greeted, as players doffed their caps and fans stood in respect. Before the game had even started, Zhana felt she had shared a religious experience with the fifty thousand others who had come.

The crowd hushed and the first pitch was delivered. It was a strike. Zhana was relieved to note that not even the pro's hit that little ball every time. On the next pitch, the Giant's hitter smashed a line drive to the left side of the infield. Zhana squealed excitedly. "He hit it!" An alert Dodger on third base hauled it quickly in, and Darrel had to explain that the hitter was "out." Darrel explained that was good — here in Los Angeles they wanted to get the Giants out. Zhana still felt bad for the hitter who was "out," although she was also glad the Dodger third baseman had been able to make a good play.

That was the way Zhana began responding to each play. She found it hard to keep straight who she was supposed to be rooting for. Her natural sense of Dazhan-conditioned empathy led her to identify with each play involved from the viewpoint of *both* teams, so that in the outcome of each play she would feel the victory of the players whose team had benefited and feel bad for the players who came out on the short end of it. The process was contagious. With his own level of spontaneous outreach at a more primitive level of conditioning, Darrel soon also found himself looking at the game from both sides. He found himself more fully involved with *all* of the players, with a new dimension of interest in an old favorite pastime.

The early innings generated enough action to hold the interest of a new fan, and Darrel was glad that Zhana had plenty of chances to see how the course of baseball activity progressed around the base paths as runs were scored by each team. By the end of the third inning, the Dodgers were leading four to three. Then both teams settled down and neither side scored through the next four innings.

As the pace of action slowed through the long middle innings, Zhana's attention began to wander.

Darrel caught a glimpse of her glancing around the various areas of the stadium, perusing the action in the stands. Darrel understood well how quickly Zhana could absorb spiritual awareness even from strangers at a distance. He, too, glanced around the crowd.

He rested his attention on a rounding, middle-aged man, well dressed and puffing on a cigar down on the ground-level seats just to the left of home plate. He was reclined back as far as he could in his seat, with his arms folded, chattering with his buddy in the next seat. Both men were dressed rather conservatively, more businesslike than the occasion would seem to require. They were enjoying themselves like little kids.

Darrel focused attentively on the first gentleman in the way Zhana and Nolak had taught him. He went through each perspective of Dazhan, step by step — appreciation of the value represented by his own consciousness; appreciation of the independent but equal value represented in the other man visualizing the scene from a detached, neutral perspective; and the merging of those spiritual perspectives. When he got to the point of really trying to identify with the spiritual value of the human individual, he put himself in the man's perspective and tried to imagine how the world must look from that point right behind home plate. He imagined the difference in the physical perspective from that vantage point; how different the field looked; the differences in sounds that could be heard from that location; the feel of the cool night air. Darrel tried to share the sense of excitement the man must feel in watching a crucial pennant contest from such good seats. He enjoyed vicariously seeing the close-up faces of famous sports personalities and of watching major-league action as close as most people would view a high-school game. Or, maybe the man had a season box down there, or was somehow involved with the team or the league, and came so often that the novelty had long worn off and it was just another important game. He couldn't know specific factual details, but he could understand and appreciate the perspective and the value.

He redirected his attention to a chubby, colorfully dressed lady out in the left field bleachers. She was trying to enjoy an exciting game while keeping two pre-teenage youths in tow.

He selected additional random faces from around the stadium. He considered for a moment the intensity of personal value represented by each one of these single individuals. One by one he thought of each person as a child, when the embryonic personality first began to take form. He imagined the chain of thoughts and feelings that shaped each life through events both great and trivial, humorous and sad, sweet and melancholy, in a dramatic pattern of intrigue unique to each of them. Each stranger he had selected became a real and vital human personality, and the perspective from which they looked out on the baseball action was just as real and vibrant as his own. As always through this process, he was awed by the potential of human exposure in just the faces of these few beings.

By now it was the seventh inning. The auxiliary scoreboard flashed a notice announcing that the paid attendance for the evening was 48,274 people. It was overwhelming for Darrel Swift to sit in the stands of that stadium, barely able to comprehend the degree of value within a few *single* individuals and suddenly try to multiply that value times forty-eight *thousand* people!

He thought again of himself — the realness of his own needs and feelings. Each one of these thousands was a being as real and dynamic as himself. Each represented the unfolding of its own incredibly complex drama, all happening completely apart from even his most remote awareness. He just wanted to know each person and love each one. He glanced over at Zhana. Is this how the happy, beautiful people of Enrisa felt all the time?

Beyond the stadium spread a great urban metropolis, with a complex mixture of personalities and cultures, rich with feelings and experiences beyond his understanding. Beyond that was a great nation, and an even more vast world beyond that. Darrel was overwhelmed. "My God!" he mumbled to himself in silent English, "each time I pass a stranger on the street or see a new face, I am exposed in that brief moment to a whole new dimension of exciting human complexity!"

At the end of seven innings, the Dodgers were still holding on to a four-to-three lead.

Darrel looked around at a few faces more nearby. There were some kids from a church group huddled playfully over by the railing. Darrel smiled, identifying with the boyish fun of each child. He remembered his own fun and antics going to watch baseball games as a child.

The kids were dropping things on people in the ground-floor seats below, planning strategies and laughing with hysterical victory at each successful "hit." Darrel laughed with them, sharing through their feelings the vicarious enjoyment of their naughty zeal. He chuckled right along with the boys as they celebrated another "hit" as a half-filled soft drink cup splattered down the face and shirt of an unwary spectator. The man grumbled furiously as he tried to brush off the sticky wetness.

Darrel could also sense the needs and feelings of this anonymous human brother who had come to enjoy an evening in the best seats at Dodger Stadium and had to endure sticky droppings on his face and clothes. Darrel's outlook immediately took on a different perspective. The man's enjoyment was disturbed by one unnecessary thoughtless act. The man shook a fist at the boys, who just laughed all the harder.

Darrel recalled Zhana's earlier explanation that there is a natural kind of pleasure in enjoying the reactions of other people, even when it is corrupted into a more cruel interest in the suffering of others. But with Dazhan, Darrel couldn't stand to see the beautiful flow of human consciousness clouded by sudden, unnecessary punishment.

The children's parents were with the church group a few seats away. Darrel wished they would do something, but they were also enjoying the humor of their children's antics. Papa was even giving helpful hints on how to release the droppings for maximum effect. Only when one of the kids, in his excitement, let out a naughty word did Mama call him back for a scolding. It seems the law of Christian love would not tolerate such an unsaintly utterance.

The other boys were excitedly preparing another dropping.

Darrel was usually one to mind his own business and would be the last to interrupt the innocent playfulness of children. But he looked down on the human targets below and could stand it no longer. He glanced around hopefully for a security officer who might come at the last moment to prevent further offense. There was no one nearby.

Darrel stood and leaned toward the railing. Without losing his feeling of closeness for the children's enthusiasm, he decided that the appropriate behavioral response would include some firmness. "Don't you drop one more thing down on those people," he pronounced with authority. The children froze with attention. "Get back away from that railing." They inched back from the railing. "All the way back." They went meekly back to their seats. Darrel sat back in his own seat with relief. His only regret was in not thinking up a more creative, pleasant way of providing a constructive alternative to the kids' inappropriate behavior, as he suspected Zhana would have done. He wished he had talked it over with Zhana first.

The Dodgers had scored another run in the bottom of the eighth. They were now leading five to three. Darrel returned his attention to the activity down on the field.

Zhana, too, was still engrossed in the progression of the game. In the natural way that she could identify so readily with each new consciousness and, coming from a culture that did not include organized sports contests, she had discovered the paradox of competitive interaction. The success of one competitor depends on the failure of another. She felt the elated triumph of a Giant hitter now on the field who singled and then scored on a teammate's double, and the simultaneous despair of the home-team crowd. Not a single play could escape that frustrating victory tempered by the simultaneous identification with defeat. "Why can't they just play the way we did?" asked Zhana innocently. "We both had fun. Each time I hit the ball we were both happy. There was no score, no rules, and no winner or loser. We just had fun!"

The Giant on second stole third and scored on a wild pitch to tie the score with one out in the top of the ninth. The batter walked on the next pitch and a new pitcher was called in for the Dodgers.

Darrel was busy explaining the importance of team sports in teaching young players to grow up and be good competitors.

"Why should they grow up and be good competitors?" she was honestly trying to understand social values from the American perspective.

"So they can be strong and successful."

"How does a society become strong and successful when its people are taught that success can only be achieved at the expense of others? A 'winner' in this competitive form of interaction seems to mean there must also be, somewhere, a 'loser'."

"You don't understand," protested Darrel. "Competition is the whole basis of a successful society. It's *natural* — it's part of human nature."

"The only reason competition in the Outside may seem so 'natural' is because it begins so early," Zhana suggested. "Or maybe that's the way humans have evolved for survival in an environment of scarcity such as the harsh Outside. But it isn't necessarily an integral part of human nature. Even if it were 'natural', there are many aspects of 'nature' such as earthquakes or floods that we label as 'natural disasters' and try to overcome."

Darrel thought for a moment. "Competition in organized sports helps develop teamwork. It means winning together. *Teamwork.*"

The next Giant struck out, followed by a dramatic home run to deep left field. The Giants now led seven to five.

"Competition doesn't mean teamwork," continued Zhana. "Competition means success at the expense of a loser. Within the same team there is no competition because competition is not productive. On the same team they all work together. That teamwork is *cooperation*. It is the *opposite* of competition. They don't compete with those on the same team; they only compete against their opponents. But why can't they just have fun without having to be opponents?"

"But competition is essential to the *economy,*" persisted Darrel. "It is just a part of human nature."

"Look at the tension, the aggression, and the viciousness that cause so much fear in your world here, Darrel," suggested Zhana.

In her brief tenure on the Outside, she had already become familiar with reports of crime and violence. Even in this very game, the playfulness of sport had been marred by desperate tempers of men who *needed* to win. "People here begin to feel threatened by imaginary, unnecessary adversity in their interactions, at the expense of all the beautiful ways they could share and all come out ahead together. Could it be that Americans have become neurotic, frustrated children trying to rationalize the two conflicting values of 'competition' and 'teamwork' that they are taught from childhood?"

The Dodgers were coming up in the last half of the ninth inning. Darrel suggested they pursue this dialogue later. He still had reservations about conceding the value of competition as an important social institution, but needed to sort out his thoughts. The Giants had come from behind to take a seven-to-five lead in the ninth.

The first Dodger swatted a long fly to deep center field. Darrel felt the excitement of the crowd and the anticipation of the batter, but he also felt the relief of the pitcher and the triumph of a center fielder who raced back to the warning track to put away the first out.

Another Dodger struck out.

The next Dodger hit a sharp grounder to third. The third baseman bobbled the ball, came up with it, and made the long throw just in time to get the last desperate Dodger. The Giants had won seven to five. The crowd was disappointed. Darrel felt happy for the Giants, but sorry the home team had lost. Still, it had been a particularly satisfying evening at the ballpark. The feelings of Dazhan seemed to add so much to every activity.

As they blended into the vastness of the outgoing crowd, Darrel found himself looking into the faces of passers-by from a new perspective. He was discovering how much more quickly he passed through each step of Dazhan after these months of practicing, and he was surprised, in the press of the crowd, how quickly he could relate to total strangers with such depth of meaning. Each passing Face, in the brief moment of encounter, reflected a dimension of consciousness and a lifetime of feelings and experiences.

The Faces of the crowd pressed in and around. He could scarcely grasp the fleeting depth in one Face, when another Face would appear, then another, through the vastness of the crowd. Surrounded by this great expanse of human treasure, Darrel's senses were alive with the kaleidoscopic awesomeness of this complex multiple awareness. He wondered if Zhana shared the same experience. He glanced at her face. She was so vibrant and alive! This teacher of Dazhan *must* feel it too — maybe in even greater intensity? They made their way to the car. Even the desperate crawl of the traffic represented a new, exciting perspective so much more pleasant than the way traffic made him feel in his "other life."

In the next few days, Darrel had frequent occasion to consider his experience at Dodger Stadium. He was particularly concerned about Zhana's feelings toward the nature of competitive sport. It seemed strange to him that an offensive side could be found to the *concept* of good, clean competition. But once the issue had been raised, it seemed to pop up again and again in every aspect of American life. And Zhana would always take the position that any kind of competitive diversion could be equally enjoyable — with less pressure and more spontaneous pleasure — if the need for a winner and loser were eliminated.

One evening they were watching TV as an international beauty contest came onto the screen. Zhana was shocked! She did not object to the admiration of attractiveness in men or women, but wondered how far reality could be stretched by these competition-obsessed Americans to turn such subjective qualities as "beauty" or "personality" into the subjects of competitive tournaments! Even Darrel began to waver on that one. It did seem somewhat arbitrary to score points for such unquantifiable æsthetic qualities. He couldn't see how women could endure month after month of cutthroat pressure through local, state and national competitions to come and stand like slabs of beef and risk it all in front of judges awarding labels for "prime" or "choice" based on a momentary or political whim.

Darrel watched the pressure build in scores of delicate human consciousnesses as twelve finalists were selected from the field of contestants. For all the others, who had worked so hard and hoped so long, it was suddenly all over. With the calling of the twelfth name, a hundred other tender hearts were broken and the dreams of these women were suddenly crushed in a painful cloud of defeat. For what? He watched as this spectacle was repeated through another round of eliminations and then turned the TV off. He wasn't ready to concede the whole issue of legitimate competitive recreation, but he could not justify this kind of degrading presentation and devastation of female human beings.

It was everywhere he turned. Activities like swimming, diving, gymnastics, or ice skating, which could be enjoyed or viewed with a free spirit of spontaneous pleasure, were distorted by the invention of point systems contrived to add structure, pressure and a semblance of objectivity to the freest expressions of human physical art.

They couldn't escape it. Even when they went out for dinner at a family restaurant, a mother was trying to get her two kids to eat faster. "Let's see who can beat...."

Zhana patted her tummy. "Our baby will grow up in the Enrisan tradition of Dazhan," she smiled. She seemed to be determined that the child born of her love for Darrel would not have his little consciousness clouded by an early environment of competitive conditioning.

Even Darrel was beginning to have some doubts. But he wasn't ready to give up on his enjoyment of organized competitive activity. "Do you mean I shouldn't play ping-pong with Alan anymore if he wants to keep score?" he half-teased.

Of course Zhana was not hard-nosed on the subject. Dazhan could never permit any rule or principle to become so important as to create frictions in the real human interactions that it was intended to enhance. Of course, Zhana would prefer to play recreational activities without the tension of competitive structures. But not everyone, especially on the Outside, could understand that. And she would never dream of ruining pleasant social activities by making a big issue out of it.

And, after all, even Zhana still enjoyed baseball. She enjoyed watching it on TV, she had enjoyed her visit to Dodger Stadium, and she enjoyed the loose, playful kind of baseball games she played with Darrel. She just did not want to get caught up in the neurotic competitive obsession to which so many Americans were addicted.

Chapter Twenty

Adversity

Zhana and Darrel burst excitedly into their little apartment together. "Let's just relax here for a moment and decide where to go out for dinner tonight," suggested Darrel, pulling Zhana close to him for a gentle kiss.

They had just come back from the doctor, Zhana's first experience with American medical science. She hadn't wanted to go. She was familiar with Enrisan prenatal health-care practices and didn't want to fool around with strange American ways when it came to her baby. But Darrel had insisted. She would be under Enrisan care soon enough. She would have her baby in Enrisa, and would be able to raise the child in Enrisan institutions and values. But it was his baby, too. With her confidence in American technology, Zhana finally agreed to see what Outsiders could do for the baby that was still inside her.

But when she got into the doctor's office and saw what was involved in the examination, she balked. She simply refused to undress for some strange man and allow him to handle her intimately, no matter who he was. An embarrassed Darrel Swift had to reschedule a new appointment with a female doctor. That done, a successful examination was completed and Darrel and Zhana enjoyed the security of a favorable early checkup.

Darrel flipped on the TV and made his way to the refrigerator. "Hey, we're all out of Diet Dr. Pepper!" he groaned. "I'll just run down to the market and get a six-pack and a few other little things we need."

Zhana noticed the evening news was just coming on TV. Darrel always liked to watch the news and Zhana couldn't always keep up with it, even with Darrel's help. She came and threw her arms around Darrel. "Let me do it!" she asked hopefully.

She was learning how to count and use American currency and to get out in the world without depending on Darrel so much. Darrel was pleased to see how much she had learned in a few short months.

The store was just down on the corner, so she could easily walk over and back. Darrel gave her some dollars and warned teasingly that he would check to make sure she added up the change right, as he sent her on her way with a little kiss. He couldn't help but notice how cute she looked in her light summery blouse and summer shorts as she disappeared into the evening. She didn't even look pregnant yet, but that would just make her all the more beautiful.

Darrel settled down in front of the TV with a glass of water to enjoy the news.

The hour-long newscast ran its course and Darrel flipped through the channels looking for something else. He found a baseball game in progress. By now it was the first week in October, and the National League playoffs were in full swing. The Dodgers hadn't made it to the finals, but it still promised to be an exciting game. Even Zhana would enjoy it. For all her dislike of the aggression generated by American competitive values, and her growing disenchantment with America's harsh social realities, Darrel knew she still enjoyed sitting down to watch a good game of major-league baseball. He hoped she would hurry back so they could enjoy the game together and then go out for dinner.

After he had been watching for two innings, Zhana still hadn't returned. She had been gone more than an hour and a half. He was a little concerned, but didn't dwell on it. She might have gotten hung up in a long line at the market. She may have found a communication problem, or taken time to make sure the change came out right. She might have just stopped to greet one of the neighbors along the way. Coming from timeless Enrisa, it was still easy for her to get distracted and lose track of Time. He didn't want to smother her in overprotectiveness. He returned his attention to the game on TV.

A couple more innings passed and Darrel grew more concerned. Where could she be? He was now too nervous to relax in his seat at the TV. He paced impatiently around the living room, glancing occasionally at the game. He stepped frequently to the door and peeked out. The night was still and quiet. Too quiet. He wanted Zhana to bounce happily into the apartment so he could scold her for making him worry.

After two more innings, Darrel was frantic. Three hours was much too long for a walk to the corner market to pick up some soft drinks. He was upset with worry over the one he loved so much. Could she have gotten into some kind of trouble or misunderstanding down at the store? He wanted to do something. Should he call the police? She was an adult free to come and go as she pleased, and he knew they wouldn't respond to an "emergency" call for someone who stepped out for a few hours in the early evening. Besides, he wasn't really sure that she was even in any kind of trouble, except in his own frantic imagination. He wanted to run down to the store to look for her, but he didn't want to miss her in case she might call by phone, as she had learned, or come back while he was out looking for her.

As the ballgame, which he had found in its middle innings, came to an end, Darrel slammed the TV off. He was sorry Zhana didn't get back in time to share it with him, but he was more concerned as to *why* she wasn't back, and he felt helplessly alone in the quiet apartment. He wanted her to bounce safely into the room, but if she did he wasn't sure if he would be glad or angry.

With the TV off, the house was too quiet. He couldn't stand it. He stood by the door waiting, pacing outside in front of the entrance where he could look around for her without leaving the apartment and without straying beyond earshot of the phone.

After fifteen more agonizing minutes of uncertainty, that seemed much longer, the gentle ringing sound of a telephone flowed out from the apartment. He made a desperate dash toward the little mechanical wonder that Zhana loved so much, with a thousand thoughts racing through his mind at once. Would he be relieved or angry? How would he compose himself enough to talk if it were someone else calling? He was a busy person, and it could be anyone. "If this is a telemarketer, I'll kill 'em," thought Darrel, in a return to the kind of feelings he had felt more often before learning and beginning to practice Dazhan.

"Hello?" he gasped breathlessly.

It was Zhana.

Her soft Enrisan words sounded weak and distant. She was fighting back tears in her voice. "Come and get me," she pleaded softly. "I'm hurt all over. Hurry and come for me, Darrel. It hurts so much...."

The soft Enrisan words were interrupted by a nurse taking over the phone in firm, crisp English. "Mr. Swift, your wife has been hurt quite badly. You'll have to get down here right away." She gave the name and address of a nearby emergency hospital, as Darrel hurriedly scrawled it down on the nearest available scrap of paper.

"What's wrong?" he blurted, stunned. "What happened to her?"

"Well, we can't tell for sure," answered the nurse. "She's not really able to tell us much because of the language problem. You'd better get down here as quickly as you can."

Darrel jumped into his car and sped hysterically through the darkened streets of Santa Barbara until he found his way to the emergency hospital. He impatiently pulled into a parking slot and raced inside. Moments later he was being escorted into Zhana's room.

As he stepped into the tiny chamber, he could see Zhana resting weakly, and could not tell if she was conscious or not. She was being tended to by a doctor and two nurses. A lady police officer was also in the room.

The doctor and the policewoman quickly approached Darrel. "What a relief to finally see you here," said the doctor. The officer echoed a similar greeting.

Darrel kept walking right past them both and hurried over to Zhana's side. He stroked her hand gently. "Sweetheart, are you alright?" he wondered.

Dazhan

Zhana's face was bruised and swollen. A puffy eyelid fluttered open as much as possible. Hearing Enrisan words and seeing Darrel, she reached for him in a painful embrace and sobbed with relief. "I'm so sorry, Darrel," she cried. "I didn't mean to have all this trouble here."

"Hey, everything is okay," Darrel assured her. "What happened?"

She lay back and tried to explain in the Enrisan no one else could understand.

"I was coming out of the market. I had bought the soft drinks and a few other things, and I was happy 'cause I did everything by myself and it was so easy. I even made sure they gave me the right change."

She explained how, as she was walking through the parking area on her way back to the apartment, she saw one of those beautifully customized vans with its sliding door opened up. Two men were relaxing inside, and motioned for her to come over. Curious about how these vans looked on the inside and, not used to turning away from any stranger, she ventured confidently over to the van.

Quickly determining that the girl did not understand English, the two men expressed their inclinations with suggestive gestures.

"Those men, complete strangers, wanted me to share physical love with them. Complete strangers!" Zhana was shocked. "I didn't have the English words to tell them I already had one special person in my life, and I really couldn't explain anything. I just made a simple gesture 'no' and backed away from them."

She continued to describe how one of the men grabbed her arm, smiled, and spoke in gentle, meaningless words. Zhana tried to pull free of his grip, but couldn't. The voices became harsher in tone. Zhana struggled harder to get away, dropping and spilling her groceries. A few passers-by slowed down to catch a glimpse of the struggle, so the men hustled Zhana into the van, slammed the sliding door shut, and sped off.

They pulled up in front of a vacant field several miles across town. Pulling the van onto the lot, they stopped back in the rear shadows of the empty field near a shrub-covered fence. The van was again filled with light as they opened up the sliding panel to face the night air.

The men fondled Zhana hungrily, pointing suggestively to her feminine features and stroking her face playfully. She drew back. The man slapped her face, hard, and began to unbutton her blouse. She felt cheap and helpless and started to cry. The man hit her face again, tugging harder at her top and ripping it. She doubled over defensively, reaching across her chest to protect herself, with one hand over the bra she had learned to wear "like the other American women." With the other hand she reached to protect her tummy, jabbering desperately in meaningless Enrisan words.

She felt weak and abused. She could not believe that a total stranger would seek such intimacy, and found it incomprehensible that the matter would be pursued so forcibly, with no regard for her consent, after the advances had been clearly rejected.

She looked into their faces and tried to imagine what painful combinations of experience could lead human beings to become such empty, vicious creatures. She was frightened as she considered the depths of violence with which human lives could be consumed.

She screamed, and a flock of curious neighbor children slowly gathered outside in the darkness. Lights began to flicker on the other side of the fence, and there were voices. The men grew impatient, then frantic. Zhana realized other people were near. She groped, in the pressure of the moment, to find her few English words. "Baby!" she cried. "My Baby! My Baby!" She clutched her tummy defensively, still doubled up.

"Now see what you've done!" snarled one of the men in meaningless English as there were more lights and more voices. He made a fist and pounded it into Zhana's face and body. He hit her again and again, ripping at her clothes. "No! No!" she cried in English.

Suddenly, they kicked her and she tumbled out of the van as they screeched backward to the street and sped away, leaving her to lie helplessly in the darkened field.

She became vaguely aware of lights, noises and a big red light circling around her. Then she became aware of the bed, and the sheets, and the medicinal hospital odors, and of calling for Darrel.

As Zhana described the painful details of her attack, Darrel was torn between a need to comfort the Special Friend he loved so much and a consuming rage against the animals who could hurt such a beautiful, gentle being. He held her closely, tenderly, but trembled in violent anger for the men who had done this. Zhana sensed both his love and his bitterness.

Weak and in pain, she choked back her own feelings and brushed an angry tear from Darrel's eye. "Oh Darrel," she sobbed. "I'm so sorry this terrible thing happened. I wish the hurt would just go away and let us be happy. Those men have done a terrible thing, but they are gone now. If they can be found, they should be dealt with properly, to protect other victims. But, haven't they done enough to us already? Darrel, don't let them ruin our lives any more. Don't let them take *compassionate joy* away from us, too. They are also our human brothers, troubled and in pain of their own. Feel compassion for them, too. They just don't understand. Just love me, Darrel, but don't let that love be poisoned in bitterness. Just love me, Darrel."

Darrel still trembled with anger as he held on tightly to the one he loved. Was he comforting her, or she comforting him? "Compassion should be for the victims, not the criminals," he mumbled softly, and in English.

Zhana seemed to hear and understand his comment. She was tired and in pain. Still, with laborious effort, she grabbed hold of Darrel's hand in hers and forced herself to speak. "Who is a victim? Who is a criminal?" She paused to rest and catch her breath between each word, but did not stop. "We have seen and read about some of the victims. Remember when we heard about the little children, taken from the parents who had beaten them, abused them physically, emotionally and even sexually. Some of those children had gone through things more horrible than what you or I could ever imagine, or possibly even endure. Remember that four-year old boy we saw on that TV show about child abuse?" Zhana paused to catch her breath again. "When you saw him, you cried. You wanted to take him in your arms and hug him and tell him everything would be okay. And we felt great happiness that he was being placed in a new home where he could receive love, encouragement and the help he needs. But what about a kid who never gets that help. We don't find him when he's four years old. We find him when he's twenty-four. We find him when he breaks into our house, or attacks us on the street. Same kid, twenty years later. Only now he isn't so cute or adorable. All he has learned is cruelty and violence. You talk about compassion for victims instead of criminals? Your prisons are filled with the victims who never got help." She paused again. "The men who hurt me are also victims. They must be stopped — they must not be allowed to perpetuate this cycle of victimization. But I have no desire to make them suffer any more. I wish we could put them in the Isolation Zone, to protect society, while *teaching* instead of *punishing* them." She breathed heavily and rested.

Darrel wept openly. He held Zhana tenderly. He loved her so much. He looked at the bruises and swelling that disfigured her cute little face. He just wanted to wave a magic wand and make all the hurt go away. But even in the darkest moments of pain and physical abuse, she was still a sweeter, happier person than himself.

Seeing that Zhana was finishing her story, one nurse moved over to care for Zhana's injuries and the other nurse guided Darrel over to the policewoman to make the statement Zhana had not been able to give. The doctor had been called out while Zhana was telling her story, but the nurse assured Darrel he would return momentarily.

Darrel sat and told her story to the nurse and police officer. The officer stopped him frequently to ask background questions or to clarify information. Darrel tried his best to remember all the details Zhana had provided so the police would have complete information about the case, but he refused to disturb Zhana for questioning, as she was now resting under medication given by the other nurse.

As Darrel was relating the factual sequence of events, the doctor stepped into the room. He motioned to Darrel to come out and join him in the hall. Darrel excused himself and stepped out into the hall.

"It appears your wife was expecting a baby?" questioned the doctor.

"Why, yes, she is," confirmed Darrel.

The doctor rested his arm on Darrel's shoulder. "I'm so sorry," he said. "I don't know any better way to say this. Your wife lost the baby. She's been through a terrible, terrible physical shock."

Darrel felt weak all over, and slumped against the corridor wall.

The doctor eased him into a seating place. "I'm so sorry, Mr. Swift."

"She had such dreams for the baby," responded Darrel, stunned with disbelief. "Please be careful how you tell it to her."

"Mr. Swift, you will have to tell her," reminded the doctor. "You're the only one who can."

Ashen-faced and stunned, Darrel made his way back into Zhana's room. She was still resting. He slumped dazedly into his seat with the nurse and the policewoman. "Zhana lost her baby," he mumbled quietly.

He took a few moments to recover his composure, and finally continued to tell the details of what happened. He felt angry and frustrated. He couldn't help himself. He just had not mastered the same happy feeling of Dazhan as Zhana had. He hoped they would catch the men, and he wanted justice rendered to the fullest extent of the law.

Eventually one of the nurses told him he would have to leave. It was after midnight and it was past the time he was allowed to visit. As he stepped out into the hall, he was greeted by the doctor.

"On your way out?" asked the doctor. "Going down for a bite to eat?"

"The nurse said I have to leave."

"Damn nurses," answered the doctor. The doctor granted Darrel special permission to remain with Zhana. Without him, they could have no written or verbal communication with the patient.

Darrel remained in Zhana's room, but was too nervous to sleep. He sat up and watched the resting form of the person who had brought so much meaning into his young life. She had brought him peace and joy in the primitive society of the cave people. He had given in return all the wonders of a mechanized civilization, which was equally primitive in its social values. Now she lay on a hospital bed, in her pain and bruises.

After several hours she stirred in bed. She sat up a little and called for Darrel. He was glad the doctor had let him stay. He hurried over to be with her. Though still in some pain, she was fully awake and coherent.

"I'm scared, Darrel," she confessed.

He held her close. "I'm with you, honey. I'm always with you."

"Is it bad, Darrel? Did they hurt me bad?"

He paused, and held her closer. "Zhana," he said with breathless tension, "we lost the baby."

"Oooh," groaned Zhana in a convulsion of agony.

Darrel held her close and wept softly with her. They cried silently in each other's arms until, at length, Darrel spoke. "Oh, how could they hurt you? How could they do this to one so gentle?"

Zhana was still aware of the painful bitterness he was trying to conceal. She was sad, yet never lost her feeling of compassion. "Darrel, we still have much beauty in our lives. Let's not lose it. Please, Darrel, it's too important that we cherish the special feelings that make our lives meaningful. We are still young. We will have more babies. And we will always have each other if we don't let them also take away our ability to look outward, beyond ourselves."

Darrel just held her close. Perhaps in time he would be able to use the compassionate joy of Dazhan to remove from others the power to take from him his happy moments, as Zhana was able to do. But for now he was still working just to add the simple practice to the every day interactions of his normal lifestyle.

"Darrel," pleaded Zhana. "Let's go back to Enrisa. I just want to go Home."

Chapter Twenty-one

Retreat

News of Zhana's attack was quickly heralded in banner headlines around the nation. While the much-celebrated cave-woman appreciated the outpouring of support the famous often enjoy, she just felt very tired. She had satisfied her curiosity about the Outside. She did not regret having come to seek new adventures. She had a whole new perspective of what the world really included, and had tasted of a broad range of eye-opening experiences far from the innocence of subterranean isolation. Now, she had tasted of the Outside and was ready to return home.

Meanwhile, her attackers had been quickly apprehended and were being held in custody. A pair of itinerant ex-convicts with a history of violent behavior, they had stolen the van from a local college student before terrorizing Zhana. They were being held on charges of grand theft auto, assault with intent to do great bodily harm, battery and attempted rape.

Zhana was easily able to identify the pair, supported by people from the community who had seen the initial abduction from the shopping area, and neighborhood youths who had witnessed the last violent activities and had come forward to provide the men's descriptions and the license number of the van, which had been used to track them down.

Faced with such massive evidence against them and unwilling to face the popular Enrisan woman in a public trial, the two men quickly entered guilty pleas to the charges of auto theft and battery, in return for which the prosecuting attorneys dismissed the other charges. Sentencing was set for later. Zhana would not find it necessary to wait around for that. By the time sentencing was to be handed down, Zhana hoped to be back in the quiet timelessness of her Enrisan home.

A feeling of compassion toward these troubled, victimized children who had grown up knowing only violence allowed Zhana to resist feelings of anger or bitterness. She felt no desire for punishment or revenge, only to undo the cruelty of all victims. She wished the Outside had an Isolation Zone where these pathetic criminals could replace their vicious learning with positive feelings. But, she also knew that it was important to remove them from the community, lest they perpetuate their legacy of cruelty.

Zhana was very encouraged by the outpouring of support that in her defense, but felt a sympathetic concern for those poor, unknown women who might have to suffer such abuse alone and forgotten. She shuddered with the thought of how much more terrible the attack might have been if it had not been interrupted and wished there was some action she could take so that no woman would ever have to be so brutally dehumanized.

By late October, Zhana had recovered from her injuries enough to travel and was eager to return to the caves. Darrel agreed that going home would give an important psychological boost to her recovery, and felt they had better get going as soon as possible.

The first snows of the harsh Canadian winter could begin to fall any time after Halloween. Even the gentlest blanket of snow could render their journey through the mountainous cliffs treacherous and deadly.

Zhana finally began trying to pin down an exact time when they could go. "Why don't you just call Alan and tell him you're ready to go," she suggested. "Alan and Lee wanted to go more than a *month* ago." The timeless Enrisan woman was becoming more comfortable with the units of Outside time measurement. "Call them now, and we'll probably be on a plane home within a few days."

With everything that had been going on the past weeks, Darrel had lost contact with Alan and Lee. He decided that Zhana was right. He picked up the phone and dialed Alan's office. Zhana listened to one side of the conversation as Darrel babbled in unintelligible English. The conversation was unexpectedly brief.

Darrel put down the phone as Zhana asked what had happened.

"They're already gone," explained Darrel. "They left ten days ago!"

"They went without us?" Zhana stared in astonished disbelief. "Without even telling us?"

Darrel, too, was stunned by this discovery. He was now concerned not only with returning Zhana safely and happily to her home, but also for the well being of the Enrisan community. Without someone there to protect the interests of the native population, Alan and Lee might feel free to do anything. "Let's get our things packed now," warned Darrel.

As Zhana went to get started, Darrel called to get flight information and reservations on the next commercial flight to Calgary, Alberta, Canada.

They packed lightly. They would need just enough clothing to get them into the caves. Once they were back in Enrisa, they would have no more need of American goods. Supplies and equipment for the actual trek to the opening of the cave could be obtained after their arrival in Canada.

Within hours, they were patiently enduring the long drive from Santa Barbara to Los Angeles International Airport. By evening they were securely aboard a jumbo jet bound for Canada.

In flight, Darrel turned to Zhana. "I knew we could never entrust Enrisan safety to the hands of greedy Americans, no matter how much they promised to cooperate with us," he said, still stunned by the unannounced departure of his erstwhile companions.

Zhana, too, had been caught off guard by the latest developments. Certainly her confidence in American moral integrity had already suffered more setbacks than she would have considered possible. Still, she was unwilling to completely write off the whole thing. "We don't know for sure that they won't cooperate with us," she suggested. "Maybe they're just getting everything ready for us."

Darrel was very curious as to just how far they had gone by now in getting things "set up." Alan and Lee had staked their claim on the cave-property several months back, and had sent up work crews who had been there all this time. He was very concerned about what might be going on in the caves at this very moment. He wished the plane would move faster.

Some of Darrel's apprehension was beginning to rub off on Zhana, but she was still able to see one positive side of the situation. "Darrel" she reminded him, "you Americans have some very exciting things. There are some fascinating wonders that I had a chance to see in your world, that you don't really appreciate 'cause you've always had them. But the Enrisans have never had those things. As long as the Enrisan people can maintain the precious social bond that keeps their lives so happy, I hope they can enjoy the new technology, too."

"So do I," agreed Darrel. "I just don't want it to turn into one of those American competitive games where one side wins and the other loses. If the Americans can share the technological skills with the Enrisans, who can offer their advanced spiritual awareness, then maybe we can combine the best achievements from each society. Each of our cultures excels in a different area. Why shouldn't we be able to have a society of compassionate joy that also enjoys the comforts and productive resources of advanced technology? I only hope that the power of the one won't be left to dominate over the simple beauty of the other...."

As the commercial flight continued into the night, Darrel and Zhana tried to catch as much sleep as their excited anticipation and an airplane seat would allow.

Zhana, relaxed and easy-going, soon fell asleep. But Darrel had more difficulty sleeping. Though tired, his mind was restless and active. His thoughts wandered across the experiences and achievements he had shared with Zhana in the Outside.

While they had not really found great success in changing the behavior and spirit of the Outside world, they had touched the lives and experiences of *some* people, and had planted the seeds for future expansion of the feelings and practice of Dazhan. They had shared scientific and sociological information about Enrisa with those specializing in such fields, and had shared the values of Dazhan with organizations contributing to specific social needs. In particular, two of Zhana's pet projects had been hurriedly set into place before they left:

First, Zhana had never really gotten over the shock of seeing homeless people in her visits to the urban areas of Los Angeles, and even in the Santa Barbara area. With Darrel, she had fulfilled her desire to meet such people, converse with them and share their stories, and try to contribute at least a brief moment of happiness in their bleak existences. More importantly, Darrel had set up a trust for the creation and operation of emergency shelters in cooperation with existing under-funded agencies, to provide low cost private rooms with dignity and self-esteem. They were also considering other plans to aid those in poverty in obtaining training in employment, living skills, and the personal confidence to make the transition into a stable and productive life.

Second, Zhana felt overwhelmed by all the problems and social unrest in the harsh Outside. She felt there must be a common denominator that underscored all the problems. She wanted to go beyond "emergency rescue" measures solving *symptoms*, to solution of the *real* problems. She was convinced that the problems of crime, violence, discrimination (on the basis of race, gender, age or whatever), economic inequality, over-competitiveness, and all the other social problems in the Outside world were just symptoms of a single deficiency: the failure of individuals to enjoy compassion. She wanted to really develop the feelings and practice of Dazhan on a widespread scale. To coordinate the implementation of those values, she had worked with Darrel to set up discussion groups and self-help organizations for those trying to implement the practice and feelings of "compassionate joy," in the mainstream of daily lifestyles and in special creative projects. It was just a start. They would have to monitor the development of those activities from the caves, to keep beginners focused on developing and continuing a pure *practice* of the steps. Real change would not happen easily or quickly. But, just as the Outsiders could share their technology and achievements with the cave people, the simple spirit and practice of Dazhan would be the contribution shared by the Enrisans in return.

Darrel looked through tired, scratchy eyes toward his sleeping sweetheart. She was so simple, so gentle, yet filled with such energy and vision! Despite all she had gone through, the wonderful new discoveries and the tragic and painful crises, her simple enjoyment of Dazhan had never faltered. He thought about the differences between practicing Dazhan in the Outside and in Enrisa. In the caves, there was a gentle environment and little economic or social adversity. The practice of Dazhan was generally accepted as "the thing to do" and, because people were generally nice and pleasant, it was easy to be nice and pleasant in return. But in the Outside, the practice had to stand on its own. And perhaps it was that very practice, if deeply rooted in spirit and habit, that could be the greatest tool in helping someone like Zhana survive so successfully in the face of greater challenges than she could have ever anticipated. Still, Darrel couldn't help but wonder if all the cave people could have survived as well. Those whose practice was only culturally superficial or who were struggling with the practice might not respond as successfully as the Zhanas, Nolaks, or other advanced Enrisan individuals he had met.

And so his mind continued to wander as the jet made its way through the nighttime sky.

The jet touched down in Calgary in the wee hours of the morning, just before the sun was readying to rise. Darrel quickly arranged for a taxi and escorted Zhana to a fine hotel near the airport. After a long night of fitful sleep, he wanted a few more hours in which to get rested and freshened for the balance of the long journey that lay ahead.

Zhana undressed and sat on the edge of the bed. She was tired from all the driving and flying. "We still have to drive up to the mining town," she sighed, recalling the sequence of the original journey. She recalled that almost a full day had been consumed in travel just between the remote village and Calgary.

"Then, we still have to trek through the mountain brush to the cave. That's a few more days. After that, we still have to go through the peripheral caves of Timera until we make our way home to beautiful Enrisa...." She was all the more exhausted just thinking about the grueling travels still ahead. She nestled into the bedding and snuggled up close to Darrel.

By the time Zhana awoke later, Darrel had unfolded an arrangement of contour maps and was gabbing away in English on the phone. Zhana quickly dressed, and greeted him with an inquisitive look.

Darrel finished on the phone and led Zhana hurriedly out of their room. "Let's go down and get something to eat," he suggested. "But we have to hurry. We've got to be down at the airport in less than an hour and a half."

"Airport?" puzzled Zhana. That was where they had just come from! She just wanted to get a hold of a rental car and get on the road toward her Enrisan home. Darrel just smiled as they hurried into the dining area. He had a different plan in mind, but didn't have enough Enrisan vocabulary to share it with Zhana.

They were soon sitting in the heliport office at the airport, as Darrel pointed to lines and figures on his maps and Zhana gazed out through large windows as huge blades spun around atop a funny-looking glass bubble with a funny tail in back. It didn't look like either a car or a plane. One always had to be on guard for new surprises in the Outside.

Meanwhile, Darrel was finalizing terms of a deal.

"Hmmm," considered the man across the table from Darrel, perusing the geographical information Darrel had brought. "We're talking about substantial mileage here, and the flight involves hazardous terrain. It is not going to be inexpensive, and I will require advance payment."

A price was quoted and "advance payment" was promptly produced in the form of a plastic bank card. In the last few days, Darrel Swift had been spending money like a man going somewhere he didn't expect to return from.

With arrangements completed, a pilot was summoned, and Darrel led Zhana under the gusty bursts of rotor-driven air into the "bubble" of the helicopter. Moments later they rose slowly, hovered, and turned to fly off into the Canadian Rockies. Zhana squealed with delight. The sensation was excitingly different than riding in a plane or jet.

In the air, Darrel explained that this "helicopter" could afford greater speed than a car on winding mountain roads, and greater accessibility to remote cliffside slopes than an airplane. Use of the helicopter would enable them to completely bypass the long drive to the distant mining town, the need for stopping in town at all, and the long trek through the mountainous terrain. They could fly directly to the opening of the cave leading down into Enrisa. Within hours, they would be at the mouth of the cave! Zhana was both pleased and amazed. The Technology she coveted for her people was more than just selfish luxury. It meant efficiency and achievement as well.

While the flight over mountains, valleys and rugged peaks was faster, more direct, and many hours shorter than the long drive might have been by car, a substantial distance was still involved. The excited cave-girl had to sit patiently through her nervous anticipation. Especially with the distant appearance of that unusual formation of jagged stones broken by uneven vertical markings that marked the opening to the caves, Zhana found it difficult to keep her enthusiasm under control.

As the distant cliffs drew nearer, Darrel felt a sharp, disquieting concern. The Canadian slopes, so rugged and undisturbed when last seen, were teeming with activity. Level places had been carved out of the mountainside at strategic locations. Temporary buildings had been set up. Everything was in motion. A highly organized and active colony of workers was buzzing around everywhere. And this was just on the *outside* of the cave. Darrel was quickly becoming nervous about what he would find *inside*.

The helicopter touched gently down onto a cleared area and, as Darrel and Zhana ran safely beyond reach of its chopping rotors, the versatile craft rose, turned, and sped away. Darrel and Zhana had returned to the Caves.

Moving unobtrusively among the busy workers, they organized the material brought in their backpacks and made their way up to where the cave opened in a narrow cleft of granite. Approaching the opening, they could see it had been substantially widened to make it more easily accessible to men and equipment.

Stepping up to the opening, they were startled by a gruff voice from behind. "Hey, you!" shouted an impatient foreman, "You can't go in there!"

"Wait a minute," answered Darrel. "We live down in those caves. We have to get back down in there."

"Orders are orders," persisted the stern foreman rigidly. "No unauthorized personnel allowed. This is private property now. Property of 'Enrisa Enterprises'. You better talk to Mr. Alan Swift or Mr. Lee Johnson before you go anywhere."

"'Enrisa Enterprises'," thought Darrel silently, not sure whether he should laugh or throw up. He answered the foreman: "I'm Darrel Swift, Alan's cousin. Where is Alan or Lee?"

"Lee has been down in the caves directing 'internal operations' for the past few weeks," came the reply. "Alan arrived from California a few days ago, and is directing operations out here."

Suddenly, Darrel turned to greet a familiar voice from behind him. It was Alan.

"Hey, little cousin," boomed Alan, taking hold of Darrel's hand and pumping it vigorously. "I saw the 'copter land and heard there was some commotion up here at the opening. Welcome back to Canada! Come on, let me show you around the camp."

Darrel explained that they were eager to get down into Enrisa, and solicited his cousin's cooperation. He also expressed his surprise that he and Zhana had not been included in the plans to return to Canada.

"Hey, we tried to call several times," laughed Alan defensively. "Once you were away on tour. A couple times there was just no answer. And last time was after the girl got hurt. All along we wanted you to be involved, to help in building successful economic relations with the natives, but we could never get you at the right time. Business is business! We couldn't wait forever. But don't worry about that. You're here now and I'm sure you're eager to get back down into the caves."

Alan summoned one of the workers. "Help these two get started down into the caves," he instructed. "Good luck, Darrel. I'll go back into camp and send a wire to Lee so he'll know you're on your way."

Darrel and Zhana followed their guide through the widened entrance of the cave. Just inside the opening, the worker threw a switch and the whole cave was suddenly illuminated by floodlights. Darrel could quickly see that a great deal of change had already been accomplished in a very short time, to make the cave more accessible.

A rope ladder, bolted firmly to the opening, reached down to the floor of the cave, making the long climb much easier. Darrel scrambled down the rope ladder, while Zhana, still more at home on the natural rock formations, danced easily down the plunging stone walls and arrived at the bottom ahead of Darrel.

They were led carefully through the remains of the original rockslide that had trapped Darrel and forced him down to his destiny in Enrisa. The area was now braced with steel reinforcements.

Where the long passageway began its plunging course deep into the Earth, Darrel was startled to find a little mining cart on a neat little row of tracks. Darrel's surprised expression preempted the need to verbalize a question.

"The actual journey from here to Enrisa is still a long one," explained the worker. It was a fact that Darrel, of all people, knew only too well. "Just to travel the passageway alone takes several arduous days on foot. With this little cart we can speed you safely through the whole tunnel in not much more than an hour. At the end of the ride, you still have to go the rest of the way on foot. But the route is now lighted, cleaned up and fortified with new equipment at strategic points, to make travel easier, safer and faster."

Zhana was pleased to find that the difficult journey she had expected would be so much faster and easier.

Darrel, too, was pleased to avoid any unnecessary delays. But the speed with which technological efficiency was being brought into the caves, by those whose greedy motives were still suspect, also left him feeling very apprehensive about what he might find at the completion of their journey.

Darrel and Zhana snuggled into the tight fit of the little cart. The worker bid them good luck and released the brake. They quickly gained momentum, hurtling rapidly down a straight, narrow corridor of stone toward their Enrisan homeland.

Chapter Twenty-two

Homecoming

Just ahead, down one last corridor of stone, glowed the narrow fracture that opened up into the great kibihni-lit caverns of Enrisa. Darrel's heart pounded with excitement, and he squeezed Zhana's hand as they raced toward their final destination.

As Alan had promised, the journey down through the broken layers of the Earth's crust had been made much easier than previous passings had been. It was almost too easy.

They hurried down the final stony corridor and stood before the narrow break that led to their home. Zhana slipped through the opening and Darrel followed.

They stood together on a ridge high above the Enrisan valleys and surveyed the vastness of the great Cavern. Darrel felt a sense of peacefulness in returning to the gentle beauty of the caves. Zhana was relieved to be back home, after having been separated these many months from the only surroundings she had ever known.

As they gazed over the panorama before them, the caves appeared as beautiful and serene as ever. In the distance, Nolak's Most High Sanctuary towered like a glittering jewel from its central position over the valley. The terraced grottoes, laced with a gentle garden of foliage, shimmered in the pale light of the exotic kibihni paradise.

But it was not entirely as they had left it. While typical Enrisan homes and structures were burrowed unobtrusively beneath the surface, and could not be seen in the distance now as before, there was now a large area strategically near the opening to the caverns, cordoned off and dominated by temporary above-surface structures. Other prominent construction projects were in the process of being set up. Directly below the ridge where Darrel and Zhana stood was what appeared to be the main camp of the Outsiders. The noisy prattle of gas-powered generators and machinery broke the quiet silence of the timeless stone-bound wonderland. Clouds of hazy exhaust hovered near the kibihni-lit ceiling of the caves. Darrel felt shaken and fearful. He took hold of Zhana's hand and followed her quickly down into the valley.

As they entered the cordoned-off area of the valley and headed toward the main camp in search of Lee, they passed the abandoned shells of burrowed-out Enrisan homes. Darrel was furious and discouraged. He led Zhana into the camp and stormed angrily into the makeshift office that Lee was occupying.

"What's going on here?" he demanded. "Get those gas engines off! Even on the Outside the air won't last forever; in an enclosed space like this the people will all be dead in a month!"

"Hey, calm down, Darrel," laughed Lee. "Everything is under control. Nobody's going to get hurt."

"The air is already turning hazy in here," protested Darrel. "And what about the people who used to live in these empty cave-dwellings? What did you do with them? You promised me safeguards to protect the Enrisan interests. So I'm telling you to get those motors off and get these people back in their homes. You may have bought the land, mister, but carbon-monoxide murder is still a punishable crime in Canada, America, or Enrisa."

"Well, Mr. Darrel Swift, the little man who always had all the money," sneered Lee. "We promised you certain rights in exchange for your cooperation. But you were always too busy to help us with your side of the bargain, so we had to do everything ourselves. Don't expect any favors from me. As far as I'm concerned, you broke off this deal a long time ago. How does it feel to be on the other side of the table, Mr. Darrel Swift?"

Darrel felt angry and frustrated. He felt a heavy weight of personal responsibility for the violation of Enrisa's quiet beauty. He stormed out of Lee's office and wandered through camp with Zhana. He was quickly able to piece together the details of what was happening from the excited workers in the camp.

With proper equipment and trained experts, it had been discovered that the mineral wealth in the caves was far greater than Alan or Lee had ever suspected. Unique combinations of pressures and temperatures miles below the outside surface had created a vast richness of known and unknown metals, precious stones and industrial minerals. At this point deep in the Earth's crust where the unusual interactions of air and water created cool enough temperatures to allow human life, the land was thoroughly layered with every kind of metal, mineral, or gem known to man, as well as many new ones. The burrowed-out dwellings of the natives were like ready-made mines, dug into the Earth at semi-regular intervals, bringing all these treasures right into the hands of those who just had to walk in and pluck them out with only minimal digging and drilling. In addition, rich layers of oil had been discovered a short distance below the surface and preliminary drilling was just getting underway. The employees of *Enrisa Enterprises* were happy and enthusiastic. Each man had dreams of instant wealth as he set about his tasks of mining, digging, building, drilling and "enforcement."

Each man had to take his shift on the "enforcement" lines.

While the cave-people had initially extended their typical enthusiastic cheerfulness and hospitality to the Outsiders, it was never enough to satisfy the intruders, who became impatient and finally felt the need to take complete control over the pace of operations. Needless to say, natives who had led quiet lives of peaceful social happiness all these years could not understand all the fuss over a few stones, common pieces of metal and some gooey black liquid. They resented being driven out of their homes as the Outsiders expanded their obsessive hunger for stones, metals and oil.

Alan and Lee remembered their earlier detention in the dungeons of Kerreih's Sanctuary, and had taken steps to avoid repeating that unpleasant experience. In addition to increased numbers of men, now close to seventy or eighty, those serving enforcement duty were protected with rifles and shotguns. Already several Enrisan natives had lost their lives as the Outsiders defended their "lawfully-staked claim."

Darrel was distraught by the tragic violations of Enrisan integrity that he had been unable to prevent. The burden of personal responsibility that he felt was intense and painful. Zhana, too, felt helpless and afraid. She had not believed Darrel's warnings of what these Americans were capable of doing.

Back when she had endured a humiliating personal assault, she had dismissed the episode as the action of aberrant delinquents. Now she realized the full meaning of Darrel's warnings: the Outsiders were just as willing to rape her entire civilization.

Zhana also felt an additional sense of pain. While she had no way of knowing which Enrisan individuals had lost their lives so far, she was familiar enough with this area of the valley to know many of the people whose homes were now found vacant. Zhana was very upset and wanted to hurry down out of the main camp and into the area still occupied by her own people.

As an American, Darrel was afraid to face the Enrisans. Yet his sense of loyalty and his feeling of personal responsibility left him willing to join Zhana and venture out into the Enrisan villages.

Zhana was not so pessimistic. "There is no need to have fear among our people," she told him. "You are one of us. No matter whatever else has happened, our people are still the people of Dazhan. They will be fair with you as an individual, not as an Outsider. They will know that of all the things that have been done, they were done by other individuals, not by you. And I will always be with you, so everyone will know exactly what Darrel Swift, the Enrisan, has done in the Outside or in the Caves, in defense of the Enrisan culture."

While Zhana's confidence was reassuring, Darrel knew only too well as he passed through the cordoned-off area around the Outsiders' camp that his decision had been made. Coming back across that line would not likely be possible. He regretted that such a choice had become necessary.

He had come to share Zhana's desire that the best could be drawn from each culture for a mutual sharing of contributions.

"What does *Dazhan* say to do when someone vicious tries to hurt others?" asked Darrel as they raced across the grottoed wonderland.

"Don't let them!" answered Zhana without hesitation. "There is a difference between the individual and his behavior. Compassion for the spiritual cripple doesn't mean you have to agree with him. It is not compassion to let someone do things that hurt himself and others. You can feel tenderness and concern even when you have to stop him."

Arriving at the home of Zhana's family, they found only Jamak at home. The child shrieked with delight when he saw his sister and Darrel and ran quickly to greet them.

"Where's Mother and Father?" inquired Zhana.

"Father is out helping find temporary shelter for the homeless," the boy answered, "and Mother is in a meeting over at the Sanctuary." Zhana and Darrel each gave Jamak a quick hug and dashed off toward the Sanctuary.

A surprised hush fell over the assembled community leaders as Zhana and Darrel entered their meeting. Kerreih quickly called a brief recess and raced with Lena to greet the two of them. As mother and daughter embraced, Kerreih chatted briefly with Darrel to quickly explore his feelings about the current crisis. Then, the young Chief Divine called Zhana aside to discuss a few important questions as Darrel visited with Zhana's mother.

As Kerreih called the meeting back into session, local sentiment quickly became apparent. While there was some suspicion from those who were least acquainted with Darrel and who had suffered abuse from American hands, a more typical reaction was expressed by Laros, the local Divine whom Darrel had befriended. "At last, here is a person who will know what to do about the Outsiders!"

Darrel felt relieved and encouraged, especially when Kerreih stood up to suppress the objections of the few who remained suspicious. "Two things a person cannot determine in life are the color of his own skin and the place of his own birth," she pronounced. "A man who speaks our language, reads our books, follows our practices and chooses to live among us is an Enrisan man." She repeated Laros' hope that Darrel's knowledge of the Outsiders' ways would enable him to help to suggest ideas for salvaging Enrisan territorial integrity.

As Darrel and Zhana joined in the discussion of the abuses and indignities suffered individually and collectively by the Enrisans, even Darrel was shocked by revelation after revelation of the Outsiders' insensitivity.

In turn, the Enrisans were shocked when Darrel painted a bleak picture of just how serious the choices they faced had become. Simply stated, if the American activity was not discontinued *immediately,* they would either have to plan a mass emigration of several hundred thousand people into a strange, harsh environment (in the middle of a Canadian winter), or face certain death as air in the enclosed chamber was gradually replaced with carbon monoxide. The Enrisans were desperate. They turned to Darrel for suggestions.

Darrel whispered a brief dialogue to Kerreih, who adjourned the session. She dismissed the Divines and the community volunteers and hastily summoned one of her fastest messengers, who was sent off to Nolak requesting an immediate and urgent audience. The Chief Divine invited Darrel and Zhana into her chambers for a meal. It was a chance for them to relax and visit informally with one of Enrisa's most important leaders. It was also an opportunity for Darrel to again enjoy the Enrisan cuisine he had previously acquired a taste for, but which had been absent from his diet in recent months.

After their meal, Kerreih sent Zhana home to enjoy a visit with her family, and led Darrel out into the tropical valley. They headed toward the Most High Sanctuary to keep their audience with Nolak.

As they made their way through the underbrush toward the cliffs that housed Nolak's massive fortress and later, as they trudged upward along the narrow cliffside trail, Darrel shared some of his thoughts and concerns with Kerreih.

"There are several hundred thousand Enrisans, from all the regions combined," he began, with facts that would already be familiar to Kerreih. "There are only seventy or eighty Outsiders, at the most, now in the caves. There is no reason any civilization with this kind of population should ever have to be intimidated by such a sparse and un-trained occupational force."

"But the Outsiders have those awful fire-sticks that make a loud noise and leave our people instantly lifeless," answered Kerreih. "One Outsider with such a weapon can just stand there and destroy an indefinite number of Enrisans who are peace-loving and have no weapons. Numbers mean nothing against the magic fire-sticks."

"Yes, I know all about the Outsiders' weapons," continued Darrel. "I even know how to use them." That remark unsettled Kerreih somewhat, but Darrel went on. "Certainly the Outsiders' weapons reduce our numerical advantage a little. But even their 'fire-sticks' have some limitations. Certainly there is no gun or rifle that can defend one man against ten thousand. We outnumber them almost ten thousand to one!"

Darrel knew what the real problem was. Isolated for centuries as a single peaceful community with a guiding philosophy of compassionate joy, the need for defensive strategies had long since ceased. Darrel was sufficiently familiar with Enrisan history to know that the Enrisans had gone through a period in their ancient history when the tribes had suffered many years of inter-tribal war and bloodshed, and that they did know the importance of resisting the violent conquests of others.

Now, as Darrel spoke reassuringly, the two of them began to share a positive optimism that, with proper training and organization, the passive Enrisans could be mobilized for a successful defensive resistance. Simple weapons could be manufactured. Enrisans could be taught to sneak into the Outsiders' camp and disable offensive weapons and machinery. Large numbers of cave-people could storm the camp and overpower the invaders. With Nolak's approval, a joint effort of all the regions could save them all. Still, Darrel couldn't help but be aware that, while his own mind kept aligning itself with *military* strategies for handling the problem, Zhana and Kerreih were receptive to such ideas but could always think of other, more peaceful solutions to permanent resolution of the *real* problems. Darrel wanted to be more like that. To be firm when necessary, but with the natural emphasis on constructive, happy solutions first.

Still, it was urgent that immediate action be taken *now*. The hazy clouds were spreading further across the cavern ceiling, and the whir and prattle of motor-driven machinery and equipment continued unabated. Men in the Outsiders' occupied territory continued to work, continued to pound new construction into the Enrisan stone surfaces and continued to pump and drill down through the layers of the cavern floor. There was no sign of stopping. The deadly cloud of poisoned air continued to expand. The pounding and digging continued. Kerreih and Darrel increased their pace and hurried faster toward the Most High Sanctuary.

As they ascended, Darrel thought he felt a slight quivering of the stone-bound trail.

It was the same kind of rumbling sensation that usually greeted him as the massive stone gates of Nolak's Most High Sanctuary were opened for his arrival, yet they were barely half way there and the great doors were not even in sight. He looked to Kerreih questioningly, but she returned an equally quizzical expression as the trail continued to shake gently.

Suddenly there was a strong, abrupt jolt. The whole cave began to shake violently. The sudden thrust of force caught Darrel off guard and he fell toward the edge of the narrow trail. Only Kerreih's alert reaction saved him from tragic consequences. With her strength and agility, she grabbed a wildly-flopping arm and threw him safely against the mountainside. She pressed him close against the inside wall of the trail, safely shielded by her own body for as long as the quaking continued. She turned only to look out over the pulsating movement that consumed the cavern paradise.

Kerreih and Darrel watched in helpless terror as the terraced grottoes buckled and split. Great folds rippled across the cavern floor and massive cracks opened in the cavern ceiling, loosening great kibihni boulders that went crashing down in various areas of the caves. Kerreih gasped in terror as she watched the rigid granite structure of her own Sanctuary collapse under the pressures of the violent Earth movement.

As the shaking gradually subsided, Kerreih leaned helplessly against Darrel, sobbing and exhausted. She imagined the sound of wailing, fearful Enrisans rising up from the devastation of the valley floor.

"Darrel," she gasped incredulously, "what was it?" Deep within the Earth, the phenomenon of massive earthquake had not been experienced within the lifetimes of the current generation of Enrisans. "What destructive powers have the Outsiders unleashed against us now?"

Darrel glanced toward the Outsiders' camp. The men, machines and equipment were now idle following the terrifying violence of the Earth's movement. Was this an act of the Outsiders or the natural release of long-dormant geological tensions? Had the Caves of Enrisa been waiting these centuries for a long-overdue quake, or had natural balances been upset by the pounding, drilling and building in the caves? Helpless and terrified, Darrel had no answers.

Kerreih, too, was shaken and afraid. But she was an Enrisan leader. She was second only to Nolak as the most powerful authority in the caves. She quickly regained her composure, directed her concerns away from her own needs and began to face this new crisis. "Darrel," she directed, "you go to Nolak. He may need your help in coping with the damage caused by the quake. In any case, we still have the Outsiders to deal with. Go to Nolak. I will return to the valley. More than anything the people who have survived will need the guidance and reassurance that I can offer."

Darrel warned Kerreih to proceed with caution as the Chief Divine turned and hurried quickly down the trail with a typical gait of Enrisan agility. Apprehensive of further danger, Darrel trudged upward, alone.

Small aftershocks continued with irregular frequency and intensity. With each small movement, Darrel froze in fearful anticipation of another larger quake.

He continued to plod upward, alone and uncertain. As he hiked, he glanced repeatedly toward the valley below. He wondered how his friends and loved ones were doing. He looked toward the now-silent camp of his cousin and erstwhile friend. He felt a deep and angry bitterness sweep over his consciousness.

Darrel thought again of his strategies for defending the caves. "We'll hit them *hard,*" he thought angrily. "They'll be sorry they ever came to Enrisa." Then he remembered Nolak. Darrel knew he would need the approval and cooperation of the Enrisan leader to complete his plans. "And Nolak will want to respond with *compassion,*" mused Darrel. How could he convince the Old Man to let him mount a really *tough* resistance? Didn't he realize what the Outsiders were capable of? Could Nolak be realistic in confronting adversity without getting taken advantage of? "Why can't they be more *practical* — like me..." Darrel couldn't complete the thought without considering the irony.

He stopped himself. "How could I think such a thing? *Nolak* should be more like *me?"* He shuddered. He thought of Nolak's ways, and the ways of Zhana. Darrel had previously observed that the Outsiders were just as willing to rape the whole Enrisan community, but he quickly remembered that it was *Zhana* they had actually tried to rape. Her response had been one of sadness, of firmness, yet of compassion and dignity. No matter what any other person could do to her, the compassion that she felt prevented them from taking control over her feelings. It did not mean she could always control situations or change the behavior of others. But because she was directed compassionately outward, she could deny them the ability to hurt her. Darrel thought of his own feelings. He was trying to learn the steps, yet when Zhana was hurt, *he* was the one who had felt bitter. When the Enrisan people were invaded, *he* was the one who was frustrated by their lack of anger in responding. He wanted them to be like him. He thought of his own bitterness. "My feelings of anger are not happy feelings. I want Nolak to listen to me, but I'm the one who needs to learn from Nolak."

Darrel thought of Nolak, up in his Most High Sanctuary. "Yes, he will want to find a happy, compassionate response. But he will not be weak. He will take whatever action is necessary to stop the wrong behavior, but he will do so with cheerful and loving compassion."

Darrel stopped and rested his head against the side of the mountain trail. He thought again of Alan and Lee. They were much as he had once been — and maybe he hadn't really progressed as much as he sometimes wanted to believe. How would Nolak feel toward them? Darrel recalled good times from the past that he had shared with his cousin and friend. He tried to understand the pressures and drives and limitations that had led them to grow in the direction their lives had taken. Sure, it didn't make it right to hurt other people. Sure, it would be necessary to make them stop. But there could be a constructive way to find the right behavioral response toward them — to reject wrong behavior but feel love for troubled, mistaken human brothers. The sharing of *their* perspectives and special value might help in finding constructive solutions. Or it might not. No matter — they would have no control over his feelings. Darrel — and *all* the Enrisans — could maintain their compassion and their dignity in the face of any adversity that others could put in front of them. Yes! He was really beginning to feel what

Dazhan was all about. It was more than just the steps. The steps, in every situation — *no matter what!* — were the building blocks of a lifestyle in which value could be drawn from all the spiritual wealth in those around us, no matter who they are or what they may do. He could see it! Nolak was right.

Darrel felt a new understanding of Dazhan and a new feeling of warmth and closeness for Nolak. And he felt a new warmth for Alan and for Lee. He felt a splash of tears escape, and then he sobbed deeply for a few moments as old, bitter feelings were poured out of his soul.

Darrel pushed himself gently away from the side of the mountain. He still had an important rendezvous with Nolak. He would share with Nolak whatever insights he could, and he would learn from Nolak whatever treasures of spiritual wealth the Old Man would offer. He faced upward and quickened his pace.

Each hour alone on the trail seemed an eternity. Finally, as he rounded the last switchback, Darrel gazed with relief on the towering citadel of Nolak's Most High Sanctuary.

But the massive stone fortress had lost some of its awesome majesty. The rigid granite structure had not been able to withstand the wrenching power of the Earth's most violent trauma. Decimated by the awful tremor, it stood broken and fragmented, like a great shattered jewel.

As Darrel approached, he felt another low rumbling, and looked to the massive stone doors. The great stone doors did not move, but the quaking grew stronger as the Earth again shook in fearsome throbs. Darrel braced himself against the mountainside for support. This was the strongest yet of the aftershocks, but was not nearly as terrible as the original quake, and the shaking soon subsided.

The stone doors remained firmly in place, which caused Darrel some concern for conditions on the other side. But it was not a problem to find an opening into the broken Most High Sanctuary. With less agility then the Enrisans, Darrel climbed around the massive structural damage, and found his way down into the broken ruins of the great hall.

The garden interior was crushed and broken by the massive columns that had come crashing down, and the gentle flows of water squirted chaotically around the main hall. Darrel gazed frantically around. There were no signs of life. The hall was bright with kibihni lights that had rolled out from their proper settings, and from gaping holes that opened up to let in light from the main cave. Granite beams and pillars were strewn throughout the hall. Darrel hurried toward the far end of the hall, climbing over, under and around the fallen, broken obstacles.

As he approached the far end of the hall, he could see that the great pillars, which displayed the text of Dazhan, were scattered in piles of rubble. Only one of the pillars even remained erect. Several of the pillars

219

had been crushed beneath a fallen area of the ceiling. Another pillar had crumbled into the central glow of fire, extinguishing the Eternal Flame. Darrel's heart pounded as he raced toward the broken pile of fragmented stone in front of the Eternal Flame where Nolak customarily sat as he conducted the business of Enrisa.

"Oh, no!" he shrieked in terror as he approached the Enrisan seat of government.

Crushed and bleeding, Nolak was sprawled silently under the massive weight of a stone beam that had fallen on him from the ceiling. Metallic "paperwork" he had been working on was strewn around in a shambles.

Darrel drew closer and looked down through the rubble. At the side of Nolak's broken body was a thin metallic page, badly bent. It was spattered lightly with the Enrisan leader's blood. A jewel-tipped stylus was still clenched in Nolak's lifeless fingers.

Ignoring a dizzy feeling of weakness, Darrel crawled down to Nolak's side. Mild, intermittent aftershocks continued to provoke fear for his own safety. Darrel rested his hand against the Old Man's head and sobbed quietly. His gaze drifted slowly upward with a desperate hope that human consciousness continued beyond the limitations of mortal destiny.

With quiet sadness, Darrel reached for the metallic pages which contained Nolak's last conscious expressions of thought. Gently, he tried to straighten the crumpled metal. He wept as he read Nolak's final expression of hope that a way could be found to befriend the Outsiders and to understand their perspective. He had hoped that such feelings might be the foundation upon which a lasting solution to the new crises could be built. More than ever, Darrel felt he understood what the Old Man was trying to say. He clutched the writing to his bosom and did not try to restrain his free-flowing tears.

Finally, beneath a text of new reflections on what the feelings of Dazhan really meant in the interactions of individuals and societies, Nolak had sketched a crowd of faceless, sexless, colorless human silhouettes. It was captioned:

Looking through the eyes of another
I find the world
Of feeling

Dazhan

Appendices

The Enrisan Text of 'Dazhan'
Translated by Darrel Swift
"Compassionate Joy"

1

The nature and purpose of human experience is to enjoy happiness.

2

The physical world is like a huge stone. It consists of elements physical in nature. This is the dimension of **things:** of *matter*. This physical dimension exists independently of wants or needs or feelings. Physical forms may vary through time, but the matter itself remains indefinitely. This physical dimension is vast and primary, encompassing the temporal space of the finite universe. The physical dimension is externally remote from conscious awareness or any subjective experience. This is the physical nature of the "External Dimension."

3

The spiritual world is like a tiny light, breaking up the consuming darkness of the surrounding physical universe. It consists of elements spiritual in nature. This is the dimension of **consciousness:** the *energy* of *thoughts, feelings,* and *experiences*. This spiritual dimension cannot exist independently; it depends on stimuli and sustenance from the surrounding environment. This spiritual dimension is tiny and isolated, confined within the individual minds of Living Beings. This is the spiritual nature of the "internal dimension."

4

Because there is no conscious awareness in the physical nature of the vast "External Dimension," *meaningful experience* can only occur within the spiritual nature of the "internal dimension," as Living Beings operate within the surrounding environment upon which their survival depends. Physical objects have no meaning or value until perceived within the conscious experience of the "internal dimension," where all meaningful experience occurs.

5

"Value" originates through the processes of interaction between these two dimensions of nature. "Value" occurs within the spiritual nature of the "internal dimension" as various degrees of goodness or badness are subjectively ascribed to the perceptions of the outside world, as individual Living Beings classify or evaluate perceptions.

6

The basis on which "value" is added to external interactions depends on the positive or negative nature of the experiences generated by those interactions. The total effect of interactions between the physical and spiritual dimensions of experience must consider the experience as a whole, including the immediate effect, the long-range consequences (including the consequences of means and methods), the number of individual beings whose experience may become involved, and the differing levels of intensity for each individual.

7

"Good" means positive experiences, or happiness. This may be enjoyed as a calm, spiritual feeling of warmth or peace, or as a bubbly enthusiastic thrill, or as a sensation of physical pleasure or comfort, or as any other positive perception of experience.

8

"Bad" means negative experiences, or misery, in any of its many forms.

9

All valid concepts of "value," including moral values, social values, personal values, or any other kinds of values, must be based on the single absolute general principle of Happiness. Additional rules or guidelines can only be relative in value, as suggestions for how this value might be applied to specific situations, according to the differing subjective experiences of each unique individual being, or of each differing culture-group.

10

Because all value originates within the consciousness of the "internal dimension," there exists a natural human tendency to pursue happiness directly, in the same way that tangible, physical objects may be pursued directly. Such efforts result in enthusiastic efforts to gratify desires of the Self as the primary objective. Such efforts may be understandable, but are counter-productive.

11

A person can never satisfy the desires that are generated by an inward pursuit of direct happiness. There is never enough to satisfy the continuous gulf between expectation and disillusionment. Self-preoccupation causes pressure, tension, and frustration instead of the intended happiness. All unhappiness represents inward-oriented concern with the Self, whether or not such inward preoccupation is voluntary or not. Physical pain causes unhappiness because it forces attention to the Self. Worry, fear, or over-sensitivity to pettiness are all unpleasant feelings which are rooted in inward concern.

12

This is the "Paradox of Happiness": Those who try hardest to make themselves happy shall be the least successful; Happiness seems to fall randomly on people who are too involved with other things to worry about it.

13

The resolution of the "Paradox of Happiness" arises out of the process by which positive or negative experiences are developed within the "internal dimension" through its interaction within the "External Dimension." The spiritual nature of the internal consciousness depends on stimuli and sustenance from the surrounding environment. Although all experience actually occurs within the "internal dimension," it has been crystallized into meaningfulness from its origins elsewhere. While certain basic personal needs must first be taken care of, the individual must ultimately reach outward to interactions with the environment in order to successfully achieve positive emotional experiences.

14

Basic personal needs requiring direct attention to the Self include keeping the physical body in good condition and free from pain, developing skills and talents so the "internal dimension" can operate efficiently within the surrounding physical environment, a reflective primary appreciation of the value of the Self, and confidence in the Self so that the "Internal Dimension" can be understood and enjoyed, and can become more effective in reaching outward toward successful positive experiences.

15

There are many ways in which the "internal dimension" can successfully enjoy happiness by reaching outward. Enjoying a variety of many outward interests or activities may generate a more total, versatile exploration of outward-oriented experiences.

16

Because the "internal dimension" is the only source of inherent value, and because the outward environment also includes the "internal dimensions" of other Living Beings, maximization of potential positive experiences involves the combinations of interactions that occur when one individual reaches outward in the sharing of experiences with another individual. The inherent value of each "internal dimension" feeds on the other, breeding new outward-oriented responses in unlimited possible combinations of experience. Life can be happy when concerns are directed toward a sharing of the inherent values of other Living consciousnesses. The key is in *sharing* among selves, not in *giving* or sacrificing of self.

17

The practice of Compassionate Joy (Dazhan) is based on this natural process of emotional sharing which exists among the individual dimensions of consciousness. There is an inborn interpersonal empathetic awareness which is innate to the process of human consciousness. If developed in an environment of negative emotions, it will be manifested in malicious feelings expressed toward others. If developed in positive forms, this natural awareness permits the enjoyment of pleasure in relating to others.

18

The feeling of pleasure from sharing the flow of consciousness among individuals requires no "give and take" nor the demand of expectation of anything in return. Because the individual is directed outward, the awareness of someone else's feelings becomes merged with self-interests.

19

The practice of Dazhan (Compassionate Joy) begins within the "internal dimension" of the individual Self. This is not the same as self-preoccupation nor inward obsession with self-happiness. This is a recognition of the value of Self and of the "internal dimension," and an awareness that even those feelings which may originate from the outside must still be experienced internally.

20

The first step in the practice of Dazhan is to respond to basic personal needs *from one's own perspective*. Physical, mental and emotional health and strength must be developed and nurtured so that the remaining steps in the practice can be successfully implemented, and to prevent the inward-oriented distractions that result from pain, illness, tension, pressure, when basic needs are not met, or when environmental and lifestyle situations are allowed to restrict or prevent the outward-oriented practice of Dazhan. When basic needs are met, an appreciation and understanding of the value of human consciousness can begin to be enjoyed through a celebration of the special value of the unique dimension of feelings and experiences that are only represented within the individual's own self through development of an understanding and appreciation of one's Self, and attention to those aspects of the Self or the present lifestyle environment which may call excessive attention to inward self-preoccupation, such as tensions, pressures, frustrations, and feelings of inadequacy or other unsatisfied emotional needs. In cases of resolving more extreme deficiencies, assistance from others (including professional specialists) may be necessary.

21

The second step of Dazhan is to re-orient the self-directed perspective into a detached, neutral perspective; to perceive one's self as part of the environment rather than as the center of it. In this detached, neutral perspective, one can become more objective and begin the process of breaking free of self-preoccupation.

22

The third step of Dazhan is to further re-orient the perspective from a detached, neutral perspective into a merging of the value of Self with the values of other consciousnesses *from the perspective of that other individual.* An individual uses the natural flow of emotions between individual consciousnesses to become acutely perceptive of another being's experiential perspective. One individual can visualize another and recognize that this other person represents an equally-unique dimension of spiritual value, as real and intense as their own. The awareness that this other being's special dimension of feelings and experiences are equally real and intense can be realized. When an individual encounters another person in an emotion-charged setting, a strong feeling of empathetic identification can occur. Deliberate cultivation of this natural process through a systematic practice can increase the capacity for spontaneous sharing of the interpersonal emotional flow, to develop an intense, deeper level of spiritual awareness.

23

Awareness is focused on the equally intense inherent value of the other person's "Internal Dimension," which is perceived as the equal value which it represents *for its own sake.* With a highly cultivated sense of empathetic union, the individual looks into the eyes of the other person. The individual imagines occupying the physical space of the other person, visualizing various objects as they would appear from that vantage point, using all the sensory perspectives the other person might be experiencing. The other person's immediate physical environment is thoroughly explored as it might appear through all the senses of that other person.

24

After completing a conscious exploration of another person's *physical* perspective, the individual carefully evolves into an exploration of the other person's *emotional* perspective. All the little thoughts and feelings of that other person's present experience are imagined through a vicarious process of empathetic synthesis — to reach outward and perceive the spiritual value of another being.

25

The fourth step in the practice of Dazhan is to find the appropriate behavioral response. The individual seeks in each situation what they can actually *do* to reach outward and make a contribution to the experiences of those around — to determine, and follow through with — the pattern of interaction (or lack of interaction) that would most contribute to enhancing the positive feelings in that shared moment of consciousness.

26

The origins of intrinsic value are developed within the spiritual lights of *every* "internal dimension." Therefore, development of maximum social happiness includes the practice of Dazhan in *all* processes of interaction, in a smooth, automatic and habitual practice.

27

Systematic and universal practice of Dazhan allows the habitual enjoyment of social happiness as an integral part of the personality, and motivates behavior toward others that will cause them increased happiness, which can also be shared through this empathetic linking-up. Mere intellectual acceptance of this concept, without this systematic and universal practice in feeling and spirit — and its effect on social behavior — would only cause the potentials for social happiness to be wasted.

Conjecture

History of Enrisa

Chronology: Approximately 20,000 BC
"Pre-Historic Origins"

As the last great Ice Age began to recede, nomadic tribesmen wandered deeper into the wilderness of the Canadian Rockies. They followed a trail of venison and other prey, gathering herbs and nuts along the way. The weather remained harsh, yet protective shelter could often be found within the caves hidden among the peaks and valleys of surrounding mountain formations.

For those tempted Northward during increasingly temperate summers, shelter, warmth, and food storage became essential for survival during the post-glacial winters. Even so, many perished.

In the early days of human life in North America, the discovery of fire and its uses long pre-dated the ability of its users to produce it themselves. Fire was carefully guarded at a central location, never to be extinguished, so it could be used to ignite other fires, and remain a continuous source of warmth and brightness. Nowhere was this more crucial than in the Far North.

The most successful of tribes, prior to the use of igloos and highly-insulated clothing materials of later centuries, nestled ever deeper into labyrinthine cave-systems, warmed by central fires and lit by torches. Some of the tribes learned to hide away in protective shelter throughout the harsh winters, and use their cavern homes as bases from which to launch hunting and foraging expeditions during the mild summers.

During this time, the Earth continued to rupture and heave in the great bursts of seismic activity that built the Rocky Mountains. In the sparsely-populated regions of the Far North, great earthquakes often unleashed their energies in remote areas, such that they were felt at most only slightly by the cave-dwelling natives. Occasionally, however, a massive earthquake might strike near a populated area, causing great disruption.

It was such an occasion, in the dead of winter, when a violent trembling began to shake across the Canadian Rockies. Nestled among the caves and tunnels of an underground labyrinth, sliced from the ruins of more ancient seismic activity, a great tribe of cave dwellers was caught unawares. As their granite shelter collapsed down upon them, most of the family groups in the main branches of the caves were trapped beneath the falling debris, causing widespread fatalities. Family groups nearest to the outside fled out into the cold, to seek other shelter or face the harshness of the sub-Arctic winter.

The family group of Mokoro and Zhikah was caught in their encampment, deep in the innermost recesses of the caverns. Mokoro called to the older children and several members of nearby family-groups, while Zhikah picked up the smallest children.

When the shaking began, Mokoro and Zhikah instinctively turned inward, to the depths of cavern tunnels that had always represented protective security. As the main chambers of caves were torn apart, they wandered deep into remote passages of the cave-system.

Suddenly, another violent aftershock jolted the mountain around them. Debris filled in the passage behind them, sealing them off from the other chambers and the outside. At the same time, in the violent trembling of the Earth, a massive fissure ripped the mountain apart.

Then, finally, all was calm.

The way sealed shut behind them, Mokoro, Zhikah, their children, and the group of survivors with them could only plunge deeper into the Earth. The great fissure created by the earthquakes, with neatly-sliced parallel walls about three or four feet wide, slanted at a vertical tilt of about forty-five degrees. In front of them the bottom dropped off sharply. Armed only with their torches and meager, hastily-gathered supplies, they forged their way downward.

After many days of wandering beyond the end of the great fissure and down through the numerous other chambers and tunnels, the little band of survivors stumbled into the Great Cavern. Illuminated by great fluorescent stones found nowhere else in the world, the Great Cavern was overgrown with lush tropical foliage, generous waterflows, and an eternally temperate environment.

Feeding on herbs, fruits, and insects, the group was able to survive and flourish. The group settled and made camp in the large area beyond the entrance to the Great Cavern.

In ritualistic, tribal ceremony to give thanks for their survival, Mokoro and Zhikah climbed to the top of a central cliff within the Great Cavern, overlooking the valley where they had settled. They prepared a great bonfire, lit by the torches that had guided them through the dark outer cave-system. The fire was to be the central flame of their new tribe, never to be extinguished. Around it would be built the Chamber of Fire and, eventually, the Most High Sanctuary around that.

Chronology: Approximately 20,000 BC to 2,000 BC
"Pre-Historic Development"

Early in the caves, life continued as a simple, pre-historic stone-age existence, except that the environment was no longer a harsh one, and survival was no longer difficult.

230

Over many centuries and many thousands of years, the handful of original survivors expanded in a gradual population growth, eventually dividing into further groupings and settling into seven regions of the Great Cavern, divided into seven distinct tribal groups based on natural boundaries of plateaus, valleys, and varying surface elevations.

Through an evolutionary development of many thousands of years, natural selection in the caves favored small, agile beings. With no large predators to defend against, nor large prey to hunt, size was no longer an advantage. With no need for the fatty protective layers that warmed them in the cold Outside; the cave-people became small and slender. Their diet of herbs, fruits, and insects encouraged their slight build and energetic activity. Without need for protection from sunlight, the skin became a half-golden, half-gray tone.

The cave people's primitive stone-age language gradually evolved its own unique linguistic patterns, isolated from the influences of other developing language groups in the outside world.

The mild, protective environment made it unnecessary to make distinctions between roles of providers and domestic care, so that the Enrisan society did not feel the need for distinctions in gender roles. Lack of harsh survival conditions also made it unnecessary to develop intense economic competition, nor the accompanying need to instill competitive values in the young through institutionalized play structures.

Chronology: Approximately 2,000 BC to 500 BC
"Early Recorded History"

With the development of tribes, common language and common legends, an early system of writing was developed, which was gradually refined into a formal phonetic alphabet,[1] written by a stylus on thin sheets of a metal alloy processed by the Enrisans.

A system of arithmetic computations, for counting, for trade, and for record-keeping, was developed in a duodecimal system, based on twelve instead of ten, including arithmetic functions, place-holders and abstract mathematic concepts.

Primitive medical practices and methods for caring for the ill were developed. Setting of bones, minor corrective surgeries, and elementary studies of cadavers to understand anatomy were introduced. The cave people experimented with and developed rudimentary birth control methods, allowing the population of the caves to stabilize around 500,000-600,000 people.

---

[1]See chapter three of story narrative, for description of the language and writing system, and Zhana's attempts to teach it to Darrel. The alphabet consists of thirty-five phonetic characters, whose shapes are determined by their sounds, so that similar-sounding words will have similar appearance. It is written from right to left.

A small Sanctuary was constructed around the Chamber of Fire, which was used as a neutral meeting site for dialogues among the chiefs of the seven tribes, and in keeping with the sacred remembrances of the site on which the first central fire was set up by the early survivors, and recalled in the handing down of re-told legends.

With the development of written language, early writings on social, political and philosophical subjects began at primitive levels. In a protective environment that required less energy to be expended for survival needs, the cave people enjoyed the luxury of being able to direct their contemplations toward more abstract concerns. Myths, legends and early writings about institutional structures were begun during this era and expanded upon by later writers and commentators.

The Enrisans continued to live in a society without day-to-day time-keeping, and life was casual and informal. With no day or night, or the time constraints of a competitive survivalist economic system, there was no need to create an artificial means of time measurement, other than the annual cycles measured by the changing of the waterflows triggered by the yearly melting of snows and increased rainfall each springtime in the outside world. While formal history was not yet recorded in numbered Watercycles, the rising cycles each year were noted and celebrated, and provided some frame of historical reference for long-term events within and beyond individual lifetimes.

Chronology: Approximately 500 BC
"The Society of Wisdom"

Around the time of the fifth and sixth centuries BC, uncounted in the timeless underground world of the caves, a great tide of worldwide enlightenment swept over the Earth. In the land of India, Gautama Buddha contemplated new ideas. In China, Lao Tse and Confucius taught new wisdom that would shape much of future Oriental thought. In Persia, the prophet Zoroaster offered new teachings. In Greece, Socrates was born. Worldwide, philosophy and science were being nurtured. Israeli prophets handed down Old Testament teachings. And far beneath the surface of the outside world, wisdom was also emerging in the caves of Enrisa.

Issanak, a student of the various early philosophical writings in Enrisa, began to establish Socratic-type dialogues with fellow cave dwellers interested in the contemplation of higher values. They called their groups the "Society of Wisdom," and sought to challenge and expand the concepts from early Enrisan writings. The Society of Wisdom, by its unfettered questioning and challenging of early ideas, was able to develop concepts of non-circular utilitarianism and resolution of the happiness paradox through outward direction of self-oriented concerns [as described in chapters five and seven of the story]. During this era, the emphasis of the early dialogues and writings of Issanak and his peers was on the abstract ideas and concepts to which the development of a *practice* of Dazhan would later be added.

The Society produced extensive writings and discussions, clearly not by Issanak alone, but rather by the Society as a whole. Because the dialogues claimed only to be the result of philosophical inquiry rather than divine origin, no deification or religious interpretation occurred, and the dialogues remained open to further discussion and evolution.

Throughout all the seven tribal regions, the early writings of the Society of Wisdom became the accepted body of cultural ethics among those who might be interested in such questions, but did not achieve widespread general popularity or official institutionalization.

Chronology: Approximately 800 AD
"Ritleh's Conquests"

The cave people had lived in general peace and harmony through the centuries of their life in their protective environment, continuing the evolution and development of their social, cultural, and scientific growth.

In time, however, one of the seven tribal chiefs, Ritleh, who ruled one of the smaller regions bordering the edge of the Great Cavern, felt confined by the limits of controlling but a single small region. He looked out over the caves, and saw an open space with six other regions, and many citizens over whom he might exercise power and control.

He mobilized the resources of his tribe, and trained them to prepare for military conquest. In the protective environment of the caves, in which there was plenty for all, the phenomenon of military adventurism was foreign to the experience of the cave people.

Citizens of Ritleh's tribe cooperated in preparing for his expansionist exploits, with appeals to their greed and promises of a better life in superiority over the other tribes after the conquests were successful.

Ritleh's tribe developed primitive weapons and strategies for training combatants, and then crossed into the territory of the adjoining tribe with virtually no resistance, killed the tribal chief, and claimed authority over the institutions and policies of the tribe.

Leaving representatives to administer the tribal affairs under Ritleh's direction, the combatants moved from tribe to tribe, repeating their bloody takeovers, and establishing tribal administrators under Ritleh's command. Soon, more than half of the tribes had lost their governments to Ritleh's usurpers.

Chronology: Approximately 800 AD to 947 AD
"Bloody Era"

While Ritleh had planned carefully for his conquests, he had little known historical precedent on which to build. His strategies were primitive and short sighted.

As he moved from tribe to tribe, Ritleh had to leave behind a sufficient number of his forces over each conquered tribe to govern and defend the conquest. After several initially easy conquests, and especially as he moved into the larger tribes, he found his resources becoming spread very thin. Simultaneously, those in the conquered tribes, while initially caught off guard, were quick to organize their own forces of resistance, seeking to regain control of their tribal homelands. At the same time, word of Ritleh's conquests spread quickly among the unconquered tribes so that, as his campaign extended, Ritleh met increasingly stronger resistance, and additional victories became ever more difficult.

As unconquered tribes sought to defend themselves, and conquered tribes sought to regain their sovereignty, bloody battles erupted throughout the caves. The centuries of Enrisan peace were broken. Violence had been introduced into the quiet gentleness of the protective caves.

Ritleh was soon defeated and executed in uprisings by his conquered victims, rebellious and eager to return to their erstwhile peacefulness. His empire fell quickly apart.

But it was not so easy to restore peace to the caves. The demon of war had been unleashed and a new precedent had been established. For now, the wars always seemed to find justification in "good causes." First, they had to fight to defeat Ritleh. When he had been defeated and killed, they had to fight over who would properly restore order and government to his now wandering tribe. Then, that tribe had to fight to defend against outside domination. Then, the other tribes whose leaders had been killed by Ritleh had to fight over who would assume leadership following the interruption of an orderly succession of leadership, and also defend against outside tribes who sought to forcibly assist them in that transition. Then, with the concepts of conquest and invasion having been introduced, others tried to imitate Ritleh's greed by developing more successful strategies and weapons. It went on and on. A great upheaval of violence and anguish consumed the quiet caves of Enrisa, and continued for more than a hundred and forty years. There always seemed to be a reason. But it never seemed to end.

Chronology: Year 949 AD — Watercycle 1
"Era of Dazhan"

The people of Enrisa became heavily burdened with the sorrows of continuous war and bloodshed for the benefit of a few greedy rulers. The caves, in all their quiet beauty and plentiful resources, cried out for peace.

In the fury of this upheaval, one of the ruling tribal chiefs named Kentah, felt compelled by the cries of his people. He looked over his tribal lands, and grieved for the rich tradition of peace that was written of in the old histories. He became a student of the old writings, including the ancient writings of Issanak and the Society of Wisdom. Ruling his tribal region in compassion and fairness, he enjoyed the widespread support of his citizens, who called him "the Divine one." They willingly resisted the invasions by other tribes, and enjoyed Kentah's policy of strict non-aggression toward the other tribal regions, which allowed them to prosper in relative peacefulness.

Citizens of other tribes heard of the peace in Kentah's tribe, and lifted up their voices in crying for the same.

Two of Kentah's neighboring tribal chiefs, weary of violence and feeling pressure from their citizens, made arrangements to meet with Kentah to form an alliance. With their three tribes united, they would have the strength to successfully resist violence by others, while establishing a framework for lasting peace that might spread throughout the caves.

In long sessions with the trio of leaders assembled together, Kentah shared with them his observations from studies of the Ancient Writings, and his outlook toward peace in the caves. In addition to combining their efforts toward peace, the three leaders also decided that it would be important to establish a system of institutionalized safeguards against violence, if lasting peace were to be maintained.

They came to the conclusion that it would be important for a single centralized government to be established, which could handle those affairs that affected the entire population of the caves. They determined that the Ancient Writings of Issanak and the Society of Wisdom must be consolidated, condensed, and systematically arranged to create a model of interpersonal values that could be instilled in their peoples to prevent feelings of greed and power from resurfacing and leading to violence.

While the trio continued their plans, battles among the remaining four tribes continued to run rampant, yet the unity of the three tribes and their ability to resist individual attacks from any of the others preserved their ongoing peacefulness. At the same time, the triumvirate continued to seek out the other leaders, to persuade them to join in the talks and to spread their goal of peacefulness throughout the caves. Through pleading and negotiating, and taking advantage of increasing unrest by citizens of those tribes who also wished to enjoy peace, two more chiefs were persuaded to join them.

The remaining two tribes were unable to fight the five united tribes, and quickly exhausting their resources in doing battle against each other. The belligerent governments quickly collapsed, and the people turned to the five united chiefs to help organize a peaceful system of government that could join in the cave-wide spirit of unity.

With all seven tribes now working together, peace was finally restored throughout all the caves for the first time since Ritleh's conquests. The seven chiefs studied together and exchanged ideas on how to preserve structures for lasting future peace. They established the following changes:

1. A central government was established, with the seven tribal chiefs selecting from among themselves a single leader, known as the "Most High Divine," who would represent the entire population of the caves. To symbolize the new commitment to social values as well as to government, the tribal chiefs were titled as "Chief Divines," assisted by various additional local "Divines." Initially, they sought to select Kentah for the new position of leader over all the caves, but he became ill, and assisted in the selection of one of the others as the first "Most High Divine."

2. The traditional Sanctuary site, in the neutral space at the central peak, which celebrated the ancestral origins of the first settlers, was renovated, expanded, and rebuilt to provide the facilities for an inter-tribe government as well as a cultural and historical center for all the tribes.

3. To implement a system of values that could be taught throughout the caves, and be instilled in young children as a part of their education, they selected scholars to work as a team in reviewing the Ancient Texts, and condensing a summary of the old teachings into a summary volume which was titled *Dazhan*, a contraction of Enrisan words meaning "Compassionate Joy." Copies of the new, shortened text were distributed and taught throughout the caves, and the original was placed in the Chamber of Fire for eternal preservation.

4. To signify the dawn of a new era, and to establish a formalized system of recorded history for the cave-wide government, chronology was to be counted in the measurement of annual Watercycles, numbered sequentially in the base-twelve counting system of the Enrisan system.

Chronology: Year 1988 AD—Watercycle 727_{12} (= 1039_{10})[*]
"Contact with the Outside World"
Darrel Swift arrives. See Story Narrative.

---

[*] Coincides with the chronological setting of the story, based on the original release date of the original publication in the 1980's.

About the Author

Douglas Dunn raised his daughter JoAnn (born in 1974) alone, as a single parent, from infancy to the teen-age years until finding and marrying his lifetime companion, Thelma. In the spirit of Dazhan which emphasizes *action,* he is active in community affairs (using his fluency in American Sign Language and Spanish to provide communication services for Deaf people, Spanish-speaking immigrants and actively supporting civil rights, women's rights, disabled rights, and equality for the LGBT community and special projects for abused or neglected children), and pursues a vigorous enjoyment of physical fitness through non-competitive recreational activities.

Doug's interest in the practical improvement of interpersonal dynamics originated from an early religious upbringing, which evolved in other directions towards other disciplines, including philosophy, psychology, Eastern religions, and other progressive approaches to applying social issues in our lives in practical ways that work in the real world

With previous editions published in 1981 and 1988, *Dazhan* uses a fantasy setting — the cave people of fictional Enrisa — to illustrate practical personal and social values, with emphasis on *how to* change behavior to increase interpersonal happiness.

Following the publication of *Dazhan,* Doug has since produced an expanded version of the non-fiction concepts into the book *Extro • Dynamics,* with more extensive analysis, examples and applications of the concepts and other resources for personal and social development.

www.ingramcontent.com/pod-product-compliance
Lightning Source LLC
Chambersburg PA
CBHW072118020426
42334CB00018B/1635